Designing
Infographics

Eric K. Meyer

Hayden
Books

Designing Infographics

Designing Infographics

Library of Congress Catalog Number: 96-78595
ISBN: 1-56830-339-4

Copyright © 1997 Hayden Books

Printed in the United States of America
1 2 3 4 5 6 7 8 9 0

Warning and Disclaimer

President
Richard Swadley

Associate Publisher
John Pierce

Publishing Manager
Laurie Petrycki

Managing Editor
Lisa Wilson

Marketing Manager
Stacey Oldham

Acquisitions Editors
Rachel Byers &
Robyn Holtzman

Development Editor
Beth Millett

Production Editor
Michael Brumitt

Copy Editors
Larry Frey &
Michael Brumitt

Publishing Coordinator
Karen Flowers

Cover Designer
Karen Ruggles

Book Designer
Gary Adair

Manufacturing Coordinator
Brook Farling

Production Team Supervisors
Laurie Casey & Joe Millay

Production Team
Dan Caparo, Lori Cliburn,
Rowena Rappaport, &
Christy Wagner

Indexer
Greg Pearson

Trademark Acknowledgments

About the Author

Eric K. Meyer teaches information design as a visiting professor of journalism at the University of Illinois in Urbana-Champaign and is founder and managing partner of NewsLink Associates, a research and consulting firm that investigates visual journalism and online publishing. He also co-edits and co-publishes with *American Journalism Review* magazine the online news resource AJR NewsLink, `http://www.newslink.org`.

Meyer has served as a researcher and consultant on design issues to more than 125 publications and telecommunications companies worldwide and has lectured to more than a dozen professional and trade organizations around the globe. Before becoming a professor and consultant, Meyer worked for 20 years as a professional journalist, most recently as news photo and graphics editor of *The Milwaukee Journal*. He has won numerous regional and national awards for writing, design and use of technology.

Dedication

Dedicated, on her 98th birthday, to a truly inspiring writer, photographer, artist and thinker, Ruth Meyer; to the loving support of Joan and Bill Meyer, who at age 72 continue to introduce the best and brightest to type lice; and to one of MIT's best and brightest, Nate Meyer-Gleason, who has demonstrated incredible good sense by choosing to become a first-generation chemical engineer and not a fourth-generation journalist.

Hayden Books

The staff of Hayden Books is committed to bringing you the best computer books. What our readers think of Hayden is important to our ability to serve our customers. If you have any comments, no matter how great or how small, we'd appreciate your taking the time to send us a note.

You can reach Hayden Books at the following:

Hayden Books
201 West 103rd Street
Indianapolis, IN 46290
317-581-3833

Email addresses:

America Online:	Hayden Bks
Internet:	hayden@hayden.com

Visit the Hayden Books Web site at http://www.hayden.com.

Contents at a Glance

Table of Contents

Part II: The Techniques

Introduction

Since the early 1980s, when information graphics exploded across the pages of American newspapers, countless volumes have fanned the flames of visual revolution. Researchers have probed cognitive constructs by which graphics are processed. Programmers have offered advanced tricks of the trade, easing the technical tasks that designers face. Artists have inspired colleagues with collections of creativity. Interaction experts have devised strategies for pairing information designers with those who create the content that they design.

What has been missing is simple tips for eager journalists, publicists, planners, analysts and illustrators—people trained in words, facts or images, not computers and information design—on how to add effective visual weapons to their communications arsenals.

Graphics have become so omnipresent that everyone should bring some knowledge of them to their job. Yet, like the majority of graphics professionals, those wishing to use graphics full-time, part-time or just for an occasional project, often are left to be self-taught.

Many begin as writers, artists, editors or photographers, but others come from professions as diverse as graphics themselves. They may be meteorologists, trying to get forecasts across, or lawyers, trying to make a case. They could be professors, reporting findings in juried journals; finance officers, making annual reports understandable; or librarians, explaining how books are re-shelved. All share with reporters, artists and page designers a need to unleash the power of information graphics.

Many try but few succeed in translating penchants for technology into skills that let them requite overwhelming passions to join the visual revolution. They learn at student newspapers, at Kinko's or in Macintosh labs, by trial and error on office PCs or by working late into the night on home computers. A few pick up skills in the classroom, if they are still in school, but the skills they learn often involve more technology or art than information and design. Worse yet, many don't learn how to do but rather how to evaluate what has already been done.

This book seeks to change that. You won't become an artist, nor will you become an expert on the Mac or PC. You won't learn the location of a magic button on the keyboard that instantly makes your work look like something out of *The New York Times* or *USA Today*. You won't even become a particularly well-versed student of the theories of visual communication. You will, however, learn:

- When a graphic is called for.
- How to find information for it.
- How to organize the information effectively.
- How to use technology to present it visually.
- How to integrate graphics into all your presentations.

Perhaps you are seeking this knowledge to pursue or enhance a career in information design or to supplement the specialties of another career—working in broadcast or print journalism, producing a newsletter or report, or making presentations that need the additional power information graphics can provide. Whatever your ultimate goal, you won't have to learn by trial and error.

In Part I, we'll explore graphics' rich heritage, look for code words that mean a graphic is needed, learn a new way to "tune" graphics for effective communication, itemize where you can find additional information and ponder the science and ethics of presenting information visually.

In Part II, you'll learn to think visually, review the computer programs that will help you, practice some basic and advanced techniques for drawing and data-presentation, and explore how these techniques come together in a finished graphic.

In Part III, we'll look at specific ways to present information visually, itemizing the strengths and weaknesses of each and offering simple yet powerful ways to easily, effectively and ethically design each major type of graphic, from bar charts to process diagrams.

In Part IV, we'll examine what it takes to join the visual revolution, the legal pitfalls to avoid along the way and how the lessons of information design extend from traditional media into cyberspace and the brave new world of publishing on the World Wide Web.

This book may be used several ways:

- If you're learning on your own, Part I provides informational tips you can review without having special equipment available. Part II introduces you to design techniques and the equipment they are practiced on. Part III provides practical reference and tutorials for each major type of information graphic. Part IV introduces you to the larger challenges of working with information design.

- If you're learning in a classroom, the book is organized into numbered sections, each of which could represent a lecture, a lab or both. Parts I and II are paired, with five lecture sections in Part I and five lab sections in Part II. By midterm, you should be able to evaluate in general terms how well a professional publication practices graphics journalism. In Part III, each of the six sections serve both as a discussion section and as a laboratory section, enabling you to concentrate on practical skills of information design. Part IV concludes with three discussion sections, letting you spend lab time completing any final projects.

- After you've mastered the skills, Parts I and IV provide consciousness-raising material that you might want to share with non-visual colleagues. Part II lets you introduce neophytes to your tools. Part III serves as a reference guide so that you and others can speak the same language. The Appendixes are available for reflection and reference.

- After you've won your "SND Gold," the Society of Newspaper Design award that many regard as the Pulitzer Prize of graphics journalism, or another award for graphics prowess from the industry you work in, this book makes a fine pedestal on which to set your trophy. Or there's always the fate listed in Chapter 5, but we wouldn't want to give it away too early.

Most of you picking up this book already understand how persuasive graphics can be. You know that graphics simplify the complex, make the unfathomable believable and present points more quickly and more memorably than text alone can. You aren't MTV-depraved illiterates; you want to learn about graphics not just to make your presentations *look* better but to make your presentations *work* better.

For a handful of hidebound journalists, however, this book should come in a plain brown wrapper. As popular and powerful as graphics have become, information design remains in some journalistic quarters as professionally respected as exotic dancers. For a serious wordsmith to be seen even toying with the idea of letting images, not text, tell a story is regarded by some as professional perversion. To them, graphics are an abdication of a moral imperative to present all the world's truth in text. They are at best a necessary evil, at worst a verification that the reading public just isn't that interested in the noble mission that they view writing as being.

A noble mission? It must be. Ask any of my fellow journalists. They'll be only too eager to tell you: The pay is lousy; the hours, terrible; the pressures, unrelenting. Deadlines come perilously close to living up to their name. The toll on private lives can be unimaginable. Worse yet, whatever we journalists do, the reading public seems less inclined to buy, appreciate or read our work. We are less happy, less trusted, more stressed and more cynical than almost any other professionals. Yet in near record numbers, students flock to our field. The sirens they answer are mythic indeed:

- For reporters, there are the historic heroics of John Peter Zenger, the magnificent muckraking of Ida M. Tarbell, the common-man compassion of Ernie Pyle and the tireless quests of Bob Woodward.

- For editors, there are the amazing mental feats of Carr Van Anda, the maniacal crusadings of Joseph Pulitzer, the popular witticisms and witty populism of William Allen White and the visionary spirit of Robert Maynard.

- For broadcasters, there are the shames harvested by Edward R. Murrow, the Hindenburg humanity of Herbert Morrison and the bombs and barbs dodged by Peter Arnett and Bernard Shaw.

- For photographers, there are the incivilities of war documented by Mathew Brady, the magazines full of life from Margaret Bourke-White and the powerful insights of Eddie Adams' portraiture and spot news.

Every journalist has his or her own heroes, and many of them probably aren't listed here. As anyone who has turned a page of Michael and Edwin Emery's *The Press and America* or Calder Picket's *Voices of the Past* knows, journalism is so full of heroic names that people as important as Walter Cronkite barely merit partial-page references.

But for graphics journalists, heroes are harder to find. To be sure, there are pioneers. But someone like *Time* magazine's Nigel Holmes, more famous for drawing rosebuds than having them as sleds, evokes nowhere near the passion of William Randolph Hearst. And graphics journalism's true heroes—some of them not human—are as likely to be vilified as they are honored.

How would you like to be thought of as someone whose professionalism is guided by a newspaper that's been called "the McDonald's of American journalism"? Or would you prefer to be thought of as someone who worships the technology of a computer named for a fruit? Worse yet, do you want to be remembered as the person whose mission it was to "break up the gray," "serve our illiterate readers" or "do whatever it is that the marketing people want"?

Is it any surprise that graphics journalism is the only segment of a glutted market in which jobs now go for the asking?

Absent a hero, perhaps the field could use a poster boy—a hero by no means, yet still someone who:

- understands how persuasive visual journalism can be

- would scarcely think of trying to convey a message, particularly a complex or controversial one, without accompanying visuals

- knows all too well that although people may gloss over verbal claims, they often regard charted data, rightly or wrongly, as persuasive and authoritative proof

Ladies and gentlemen, information graphics' ersatz hero: billionaire businessman and amateur politician H. Ross Perot, who spent most of his two presidential campaigns showing the electorate his homemade infographics.

You don't have to admire his politics. Many don't. But you do have to admire his visual skills. An unprofessional orator, he might well have been confined to the same sort of anonymity that befell his 1992 running mate. (Quick: What was his name?) But Perot, unlike forgettable vice presidential partner, retired Adm. James B. Stockdale, knows the power of visual communication. Producing chart after chart to support his voluminous contentions, he appropriately or inappropriately emerged to score an amazingly credible percentage of the popular vote.

While his appeal might not have been inexorably linked to his graphics prowess, Perot nevertheless demonstrated for a profession desperately in need of heroes that the future of American thought and persuasion lies not so much in words as it does in images.

A Brief History of Information Graphics

Popular perception is that information graphics did not come into substantial use until Allen Neuharth's dream of a national newspaper, *USA Today*, took form in 1982.

Popular perception, as usual, is wrong.

With its colorful weather pages and "Snapshots" trivia, what became known as "McPaper" left many talking about graphics. To find the first people actually *doing* something with graphics, however, you must travel beyond the pyramids and hieroglyphics to cave drawings and pictograms that became the symbols upon which the first alphabets were based.

We won't spend a lot of time on a theoretical look into how people perceive things, nor will we offer a dissertation on the history of graphics. But if you've ever cringed at the thought of having your finest work being labeled a "Big Mac attack," you may want to read on. You'll quickly learn that graphics have a solid position in history. For centuries they served not as trendy, artsy fluff but as powerful, serious communicators.

Not all text is poetry, and not all graphics are art. This point certainly wasn't lost on some of the greatest thinkers in the history of Western civilization. Many of them routinely included information graphics in their written works. And seldom did anyone accuse them of pandering to MTV-depraved, illiterate masses.

The Medium

The Techniques

The Forms

The Profession

As you'll learn in the next few pages, graphics predate not only today's graphics-laden media but also written language itself. Graphics influenced the prehistoric development of writing. From ancient years to the Renaissance, authors effortlessly mixed visual and verbal forms as they crafted the documents upon which Western civilization was founded. Only when technology intervened in the form of moveable type did visual expression become something done only by artists.

This technologically induced split of the verbal from the visual led many to regard words as serious and graphics as frivolous. But it also led to a honing of visual tools. As industrialization began, graphics designers invented more powerful techniques for presenting large amounts of data in charts and maps. They even began exploring how graphics could be more efficient than text in showing readers the "big picture" of what large collections of data meant.

At the dawn of an information age in the 1980s, newspapers began calling for tools capable of doing what graphics could—helping readers once again see the "big picture." At first, efforts became mired in confusion lingering from the technological separation of visual and verbal expression. Artwork, not graphics, answered the call. In the 1980s and '90s, however, desktop publishing re-created the ability to mix visual and verbal forms. In the process, a golden age of information design was born.

In the Beginning...

Prehistoric forerunners of both verbal and visual journalism coexisted in cave drawings of the Paleolithic and Neolithic eras (35,000–4,000 BC). Without a prehistoric Rosetta Stone to suggest the drawings' true purpose, scholars may only speculate why pre-civilized humans inscribed these elementary symbols or pictures, called petroglyphs, on their dwellings' walls. The fields of archaeology, anthropology, prehistoric linguistics and art history all debate the images' meaning and their links to modern concepts of art and language.

Were the ancient cave dwellers, by drawing animals and placing markings next to them, deifying beasts in the way indigenous American populations did 1,000 years ago? Were they decorating their homes with familiar images and simple patterns, forming treasured icons? Or were they, in graphics journalism fashion, preparing training rituals for their young, reporting the results of bountiful hunts or otherwise recording day-to-day history in what today would be known as a "visually literate" style?

Whatever their true purpose, petroglyphic symbols such as those in Figure 1.1 became simpler and more stylized as they evolved into separate communication forms—pictorial art and linguistic writing. These two components would reunite millennia later in the modern practice of information design.

1.1

Petroglyphic symbols such as these have been found world-wide.

The ABCs of Graphics

Alphabets began to appear when symbols that looked like the objects they represented got so simple or stylized that their resemblance to reality was no longer apparent. These symbols began being associated with sounds—initially, with the sounds the symbols might have made. Imagine the word splash, which even today sounds like what it is, and a symbol for it that looks something like a splash of water. In some now-forgotten cave, such a symbol might have become only a wavy line, such as the letter S. When a similar-sounding word such as "splice" came along, it too might have been denoted by a modified version of the same symbol. Abstract concepts also had symbols and words to express them. Slowly, the collection of what originally were sound- and picture-based symbols became "letters" that could be used to spell out unrelated words. Although no one thinks this is actually how the letter S began (in fact, the suggestion here could not be true), the analogy shows how visually semiotic representations of onomatopoetic sounds may have created our alphabet out of pictures.

An ancient precursor of information graphics may have existed among Egyptians, who combined Sumerian "letters" and their own pictures to form hieroglyphics from 3100 BC–AD 394. It was not until 1799, when the Rosetta Stone translation of a common text into known and unknown languages was discovered, that this combination of symbols and letters was recognized as illustrated writing, in many ways similar to icon and text combinations used in information graphics today.

Illustration and writing continued along frequently crossing paths through Greek, Roman and medieval times (600–1500 AD). This is perhaps represented best in the prized illuminated manuscripts of medieval Christians, described by design historian Philip B. Meggs as "cinematic graphic sequences, not unlike comic books of today."

Putting the Graph into Graphics

Toward the end of this period came the first works in which graphics began to be used not merely for pictorial representations but also as representations of quantitative data—as the charts and graphs we know today.

One of the first to use such methods was Nicole d'Orseme (1352–1382), bishop of Lisieux, who combined figures into groups and graphed them. Another pioneer in this, as in many other fields, was Leonardo da Vinci (1452–1519), who charted astronomical, mathematical and geographical information. Simple but effective diagrams and pictures were featured in da Vinci's texts, wherever points that could benefit from visual elaboration were raised, as in Figure 1.2. Philosopher René Descartes (1596–1650), the developer of geometry, also made substantial use of graphs in his texts. Sir Isaac Newton (1642–1727), who documented gravity, continued the trend in his handwritten work.

1.2

Leonardo da Vinci mixes graphics and text in his *Treatise on Painting*.

Before industrialization, illustrations and text were handwritten. The introduction of moveable-type presses by Johann Gutenberg (1400–1468) spelled the beginning of the end to this trend and to the easy integration of text and images. To be reproduced on mass-market presses, images had to be hand-etched. The etchings were then mounted on blocks, making them difficult to insert into intricately arranged, pre-manufactured type. Text and graphics thus came to be physically separated into different parts of published works and, as a result, had separate roles. Technology, in modern times regarded as a great exponent of graphics, was at this point in history its enemy.

Segregation of verbal and visual expression has persisted in one form or another ever since. It may in fact have led to a subtle intellectual disdain for visual communication that exists today. Researcher Albert D. Biderman, lamenting the impact of this segregation of information graphics, concludes:

> *The exigencies of typography that moved graphics to a segregated position in the printed work have in the past contributed to their intellectual segregation and marginality as well. There was a corresponding organizational segregation, with decisions on graphics often passing out of the hands of the original analyst*

and communicator into those of graphic specialists—the
commercial artists and designers and audio-visual aids shops,
for example—whose predilections and skills are usually more
those of cosmeticians and merchandisers than of scientific
analysts and communicators.

"Cosmeticians and merchandisers"—Biderman's words for artists and salespeople—were indeed the most significant users of graphics after Gutenberg, but scientific "analysts and communicators," as he calls them, also used graphics during this period. Although the term "graphic designer" was not coined until 1922 by artist William Addison Dwiggins, specialists in presenting information visually began appearing in the 18th century. Confined to visual tools alone, these visual information specialists were forced to forge new tools, enabling visual expression to effectively convey complex messages.

Appropriately, one of the first of these pioneers was a contemporary of America's founding fathers: William Playfair (1759–1823). Contemporaneous to the birth of modern journalism, scant years after the John Peter Zenger trial (1734–35), before the adoption of the First Amendment (1791) and amid the rise of the Fourth Estate, Playfair began a type of graphics journalism that many did not believe to exist until the founding of *USA Today*.

The Quest for a Graphical Eden

William Playfair spent most of his life in the shadow of his older brother John, a leading Scottish mathematician, geologist and geographer whose quite banal accomplishments still merit a mention in *Webster's Biographical Dictionary*. William, the closest thing that graphics has to a hero, remains unrecognized in the word-filled world of *Webster's*.

Impatient with the academic rigors of his chosen trade, industrial drafting, William set off at age 25 to create a new journalistic form: the information graphic. The fruit of his labor was *The Commercial & Political Atlas,* published in London in 1786 and including 44 graphics, most of which were line (or fever) charts, as in Figure 1.3, or bar graphs. Among them was the first known series of charts representing changes in data over time, a classic source of graphics material today.

1.3

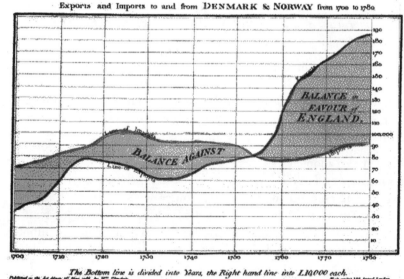

Exports and Imports to and from DENMARK & NORWAY from 1700 to 1780

The Bottom line is divided into Years, the Right hand line into L10,000 each.

William Playfair's *The Commerical & Political Atlas* includes this hand-colored graphic detailing Great Britain's balance of trade with Norway and Denmark.

Statistician Edward Tufte writes that Playfair "developed or improved upon nearly all of the fundamental graphical designs, seeking to replace conventional tables of numbers with the systematic visual representations of his 'linear arithmetic.'" Playfair also possessed an uncanny sense for his creations' usefulness, attraction and memorability, writing in a note accompanying one of his charts:

> *The amount of mercantile transactions in money, and as profit or loss, are capable of being as easily represented in drawing, as any part of space, or as the face of a country; though, till now, it has not been attempted. Upon that principle these Charts are made; and, while they give a simple and distinct idea, they are as near perfect accuracy as is any way useful. On inspecting any one of these Charts attentively, a sufficiently distinct impression will be made, to remain unimpaired for a considerable time, and the idea which does remain will be simple and complete, at once including the duration and the amount.*

Playfair went on in subsequent works to create other new forms of visual expression. In his *Statistical Breviary* (1801), he represents quantities as different sizes of circles in what are regarded as the first instances of area charts. He then divides circles into component pieces in his *Statistical Abstract of the United States* (1805), creating the modern pie chart.

By abandoning a literal, metaphorical approach that likened data to piles of items, Playfair "broke free of analogies to the physical world and drew graphics as designs-in-themselves," Tufte notes. In doing so, he furthered the quest, begun in Paleolithic times, for symbolically representing ideas rather than simply depicting items.

Playfair also adopted a strategy of adjusting monetary totals to account for inflation and developed a cleaner look to his charts, emphasizing data and de-emphasizing technical accouterments. He added color by hand and evaluative labels at key points, and commented in his text: "By this method, as much information may be obtained in five minutes as would require whole days to imprint on the memory."

Despite his uncanny sense for what scientific research later would prove, Playfair's revolutionary ideas failed to cross the Atlantic and affect American journalism for more than a century. The first inklings of interest, fellow Briton Nigel Holmes notes, came after the Wall Street crash of 1929 produced a soaring preoccupation with financial data.

New Ways Flourish in Old World

While the industrialized American press was unwilling or unable to invest in the laborious methods Playfair employed, Europe embraced his approach. Among the early adopters of Playfair's techniques was French engineer Charles Joseph Minard (1781–1870), who advanced the data map, linking geography with statistics and history. Without digressing too far into a history of cartography, suffice it to say that before Minard, data maps had stressed geography, not data and its relation to it. As early as 1100 AD, China had produced data maps such as the Yü Chi Thu, or Map of the Tracks of Yü the Great. Europe saw its first data maps of this sort after 1550 AD. Among them was John Snow's map locating cholera deaths in London, a map that led to the identification of a contaminated well, saving many lives. What Minard did to change this field was to create a new form of data map that stressed data over geography.

Representing not merely locations, Minard's maps reported in time and amount. Using lines of proportionate thickness, he charted trade routes and trade volumes simultaneously. Using multiple chartings integrated with geography, he told the story of Napoleon's 1812 Russia campaign, creating a graphic that Tufte says "may well be the best statistical graphic ever drawn."

Keep It Simple

Minard's work was loaded with data—too loaded, perhaps, for today's standards and certainly too loaded for the style of the Modernists who followed him.

Sociologist Otto Neurath (1882–1945) led this movement with the development of the "Vienna method," a style that placed a premium on simple images. A classic example of this style, which banned "irrelevant, decorative elements" and instead used simple pictograms (or icons), is shown in Figure 1.4. Under Neurath's direction, the Vienna Museum of Social and Economic Studies undertook a massive visual reference project, reporting in graphic form virtually every topic documented in statistical data.

1.4

The simple pictographic style of Otto Neurath's "Vienna method" is used to compare German marriage rates in the 1910s and '20s.

Upon relocating to Holland in 1934, Neurath expanded his quest to
include a search for a world language without words. This pictographic
communication system became known as the International System of
Typographic Picture Education, or Isotype movement.

Isotype, coinciding with the Modern Art movement, had a profound
impact on graphics and design world-wide. The influence continues to
be felt today in such things as road signs and international symbols on
office equipment and machinery, which are discussed further in
Chapter 6. In style and substance, graphics created in Neurath's Vienna
project are indistinguishable from newspaper graphics today. Many
enduring works emerged under the influence of his method. In 1933,
draftsman Henry C. Beck won a design competition by creating the
world's first intentionally schematic map, which stressed, as Isotype
would, function over precise geography. The map survives to this day as
the basic route guide, posted in each station, for the London Underground, shown in Figure 1.5.

1.5

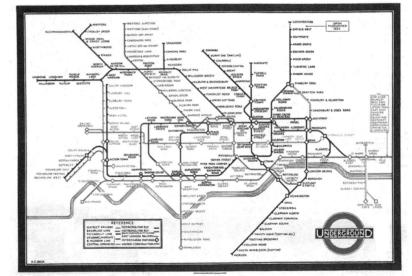

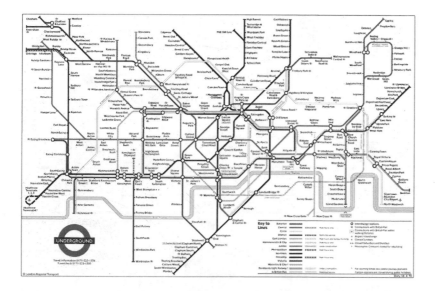

Today's London Underground route map retains the basic simpicity of Henry C. Beck's original route map, stressing function over geography.

While Neurath saw symbols as ways to increase communication, his successors took graphic design beyond mere semiotic icons. Piet Zwart (1885–1977), who called himself a "Typotekt," or typographical architect, stressed design as a means to improve communicative efficiency. Ladislav Sutnar (1897–1976) synthesized the two approaches into a movement for functional design.

In the graphically isolated US, however, a purely artistic mode of traditional illustration remained pre-eminent. This changed, however, with the market crash of 1929 and European immigration of the 1930s. Another key event was a seminal trip by Sutnar to New York City to design material for the 1939 World's Fair, regarded by many as a pivotal point in the development of US culture.

Praised for having a Continental flavor, graphics like Sutnar's began catching on in the States. The same year as the fair, *Fortune* magazine published a page of bar charts (see Figure 1.6), highlighting results of a business survey. The *Chicago Tribune*, a pioneer in graphics use, likewise published a page-wide graphic exploration of the Maginot Line. While neither presentation was totally representative of the Isotype movement or of Sutnar's invocation for functionality, each makes use of Isotype-style pictograms, even if many are rendered in the more illustrative style that dominated American artwork.

1.6   LABOR UNIONS

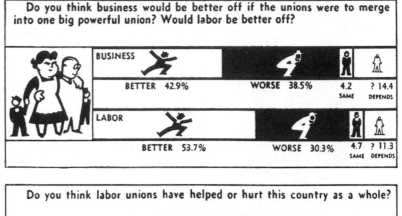

FOREIGN TRADE

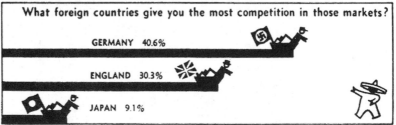

Fortune magazine used a chart to report the results of a 1939 survey.

Even the matron of American journalism, *The New York Times*, was using graphics in the era between the two World Wars. As a cultural leader, it did not wait for Sutnar's visit to employ elements of his Continental style. In the 1920s, when even photographs were unusual on its front page, the *Times* was far from unacquainted with information graphics. As shown in Figure 1.7, the November 3, 1920 front page features a large shade-coded map, a standard of post-election coverage, reporting state-by-state how Warren G. Harding had won the presidential election. In a chronological *Times* retrospective, the surprisingly modern graphic appears several pages, and several years, before the first photo, a startling image of the Hindenburg disaster.

1.7

Warren G. Harding's victory in the 1920 presidential election was reported graphically by *The New York Times*.

The players thus were ready and the stage clearly was set. Only one obstacle remained to be conquered before informational graphics were to become part of the regular fare in American newspapers: time.

The Challenge of Serpentine Growth

In the decades before desktop publishing, producing information graphics remained a laborious, virtuoso effort, employing time-consuming techniques not much advanced from Gutenberg's day. An artist armed with a Rapidograph pen would draw each line by hand. Type would be set and proofed so it could be pasted onto the drawing, and the finished graphic, with each shaded panel cut by hand, would be photo-mechanically etched onto a printing element.

Only the largest newspapers, and those committed to information graphics, could afford the luxury of this low-tech process. As a result, little attention was paid to the field by newspapers without the re-sources of a Chicago or New York giant. All the while, the American art community, influenced in the 1930s and 1940s by Modernism and Sutnar's work, began moving toward more emotive artistic styles, discarding the calculated style of functionalism. While immigration brought to the US "the Modernist tradition that was the product of the visual, social, and scientific revolution in Europe," as art historian Mildred Friedman notes, so too did it bring other artistic approaches less concerned with communication science and efficiency.

In revolt against the Industrial Revolution came the throwback ornamented style of William Morris (1834–1896), the cubism of Pablo Picasso (1881–1973), the rule abandonment of Dadaism, the figurative and ornamental appeal of Art Deco, the neo-classical Futurist move-ment and the Freudian-inspired Surrealist style. These arrived in an art community pre-disposed, historian Angela E. Davis notes, to "elitist 'fine' or 'high' art" and disdaining commercial art, which was regarded derisively as dealing with "the common life of society, a process centered increasingly around the concept of mass communication." Approaches such as functionalism and its associated Bauhaus or Swiss methods fell out of favor.

As designer Paul Rand commented, the history of graphics in America is "the history of a struggle between the craftsman and the creative artist, between common sense and sentimentality." As America advanced from the postwar era to the Vietnam era, creativity and sentimentality held the upper hand.

Nevertheless, pressure for common sense graphics and efficient communication was mounting. As early as 1962, researchers Arthur T. Turnbull and Russell N. Baird asserted: "Graphic communication today is the lifeblood of our economic, political, and cultural existence." Invoking newly formulated information theory, they valued the role graphics could play in facilitating the decoding of messages. Graphics, they noted, caused the messages to rise above the "noise" of distractions:

> *We know, for example, that readers will overcome formidable graphic obstacles to get information they strongly desire. Students scan a monotonous list of scores presented in small type to find the results of their school's football game. The interest in content is so great that the graphics play only a secondary role. On the other side of the coin, however, rests the wastebasket fate of vast quantities of printed material. Tests have proven that material of the same content has been received, read and acted upon in one form, but discarded in another. These examples, coupled with the knowledge that every reader is offered much more than he can ever assimilate, assert that graphic techniques are too important to be ignored.*

Little did the authors know how prophetic their words would be. At the time there was no Internet, no CNN, no cable TV. In many markets, national and local newscasts were 15 minutes long and occurred only twice a day—less often on weekends. Typically, no more than three TV channels were available per city, and daily newspapers' circulations were at all-time highs. By the 1980s, however, this information explosion (see Figure 1.8) was putting even more "noise" between message and receiver. The need for efficient graphics became even more imperative. No longer did readers seem willing to scan "monotonous lists," as Turnbull and Baird had called them; alternative media provided the same information with fewer obstacles. News was available day or night, and in quite visual fashion. Even hard-core "news junkies" could overdose on the offerings. Circulations plummeted as newspapers' "monotonous" yet comprehensive fare increasingly fell victim to visual yet incomplete offerings of rival media.

1.8

1960s   TV evening news
             "60 Minutes"
             Expanded local newscasts
1970s   All-news radio
             National Public Radio
             Cable superstations
1980s   Computer bulletin boards
             C-SPAN
             CNN Headline News
1990s   Fax newspapers
             Court TV
             Internet newsgroups
             World Wide Web

An information explosion has increased the need for graphics.

The resulting progression of efficient graphics for newspaper use is documented in the works of the premier US visual journalist of the 1960s through early '80s, Edmund C. Arnold. Arnold, despite being strongly influenced by Sutnar's concepts, makes no meaningful references to information graphics in his 1968 book, *Modern Newspaper Design*. In 1981, however, a full year before *USA Today* was born, he acknowledges the field, in his final major work, *Designing the Total Newspaper*:

> *A popular but rather vague term is graphics. 'Graphics' seems to mean—as Alice was informed in Wonderland—'just what I want it to mean.' And it seems everyone who uses the word wants it to mean something a little different from other user's meanings. Harold Evans of the* Sunday Times *of London divides graphics into 'information' and 'flavor' categories. A flavor graphic is primarily an ornamentation, a mood-setter; the information graphic transmits specific information. American typographers often use 'graphics' to describe not only a single pictorial element but more often also the grouping of elements in a striking or unusual fashion. If you have a good definition of 'graphics,' please turn to the glossary at the end of the this book and write it down there.*

The functionalist Arnold's frustration with definitions reflects the confusion that abounded in 1981. Sensing a need for graphic elements, as Turnbull and Baird had predicted, newspapers turned to artists as never before. By the end of a 1980 *New York Times* retrospective of its most famous front pages, graphics, particularly maps, appear to have become near fixtures on the paper's otherwise less-than-visual front page: A modern sequence map shows the failed US effort to rescue hostages from Iran in 1980 (see Figure 1.9). An bar chart summarizes poll results as a preview of the Gerald Ford–Jimmy Carter presidential election in 1976 (see Figure 1.10). A sophisticated pictogram of US and Soviet nuclear arsenals accompanies a 1972 story about the signing of arms accords (see Figure 1.11). A stylish sequence graphic tells of the Gemini 6 space rendezvous in 1965 (see Figure 1.12).

By 1981, other newspapers were using graphics as well. While some remained relatively true to the efficient and functional Modernist approach of Sutnar and Isotype, others—more influenced by art trends than by traditions of communication efficiency—looked for other models like those found a year later by *USA Today*. Credited with creating a trend that began long before its birth, *USA Today* was still among the first in the United States to commit to using graphics every day. Yet with such mind-numbing Page 1 offerings as the type of bread—white, wheat or rye—preferred by members of Congress, this "new form" newspaper may have served more as an anti-hero than as a trailblazing pioneer in graphics use. Part of the reason may have been its conscious decision to model its graphics after the whimsical "chartoons," or cartoon charts, popularized in the '60s and '70s by *Time* magazine designer Nigel Holmes.

Holmes, a Briton, was influenced by post-Isotype trends that emerged in Europe in the mid-'50s. A main influence was the German newsmagazine *Der Spiegel*, which broke with Isotype's disdain for "confusing" three-dimensional artwork (see Figure 1.13). It began publishing more artistic graphics and became the forerunner of the illustrated style developed by Holmes and furthered by *USA Today*.

1.9

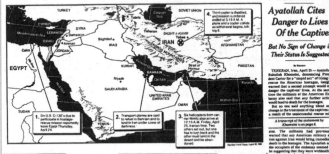

1.10

1.11

The New York Times

VOL. CXXI...No.41,762   NEW YORK, SATURDAY, MAY 27, 1972   15 CENTS

U.S. AND SOVIET SIGN TWO ARMS ACCORDS TO LIMIT GROWTH OF ATOMIC ARSENALS; TRADE PACT DELAYED, TALKS TO GO ON

Joint Commission Set Up To Resolve Trade Issues

By ROBERT B. SEMPLE Jr.

MOSCOW, May 26—The United States and the Soviet Union announced today a joint commission to devise a comprehensive trade agreement that has proved impossible to reach during President Nixon's visit to Moscow.

U.S. TRADE DEFICIT BIG AGAIN IN APRIL

Imports Exceeded Exports by $699-Million, Second Largest Gap on Record

By EDWIN L. DALE Jr.

WASHINGTON, May 26—The United States recorded another huge deficit in its foreign trade in April, the Commerce Department reported today.

FOE PUSHES FIGHT IN TWO KEY AREAS

Losses Heavy, but Enemy Clings to Small Gains at Kontum and Hue

SAIGON, South Vietnam, Saturday, May 27—North Vietnamese soldiers hurled themselves against Government defenses in the Central Highlands city of Kontum and near the northern city of Hue through the day yesterday.

A First Step, but a Major Stride

By MAX FRANKEL

MOSCOW, Saturday, May 27—The nuclear age gained its first strategic arms limitation treaty in the Kremlin last night.

CEILINGS ARE SET

Nixon and Brezhnev Pledge to Abide by Treaty at Once

By HEDRICK SMITH

MOSCOW, May 27—President Nixon and the Soviet Communist party leader, Leonid I. Brezhnev, signed two historic arms agreements last night.

LAIRD DISCOUNTS BIG ARMS SAVINGS

Reaction to Pact in Capital Mostly Favorable but Some Conservatives Are Critical

By JUAN M. VASQUEZ

WASHINGTON, May 26—Defense Secretary Melvin R. Laird today hailed the United States arms agreements with the Soviet Union.

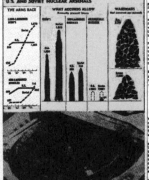

AFTER SIGNING: President Nixon and Leonid I. Brezhnev exchange treaty copies at Kremlin. In center, Soviet President Nikolai V. Podgorny.

Lindsay Aide Says Council Must Raise Taxes on Property

By FRANCIS X. CLINES

Court Throws Out Jersey Law Barring Primary Cross-Voting

NEWARK, May 26—New Jersey's primary election law prohibiting enrolled voters from casting ballots in other party contests was declared unconstitutional today by a three-judge Federal panel.

U.S. AND SOVIET NUCLEAR ARSENALS

Von Braun Will Leave NASA For Job in Aerospace Industry

By HAROLD M. SCHMECK Jr.

WASHINGTON, May 26—Dr. Wernher von Braun, one of the chief architects of man's first landing on the moon, is retiring from the National Aeronautics and Space Administration.

1.12

The New York Times, which published graphics like these from 1965 to 1980, has a far better claim than does *USA Today* to being the initial proponent of American newspaper graphics.

1.13

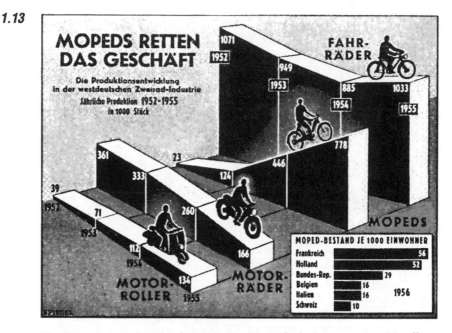

The German magazine *Der Spiegel* veered from the Isotype movement to offer more artistic, three-dimensional graphics, like this one on moped, motorcycle and motor scooter registrations in 1956.

Similar transformations were present in other areas of graphic design as well. Rand, a longtime Modernist, is credited for example with founding the New York School, stressing whimsical but still universally understood symbols like those of Holmes (see Figure 1.14). Reflecting the self-absorbed social attitudes of the 1970s, this movement eventually broadened to become Post-Modernism—a more personal, less technical style that sacrifices legibility for the sake of artwork and a sense of "feeling right," something that Isotype and functional design would reject.

1.14

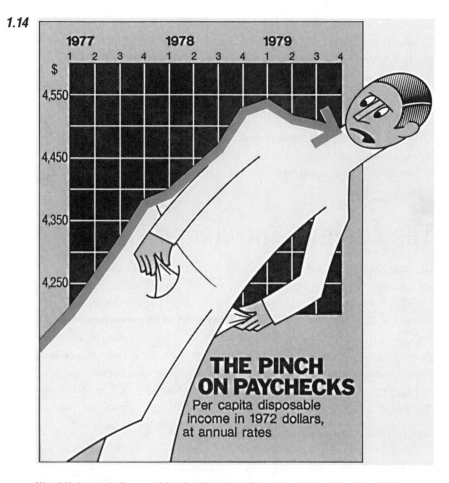

Nigel Holmes, influenced by the New York School, added whimsy to 1970s graphics in *Time* magazine.

Information designers approaching the profession from art backgrounds brought New York School and Post-Modern ideas into the 1980s. Designers approaching the profession from more traditional information analyst or journalistic backgrounds remained rooted in the Isotype approach and the principles of functional design advocated by Sutnar and Arnold, "the grandfather of newspaper design."

Meanwhile, new-age designers such as Robert Lockwood and Mario R. Garcia began adopting different approaches, based less on information theory, which had driven functionalism, and more on semiotics and the subtle dissonance of familiar images and color. The result was an unusual state of concurrently competing design strategies among America's traditionally designed newspapers. On newspaper weather pages, where *USA Today*'s influence is most frequently cited, little response was noted among the nation's 230 largest newspapers. However, small, group-owned dailies emulated the look and feel that Holmes, Rand, and *USA Today* had inspired.

Different approaches continue to this day, and the differences probably would have been exaggerated as graphics became increasingly prevalent—save for another development that fueled the use of graphics: the personal computer.

The Apple of Knowledge

In September 1982, while *USA Today* was being brought to life, a technology was emerging that would revolutionize graphics production. Invented in 1974 and mass-marketed in 1978, the desktop computer afforded tremendous capabilities. While newspapers were published using typesetting equipment driven by room-size, 8-bit processors equipped with 32 kilobytes of memory (less powerful than pocket calculators today), personal computers provided more digital horsepower and put it all under the reins of a single user. The introduction in 1985 of the first inexpensive laser printer, capable of reproduction-quality output, completed the revolution. "Desktop publishing" became more than just a casual phrase.

Before the desktop computer, multi-million dollar systems and printers received initial use at newspapers like *The New York Times,* where art department workloads were reduced by 15 to 20 hours a week. The advent of inexpensive, easy-to-use desktop machines like the Apple Macintosh, introduced in 1984, led to even greater time savings and more affordable graphics. With a half-megabyte of memory, a 16-bit processor, a small black-and-white screen, an external 20-megabyte hard drive and bundled software called MacDraw, the Mac and, in particular, its Apple Laserwriter printer, put quick and easy graphics within the reach of every newspaper.

By 1988, the rush to adopt new graphics technology reached breakneck speed. Newspaper art departments clamored to convert, and editors predicted tremendous growth in graphics use. Wire services quickly entered the race. Moving from telephone lines to satellite delivery systems, the Associated Press, the Knight-Ridder-Tribune News Service, the New York Times News Service and the Gannett News Service began offering graphics just as they offered news stories by wire. By 1989, each was distributing half a dozen or more infographics to newspapers world-wide every day.

No longer was it necessary to have staffs of skilled artists, each experienced in the complicated techniques of hand-drawn art. A single journalist, even one incapable of drawing a straight line with a Rapidograph, could out-produce a typical art department by using a single Mac and graphics offered by the news services. More important, graphics creators could concentrate not only on the art of their graphics, but also on their graphics' news value—on creating "information" rather than "flavor" graphics. At some newspapers, artists trained in sketching and technical drawing were replaced by more traditional journalists, using technology to make up for lack of technical art skills. Similar developments occurred in other fields as desktop publishing revolutionized the industry and brought what formerly had been communications specialties within the reach of non-communications businesses.

The trend continued as the technology improved. Computers grew to include 32-bit processors, 64 MB of memory, 2,048 MB of storage and scanners capable of electronically rendering photos and artwork. Even the most cynical of traditionalists began being won over. Graphics editors became powerful forces within newsrooms and graphics became so popular that readers following significant stories asked for printouts of unpublished graphics that had been cut due to space limitations. Requests were made for information graphics to be recognized by the Pulitzer Prize committee.

Initial offerings by non-artists were at times simple, boxy graphics, revealing a lack of the visual training that their artist predecessors possessed. As the '90s arrived, the divergent talents of artists and writers were combined, as they created graphics side-by-side, and the modern age of newspaper information graphics began.

Statistician Tufte's writings reflect this trend. In his self-published 1982 work, *Visual Display of Quantitative Information,* Tufte advocates a strictly statistical, almost clinical approach to visual communication, disdaining tenets of the Isotype movement. While he does not advocate liberal use of artistic humor in graphics the same way Holmes did, Tufte's 1990 work, *Envisioning Information*, reveals Tufte to be enamored of more sophisticated approaches. In that work, released even as he moved from Connecticut to Illinois, he urges graphics creators to "escape from flatland."

Supporting this transformation came a growing appreciation for the communicative powers and limitations of visual journalism. In 1990, Eye-Trac research conducted by the Gallup Organization for Garcia and the Poynter Institute concluded that visual elements possessed greater power than originally thought. Using computerized headgear that recorded what readers saw on a page, researchers persuasively demonstrated how visual elements attracted tremendous attention. More important, in follow-up comprehension studies, researchers at Poynter and elsewhere discovered that visual elements produced more memorable impressions than presentations consisting of words alone and conveyed information more rapidly.

What Poynter billed as the most significant finding was perhaps most telling:

> *There's no doubt color and compelling design attract readers to newspapers and advertising, but it's the editor's imaginative approach to articulating and presenting the news that makes the difference.*

Manifestations of the importance of that difference were reported from other studies. Chartoons, such as Holmes' (see Figure 1.17), produced mixed results, faring poorly in some studies. Graphics containing mostly decorative, non-informative icons met with similar results, and complex images were found to confuse readers. More clues than mere visual representations were needed, and three-dimensional artwork, while pleasing to the eye, often proved disastrous to comprehension.

Such limiting factors came as no surprise to researchers at the Institut für Kommunickations-Forschung Beate von Keitz at Saarbrucken, Germany, who warned earlier that conclusions based on Garcia's Eye-Trac research swept too far. Working from what theoreticians call a Gestalt perceptual perspective, they had similar eye-tracking gear for nearly a decade, noting how photo captions, headlines, news summaries and indexes attracted far more attention than anything else on a newspaper page. Rather than merely compelling attention as readers explored pages, graphics, they theorized, must effectively convey information during separate orientation, processing and reading phases for each page.

While investigation is needed to confirm preliminary indications of how this can be done most effectively, a trend toward smaller graphics, along the lines of da Vinci's and Playfair's, is underway. Several major newspapers, including such early adopters as *The New York Times* and the *Chicago Tribune,* are leading the move in this direction.

Even Holmes, father of the "chartoon," has been drawn to this way of thinking, foreseeing what he terms "a backlash against overproduced things." Graphics, he predicts, will get simpler and start to play more of "the explaining role they ought to do"—the same role they had on the walls of Paleolithic caves more than six millennia ago.

To Help You Think Visually

To see how prevalent graphics really are, pick up a copy of your favorite daily newspaper and note the first five things you find that are not headlines, paragraphed text, photographs or advertising. You can do much the same going through an annual report, a magazine, a research white paper or a flyer promoting a new product and its specifications.

1. How many pages did you have to go through before finding them?

2. As you were leafing through the pages without reading them, did the information from the graphics seem to be more prominent than the information in the text?

3. In your opinion, did the items you found justify their use of space?

How to Tell When a Graphic Is Needed

If the sun rises in the east, it's not a story. If the sun rises in the west, break out the end-of-the-world type for a banner headline. Even if you're not a journalist, it's easy to determine when news stories are needed. It's far less easy to determine when graphics are needed.

Almost anything that appears in a newspaper, a newsletter or any type of report can have a graphic. Not all need one, however. Your ability to decide which do need a graphic and which don't may determine whether you someday find yourself driven to an early grave or to an awards banquet honoring your prowess as a visual communicator.

News stories try to answer the five Ws and two Hs—who, what, when, where, why, how and how much. Sometimes the first clue that a graphic may be needed is when one of these questions seems more important than the others in explaining what's new. Rank each tidbit of information hierarchically, with the most important new tidbits first. Then see which of the five Ws and two Hs is answered by the most important point. That's the kind of story you'll be telling and it could give you a clue as to the kind of graphic that may be needed:

A "who" story	A **bio box** of the person profiled or breakout of the cast of characters (See Chapter 11)
A "what" story	A **breakout** of the provisions (See Chapter 11)
A "when" story	A **time line** of the history or schedule for the future (See Chapter 13)
A "where" story	A **map** (See Chapter 14)
A "why" story	A pro-and-con **breakout** (See Chapter 11)
A "how" story	A **sequence** or process graphic, flow chart or **diagram** (See Chapters 13 and 14)

Are you surprised that only if the story focuses on the often-ignored "how much" do traditional bar, fever and pie charts come into play? You shouldn't be. The assumption that numbers are the only thing that graphics are made of is one of the first mistakes that neophyte information designers make. Only if a set of numbers actually **tells** the story is a graphic featuring numbers (discussed in Chapter 12) in order. Otherwise, you fall victim to the same knee-jerk style of decorative design that has people clamoring to get photographs of every person mentioned in an article.

If, for example, a company's stagnant sales explain why its board has hired a new chief executive, sales data would be the most informative graphic. But if there's no link between sales and the hiring of the new CEO, why include such a graphic just to have a chart with your report?

Because *USA Today* and the business section of your local newspaper might do so does not make it right. Knee-jerk graphics add nothing more than needless decoration. This hearkens back to a newspaper map a few years ago that located Waco, Texas, scene of the Branch Davidian religious cult standoff. Included with the map was a statement that everyone now knew where the town was located, thanks to months of recent news coverage. A graphic that re-reports the obvious is no more important than a story about the sun rising in the east.

Graphics often are created after text is written, yet readers are likely to read graphics before, not after, looking at the text. If a graphic doesn't tell the story, readers may decide, without ever sampling the accompanying text, that it doesn't either.

If the Acme Furniture Company is trying to market a new suspension system for its sofas, the product brochure it creates probably will discuss how the system works and why it is better than a competitor's. Graphically, the brochure might include a pro-and-con table, comparing the two systems side-by-side (a "why" graphic). It might include a diagram showing its construction (a "how" graphic) or a breakout highlighting its advantages (a "what" graphic). Better yet, it could combine all three into a single graphic that would answer the questions of what, how and why. What the graphics should not focus on is where the company is located, who its CEO is, how much it earned last year—things that aren't important to the story. A designer might work up a really nice chart from the numbers, but the numbers would not tell the story.

So if numbers rarely tell stories, what does?

Here's a list of code words that you can use to remind yourself when a graphic should be used. If these phrases appear in the first paragraphs of a news story or report, think about telling the story visually:

"Who" code words	Key players	The victims
	Who's next	The heroes
	Who's who	Joins an elite group

continues

"What" code words	Key points	Plan
	Agreement	Record-breaking
"When" code words	Chain of events	Key dates
	What's next	Looking back
	Chronology	Looking ahead
	Schedule	
"Where" code words	Police chase	Expansion
	Escape route	The neighborhood
	Trail of evidence	The region
"Why" code words	Pros and cons	The reasons
	Debate	The background
"How" code words	Plan of action	Reorganization
	Organization	How to
	Agreement	Step-by-step
"How much" code words	Budget	Projections
	The figures	Market share
	Expansion	

This is, of course, a cursory list. Add your own to serve as personal reminders, based on areas you deal with frequently. If, for example, you work in health care, you might add "physicians" to the "who" list, "medications" to the "what" list and "appointments" to the "when" list.

A good way to develop your personal list is to examine impressive, informative graphics. Look for code words in the text that accompany the graphics and add those words to your list in the appropriate category. If you frequently create graphics to accompany other people's text, you might want to forward your list to the writers you work with so that you can encourage them to alert you when code words come up.

Keep in mind that what is regarded as dull-but-important information can be enlivened by a graphic. Details of how Acme's new suspension system works might merely bog down a copywriter's sales pitch. Likewise, a well-written tale of a small town's fight not to succumb to environmental regulation over an endangered earthworm could suffer from having to include details about the worm. In the sales piece, an interesting graphic could enable the copy to make a less technical sales appeal. In the environmental story, the worm's tale could be turned into an engaging graphic, leaving quotes a reporter received to function as the story's narrative. Neither text nor graphic needs to tell every aspect of a story. Each can present what it tells best.

Different Graphics for Different Stories

Practice thinking visually by running down a list of topics from the front page of today's newspaper, the lineup of stories on this evening's television news, or the table of contents of your favorite magazine. Come up with at least one idea for a graphic for each of them.

We'll get you started with a few examples. As you'll see, there are many different ways to tell a story graphically. The one you choose depends on which part of the story is the most important.

Graphics are like wildflowers. When a graphic is appropriate to its information environment, it's beautiful. When it's out of context, it's just another weed. Each of the graphics in the next set of examples is an informational blossom within the context of that specific example, but an informational weed in the context of the others. Graphics that help tell the overall story make a contribution. Graphics that don't tell that story serve only to distract from the main point and should be weeded out.

> "Smallville Savings & Loan, the troubled local thrift that narrowly averted takeover by the Federal Deposit Insurance Corp. last year, today fired Jonathan Kent as its general manager and named Metropolis financier Lex Luthor to lead its attempt to recover from near bankruptcy."

A knee-jerk graphic might be to chart the S&L's historical woes. But that was yesterday's news. Today's news is more a "who" story, and the key people are Kent and Luthor. But watch out. A simple biographical sketch including his age, the college he went to, and how many kids he has might tell us who Luthor is, but it's more important to show exactly what he has done in the past that has a bearing on what he will do in the future. Keep in mind the advice of résumé specialists who emphasize structuring your résumé to focus on the individual job you seek. The bio box "résumé" you create for a newsworthy subject should be no different. It should briefly recount the key points of experience or ideas that pertain to the task at hand—in this case, the experiences Luthor has had in turning around financially troubled institutions.

If you want to tell the story graphically, you can take this a step further (see Figure 2.1) by detailing the amount of experience, or lack thereof, that his predecessor possessed in the same areas. Now you're telling the whole story—who's in, who's out, and why. If you can't answer these questions easily in a graphic, chances are there's more to this than you have uncovered.

2.1

A *USA Today*-style "bio box" highlights key differences. Note how essential words such as "Metropolis Savings," "6 banks," "farmer," "general store" and "Coyotes" are "punched" into bold type to make them stand out. Also note the graphic's vivid quality. More on these techniques in Chapter 3.

"Smallville Savings & Loan's new general manager unveiled a restructuring plan today that features a stringent crackdown on delinquent loans, divestiture of assets not producing income, and increased fees for most bank-related services."

The saga of Smallville's nearly failed thrift has now become a "what" story, with some "how much" elements as well. What's in order is a listing of the key actions proposed, highlighting their impact on the community. Like the "bio box" for the first-day story, this is another form of glance box, this one called a "breakout box." Key proposals are broken out of the story, and the graphic (see Figure 2.2) is organized hierarchically so that detailed information about each one is readily available.

Instead of forcing readers to wade through seven or eight more paragraphs about the restructuring, Figure 2.2 gives them a graphic that lets them instantly check what will happen to specific fees they pay or whether the loan they are late on will be accelerated. In many ways, breakouts are the graphic equivalent of what journalists call "nut graphs"—the essential meaning and impact of a story in a nutshell.

Breakouts are among the most powerful of what communications researchers and designers refer to as entry points. In many ways, they are like miniature headline-and-text combinations. Just as readers can skim a front page to determine which stories are of greatest interest to them, they can skim the main points of a breakout box in search of smaller pieces of information they want to retrieve. If produced in the inverted pyramid style explained in Chapter 3, breakouts are closer to outlines—with separate main, secondary and tertiary points—than they are to lists. As such, they alert readers to important factors that might not otherwise have received prominent mention in a headline or text.

In this example, the "what" breakout could easily be enhanced by adding "how much" elements to it. How much, for example, will each of the steps Luthor proposes save the S&L? How much will each of them cost an average S&L customer? Follow this line of thinking and once again you begin

2.2

A simple graphic itemizes key points that might not stand out in the text. Note again the "punched" bold. Organization, not vividness, is stressed is in this graphic. More on that in Chapter 3.

telling the whole story. In the process, you can make sure that the entire reading public, not just those attuned to corporate maneuvering, sees what is important about the story.

> "Smallville Savings & Loan's recently enacted restructuring plan is ahead of schedule, general manager Lex Luthor told the board of directors today. By next year, Luthor said, the troubled thrift looks to have its first profitable quarter in more than five years."

Obviously, this is a "when" graphic, with "how much" overtones. The trick is to avoid getting caught up in the past. We know the S&L has had its problems. Recounting them is old news. The real news is that the future looks brighter. Although you might want to include past troubles as secondary points, as explained in Chapter 3, the main point of the graphic should be the turnaround. In the process, the graphic can perform a valuable service by evaluating the general manager's claims.

Some of the general manager's changes already have been implemented, creating a track record that shows how well they have performed. A time line like the one in Figure 2.3 is what is needed. It can report each change and how much it has saved, and show how each change relates to the total savings goal. Such a graphic focuses attention not merely on Luthor's claim but also on the facts underlying it. If two months of higher fees have produced negligible results, can we trust Luthor's claim that the results will be tangible after a few more months? Our graphic might not contain the answer to that question, but it certainly could raise valid questions to prompt information gathering.

An excellent example of a graphic uncovering news happened a few years ago in a story about ozone pollution. "When" was the crucial angle. A graphic artist assigned to the story wanted to show how commuting's contribution to the problem had been alleviated. The chart he used was ozone levels by hour, which demonstrated that industrial pollution, not automobile pollution, was the main culprit. In his research, however, he discovered something that the newspaper's environmental reporter had not found: that hourly readings taken by state officers stopped at 4 p.m. each day, an hour or two before peak ozone pollution from evening drive time. It turned out that the state, in violation of federal rules, had been monitoring pollution only during normal office hours. When the US Environmental Protection Agency ordered that the monitoring be expanded, the state set a record for the number of ozone alerts called in one summer. Almost all of the alerts occurred because of readings taken after 4 p.m. A graphics journalist's diligence resulted in stricter emissions checks for autos and much cleaner air for the region.

2.3

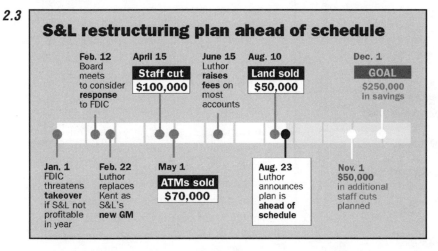

This timeline focuses on key facts by making them bigger and bolder. Non-essential material is eliminated.

"As part of its lagging restructuring plan, troubled Smallville Savings & Loan announced plans today to close seven of its 19 branches, including all three serving Smallville's central city."

"Where" is the question, and the answer is a map. But don't stop there. Locating branches that are closing doesn't **tell** the story; it only **illustrates** it. To truly tell the story, you need to show not only the branches that will close but also those that are staying open, as shown in Figure 2.4. More important, you should create a map that is shade-coded to show per-capita income in city neighborhoods. (Data to do this is available online from the US Census Bureau's TIGER map service, mentioned in greater detail in Chapters 4 and 13.) Chances

2.4

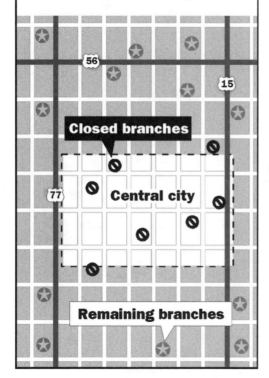

S&L closings hit central city hardest

All seven of the Smallville Savings & Loan branches being closed are in or near a 21-square-block area that the U.S. Census Bureau reports is the city's most impoverished neighborhood.

Closed branches

Central city

Remaining branches

This map answers the questions of "where" and "why." Note how background detail is kept to a minimum while key points are clearly labeled.

are, all seven of the branches being closed serve areas of below-average income, whereas all 12 of those remaining open serve areas of above-average income.

The secret of success for information analysts is never to lose track of their single most powerful investigative tool: human intuition. The mind is, after all, the world's most efficient analog computer. It instinctively sees patterns and trends that the biggest digital supercomputers have difficulty identifying. Yet all too often when we analyze information we get so caught up in methods and procedures that we fail to do what comes naturally. When presenting facts, we write such things as: "In response to reductions in federal Urban Development Action Grants, the Podunk Common Council voted five to four Thursday night to increase fares on the Podunk Area Rapid Transit System by an average of 25 percent," when what we really mean is: "Bus fares are going up 25 cents. Federal cuts are why. The vote on increasing fares was very close, 5-4."

The oldest rule of writing is to focus not on the task of writing but on what you have to say. You just saw something exciting and raced home to tell someone. The first words you write should be the first words you would say right after "Guess what I just saw?"

The same spirit should guide you to find the hidden story behind the facts. Rather than examining common threads, consulting additional data sources or spending time putting everything into a spreadsheet program, imagine that you're talking about the story with your hair stylist. When the conversation gets to the point of "Yeah, and I'll bet that means...," you'll know what needs to be followed up.

Graphics are great tools for quantifying what seems intuitive. They can, in a case like this, transform something that might sound like community whining into a provable assertion. It's not that the S&L hates central city residents or that its branches there are old and in need of repair; it's that the S&L doesn't want to do business with poor people, no matter where they live.

Graphics can be enterprising in other ways, too. Instead of charting just the Smallville S&L closings, why not go back a few years and add information about other financial institutions that have closed within those areas? By doing so you have a chance to go beyond the basic day-to-day story and report visually on a trend with larger implications.

> "In response to public outcry, a consortium of major lending institutions led by Smallville Savings & Loan today announced plans to provide special lending programs targeted at homebuyers and business owners in low-income areas of the city."

The graphic accompanying this story should show how these new programs work. A process graphic like the one in Figure 2.5 should quickly outline the steps that a home buyer or business owner must go through under the program. Such a graphic should specifically highlight how the program will or won't make it easier for these customers than other customers. Focusing attention on the process makes it difficult for lending institutions to get away with a smoke-and-mirrors campaign. If there's nothing to highlight, is there really a program?

Process graphics are difficult to construct because they require intimate knowledge of the procedure in order to simplify it so that key points can be emphasized. This requires much work but tends to be worth it. Producing a process graphic forces you to look beyond the hype for the concrete reality. It is much better journalism than increasingly common "he said, she said" litanies of reportage, which in the end are nothing more than rewrites of speeches and news releases.

Also appropriate for a story such as this would be a "why" graphic, outlining the pros and cons of increasing lending to impoverished areas.

2.5

Faster, easier loans proposed

Application
Shorter form requires only 10 minutes to complete and may be obtained and returned **by mail**.

Review
Rather than wait for loan committee to meet, banks will have one branch officer review form **within 24 hours**.

Approval
O.K.
All applications from central city will be **group-approved** as if they were for a single loan, combining all collateral.

Payout
Proceeds of loans will be paid **not to borrowers** but directly to seller of what's financed.

Process graphics answer the question of "how." Note yet again the use of "punched" bold and the reliance upon icons to identify topical areas.

"Citing its innovative program to encourage central city lending, Smallville Savings & Loan today announced record profits that complete its turnaround from near bankruptcy little more than a year ago."

Finally, you reach "how much," which in this case requires a graphic plotting profits, as in Figure 2.6. The storytelling nature of the graphic can be enhanced by highlighting when each policy changed. This emphasizes and evaluates the reported causal role each change had in completing the turnaround. Because the story has a strong "when" element, you also have an opportunity to merge "how much" data into a "when" timeline of the S&L's recovery.

As these examples indicate, graphics serve a much larger role than merely reciting data. You wouldn't think of putting footnotes in headline-size type, yet that's exactly what happens if graphics merely recite data rather than presenting deeper, essential messages.

A good test of a graphic is whether you can describe what it "tells"—not merely what it is about or shows. A weak graphic is about how a touchdown was scored; it shows the winning play. A strong graphic "tells" how the left guard made the key block that led to the winning score.

Make certain you focus on the main point and remember that graphics are beautiful only when they grow within that field. Anywhere else, they're just weeds.

In this world of information overload, we don't need graphics to present even more information. We need them to present evaluations of what that information means. They are too powerful a form of communication to waste on non-evalua-tive recitations of footnote material. Just as we don't put our footnotes first, we shouldn't let our graphics, which readers look at before text, convey anything less than the most impor-tant information. Simply put, graphics should report not the details but the story itself. If we as graphics professionals dedicate ourselves to this proposition, we can quickly eliminate the need for keeping books like this in plain brown wrappers.

2.6

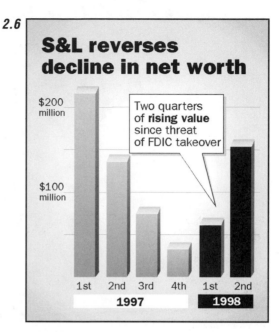

A chart like this tells "how much."

To Help You Think Visually

Return to your favorite daily newspaper or other publication and find five packages of text that do not have graphics but probably could have. Make sure each would involve a different type of graphic. For each of them, answer these questions:

1. What type of graphic would you envision for the story?

2. Why do you suppose the publication chose not to create such a graphic?

Chapter 3

Getting a Point Across

Historians tell us that journalism's peculiar form of narrative—putting the most important facts first and the least important last—is a Dow Jones-inspired legacy of the telegraph era, when no one was sure how long a connection would last. It continues today, when layout editors are unsure how long their news space will last. And it projects well into the future when, researchers tell us, we won't be sure how long a reader's attention will last.

Inverted pyramid, as this style of writing is known, has a simple credo: If you want to make a point, make it quickly. This is as true for graphics as it is for news stories.

- **Start with the main point.** If you're doing a graphic on consumer prices, make sure the latest movement in the price index is loud and clear.

- **Go on to the secondary point.** Cut the visual volume a bit and show how the latest number fits in with recent trends.

- **Offer supporting details.** Reduce the volume and provide actual figures for each month along with such information as the source and other lesser facts.

As publications have become more "designed," graphics and other visual elements increasingly have provided the inverted pyramid clues that text used to be relied upon to provide. Years ago, readers could read the first paragraph or two of a story to decide whether its main point was interesting. Now, if you believe Eye-Trac studies, readers tend to look at headlines and graphics for such information, getting to the text only after they have made up their minds on whether the topic is interesting.

This has liberated writers to pursue more narrative approaches, which do not demand that essential facts be placed in the first paragraph. These writing patterns, however, place considerable responsibilities on graphic designers to efficiently convey important information without letting less important material get in the way.

Such responsibilities aren't confined to journalistic designers, either. Copywriters, teachers, researchers—any communicator knows that subtlety is rarely the best policy when readers are looking for specific information. Remember the last time you tried to assemble one of those "some assembly required" projects that any 10-year-old is supposed to be able to put together? What was the first thing you looked at: the words on the instruction sheet or the sketch of what the finished product was supposed to look like? The main point needs to get across first and foremost, whether you're working for a newspaper or a toymaker.

The Main Point

Nigel Holmes, who after more than 15 years recently left *Time* magazine to become a consultant, explains that a good graphic should have a beginning, a middle and an end. Just like text, a graphic should tell a story. If so, the graphic's main point—the visual elements that convey its essential information, as explained in Figures 3.1 and 3.2—becomes the equivalent of a news story's headline and lead.

3.1

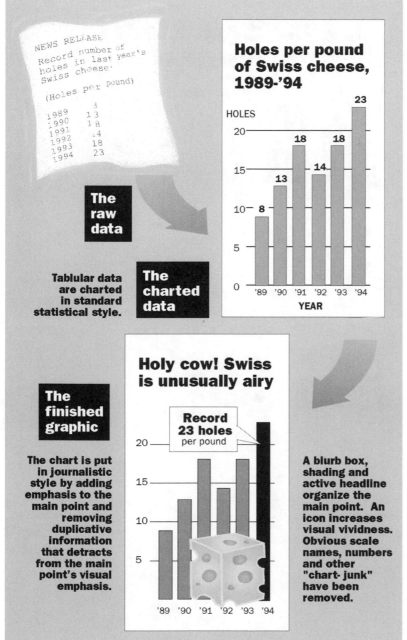

NEWS RELEASE
Record number of
holes in last year's
Swiss cheese.

(Holes per pound)

1989	8
1990	13
1991	18
1992	14
1993	18
1994	23

The raw data

Tablular data are charted in standard statistical style.

The charted data

Holes per pound of Swiss cheese, 1989-'94

HOLES

23
20
18   18
15
14
13
10
8
5
0
'89 '90 '91 '92 '93 '94
YEAR

The finished graphic

The chart is put in journalistic style by adding emphasis to the main point and removing duplicative information that detracts from the main point's visual emphasis.

Holy cow! Swiss is unusually airy

Record
23 holes
per pound

20
15
10
5
'89 '90 '91 '92 '93 '94

A blurb box, shading and active headline organize the main point. An icon increases visual vividness. Obvious scale names, numbers and other "chart- junk" have been removed.

3.2

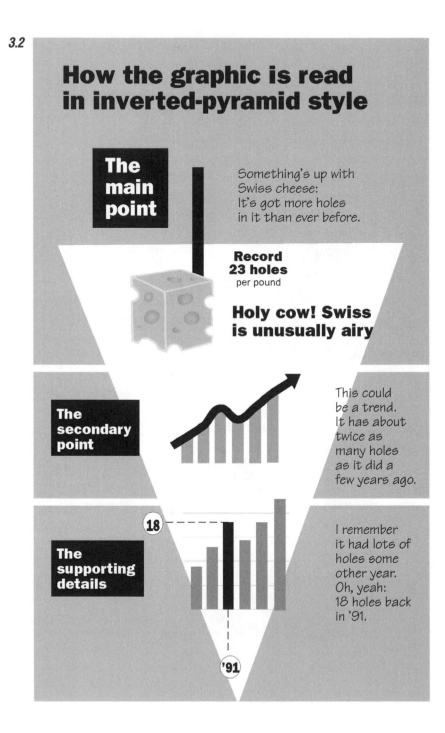

How the graphic is read in inverted-pyramid style

The main point

Something's up with Swiss cheese: It's got more holes in it than ever before.

Record 23 holes per pound

Holy cow! Swiss is unusually airy

The secondary point

This could be a trend. It has about twice as many holes as it did a few years ago.

The supporting details

18

'91

I remember it had lots of holes some other year. Oh, yeah: 18 holes back in '91.

A graphic's main point should be brief and, as its name implies, to the point. It should convey essential information and make ample use of visuals, an active headline and a pointer box. Each should tell not merely what the graphic is about but specifically what the graphic says.

Visual communication is powerful because our minds process and store symbols more easily than they can decode text. In a perfect world, a graphic's main point should be understood even if the reader cannot speak the language of the graphic's words. Such a goal may not always be attainable, but it is within reach in most cases. A graphic on consumer prices, for example, could contain a price-tag backdrop with a clear, bold bar indicating how prices have increased. Although some words might be needed to convey the full meaning, the gist of the graphic could easily be obtained without ever reading a word.

Readers today are likely to skim rather than read most things they look at. In fact, Urban and Associates estimates skimmers outnumber readers four to one. Reflecting this, Eye-Trac studies indicate that a person viewing a page spends only a fraction of a second on the main point of a graphic—just long enough for a skimmer to decide, on the basis of image, whether the topic is interesting enough to read. The beauty of a well-done graphic is that it can inform even on this fundamental level. The visual image of prices going up might be all the information that the viewer needed. A well-crafted graphic can convey this in the blink of an eye.

Of course, it may not be possible to always make a graphic's main point understandable to a non-speaker of your language. Suppose your graphic is text-based: a breakout on the pros and cons of a new legislative plan. Legislation is hard enough to explain in words, much less in the limited vocabulary of images. But just because a topic doesn't lend itself to a visual scenario doesn't mean you shouldn't try. Try to devise ways in which to make the key points stand out visually. Don't abandon your chance to inform by creating a large icon that merely labels the topic. Instead, create small, topical icons and boldface an essential word or two, as was done in our Smallville process graphic, shown again in Figure 3.3.

3.3

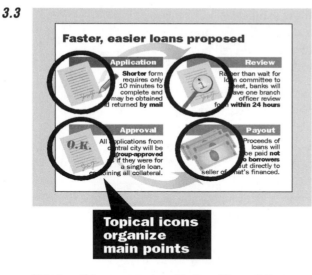

Note how this sequence graphic from Figure 2.5 uses topical icons and punched bold to get its main points across.

As was mentioned before and shown in Figure 3.2, a graphic's headline, although not visual in a purist's sense, still counts as helping to convey a graphic's main point. Though attracted mostly by images, readers may still process a word or two of the biggest or boldest type in hope of finding information. For this reason, headlines, like images, should actively communicate facts, not merely serve as labels. "Consumer prices soar in June" is an active headline that gets the main point across. "US Consumer Price Index, 1994-96" is just a label, better used in an economic text. Professional journalists disdain label headlines on stories. Information designers should be no less disdainful of them on graphics.

Another element of text commonly counted in the graphic's main point is a pointer box—a graphic callout that points to and summarizes an important fact. Rather than state that a specific item is shown, a pointer box should also contribute significant information. The best pointer box is an extension of the graphic's headline. It should relate back to the headline and convey a specific detail that adds to the headline's message. If the graphic headline says "School leads state in SAT scores," the pointer box might add: "Average score of 1200 is 15 percent higher than any other school's."

Realize that readers will understand the graphic's main point if it is presented clearly. Whether they go any further depends on how interesting the topic is and how efficiently you present it. If your graphic makes the main point seem limited or invalid—a footnote, for example, might say that the government thought the latest consumer price figure was an anomaly—you probably would need to hedge the main message as well. Without precautions against misleading, a graphic can become the visual equivalent of a long-ago *National Enquirer* story. The story's headline offered to reveal Lawrence Welk's hidden, passionate relationship. On the third jump page, in very small type, the relationship was revealed to be the champagne musician's marriage of several decades. One wonders how many great-grandmothers had coronaries before getting that far.

Simplifying material to the point that you have isolated just one main point is a worthy challenge. In all likelihood, you already will have boiled down the information to fit it into the graphic. Boiling it down further to its most essential handful of words is a knack you must develop.

You can practice simplifying material by taking a typewritten page and reducing the text in half, losing as little meaning as possible. Delete words as if you were trimming a personal ad to fit the allowed space. After you've cut the text in half, cut it in half again, making it only one-fourth as long as the original. Then cut it to one-eighth, then one-sixteenth. Keep cutting until you get down to four essential words. This paragraph, for example, could be reduced to just two words: practice and simplifying. These words could be set in boldface to make them stand out for skimmers as the main points. The words that remained right before we narrowed the field to just those two would survive in lightface type as secondary points. The rest of the text is nothing more than supporting details.

Secondary Points

One of the best information designers I know keeps the three most important things he does to every graphic that comes along pasted onto the edge of his computer screen. His list:

Organize

Organize

Organize

Separating the secondary points—the "middle" of the graphic—from the primary ones and the supporting details is one of the main challenges of organization. In a well-designed graphic, the secondary points must not compete for attention or fade anonymously away. This is why tables almost always make bad graphics. They're details, not overviews. For a graphic to succeed, it should be an overview. In an information age, anyone can get access to all the numbers if he or she really wants. What you're selling is your evaluation of the numbers. And to be evaluative, you must be organized.

3.4

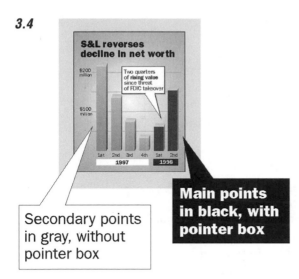

This graphic uses black bars and a pointer box to draw attention to its main points, while gray bars without pointer boxes convey secondary details.

3.5

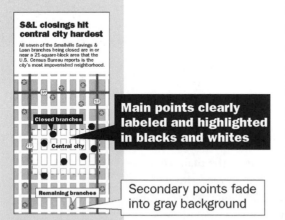

This graphic uses solid blacks and whites to draw attention to its main points, while secondary points fade into the gray background.

In charted data, the main point is identified by filling the bars of data solid black; the secondary points are made by bars shaded in a much lighter gray, as in Figure 3.4. In a map, the main point is made in a pointer box directing attention to a specific area; secondary points are other major sites that put the key site in perspective, as in Figure 3.5. In glance boxes, main points are made by icons, headings or boldface words; normal-size type in light face makes the secondary points, as in Figure 3.5. All these techniques are explored in greater detail in Chapters 11 through 16, which offer specific tips on each type of graphic.

"Generally," Mark Feeney writes in *Design* magazine, "the better the graphic, the more rewards there are to be gained by devoting time to it. While a graphic that must be puzzled out is, by definition, a failed graphic, a graphic that lets you take in at a glance all the information it contains is an extremely limited graphic."

The secondary points should be the keys that readers need to unlock the additional informational rewards.

Secondary points of a graphic commonly report underlying patterns. The main point could be, for example, that consumer prices went up 0.3 percent in October. The secondary point is that consumer prices have been rising at a much lower pace in preceding months. In Figures 3.1 and 3.2, the rising number of holes in recent years is secondary point. In Figure 3.4, it is the bank's previous profitability. In Figure 3.5, the bank branches that won't close are secondary points, whereas in Figure 3.6 the actual details of each planned change are the secondary points.

Secondary points often are not stated in text. If they are, they tend to be stated in the "chatter"—a small, unemphasized block of text that appears beneath the headline. (See Chapter 10 for more on parts of a graphic and their purposes.) If the headline says: "School leads state in SAT scores," and the pointer box adds: "Average score of 1200 is 15 percent higher than any other school's," the chatter might go in a related, but different direction: "Only one city school, Meir, made the top 10 list, which was dominated by suburban districts." The graphical support for this would be the unemphasized bars.

The Supporting Details

Oddly enough, the "end" of the graphic— the supporting details—is where the actual numbers go in most charted data. In a chart, one key element is highlighted to give the main point. The other elements contribute the secondary points. The least significant points, because you already have shown visual relationships among the items, are the actual numbers supporting these relationships.

As third-level elements in the visual inverted pyramid, numbers occasionally are added in small type, but more often they are left to be inferred. Note how Figures 3.1, 3.2 and 3.4 include no specific figures at all. Readers concerned enough about a topic to plumb a graphic for its supporting details are motivated information-seekers. Unlike skimmers, information-seekers are willing to put up with inconvenience. A graphic can enable information-seekers to figure out supporting details by consulting scales. The main and secondary points

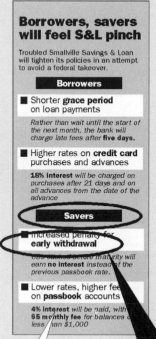

Borrowers, savers will feel S&L pinch

Troubled Smallville Savings & Loan will tighten its policies in an attempt to avoid a federal takeover.

Borrowers

■ Shorter **grace period** on loan payments

*Rather than wait until the start of the next month, the bank will charge late fees after **five days**.*

■ Higher rates on **credit card** purchases and advances

18% interest *will be charged on purchases after 21 days and on all advances from the date of the advance*

Savers

■ Increased penalty for **early withdrawal**

*CDs cashed before maturity will earn **no interest** instead of the previous passbook rate.*

■ Lower rates, higher fees on **passbook** accounts

4% interest *will be paid, with **$5 monthly fee** for balances of less than $1,000*

Main points in labels and punched bold

Secondary points in lightface text

Boldfaced words and labels draw your attention to its main points. Normal text presents the secondary points.

need not be cluttered by details that would slow down skimmers and other information-browsers. If the main and secondary points pique their curiosity, they could begin looking for details themselves. Just as graphics serve as "entry points" into text, the main points within graphics serve as "entry points" to the secondary and supporting details.

Although Eye-Trac studies indicate that the average reader checks out the main point in the blink of an eye and may spend a second or two getting the secondary points, interested readers may choose to study the supporting points in great detail, as illustrated by the example at the bottom of Figure 3.2. Instead of holes in cheese, let's say our chart was of consumer prices over the past 20 years. Particularly interested readers might compare annual changes in their salary to each year's figure. Not many would do so, but those who do would appreciate it if the graphic contained substance they could pore over after quickly getting the gist. The challenge in creating such a graphic is to avoid letting the details get in the way of the main message.

Our sample graphic on bank profits, shown again in Figure 3.7, offers a perfect example of important third-level information. Once you notice how profits have been rising (the main point) and how previously they fell (the secondary point), you can see how the reversal of fortunes still has a long way to go before profits return to their previous levels. This is a prime example of information for which an interested reader would be willing to search.

3.7

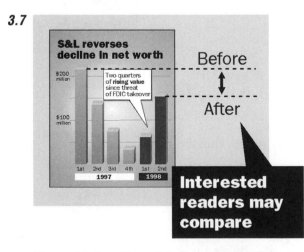

The graphic from Figure 2.2 gives more than the main and secondary points. During the third level of reading, viewers can study details of specific data relationships.

Supporting details are less abstract than primary or secondary ones. Suppose you are creating a sports graphic on a record broken by a local athlete. The new record is the main point; the old record is the secondary point. The list of how closely others have come to breaking it forms the supporting details. As done in Figure 3.8, you could use a bold reverse on the main point, still-sizable black-on-white type for the secondary point, and smaller type, fading into gray, for the tertiary details.

What you would *not* want to do is list all three points the same way.

The first mission of a graphic is to be read at a glance. That's how glance boxes get their name. Make sure yours don't become "stare" or "gaze" boxes instead. At the same time, be sure, as Feeney advises, to provide enough unemphasized information so that an interested reader can spend time mining your graphic for additional information.

3.8

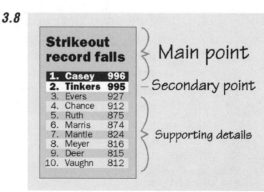

Even a tiny "entry point" such as this table needs to be organized in visual inverted pyramid style.

Tuning Your Graphic to Reach Its Likely Audience

How a graphic is designed—whether it is highly visual or only modestly visual, very organized or only modestly organized—has a profound effect on whether readers come away with the graphic's main information.

Whatever topic you are dealing with, readers tend to fall in one of two camps: those who have a personal stake in the issue and those who do not. If you, as a reader, believe that something will affect you personally, or that you can personally affect it, you will approach information about the topic systematically—that is, you'll carefully pore over the details. If, on the other hand, you believe that the issue is likely to have little personal impact on you or that you have little control over it, you'll approach the topic in what researchers call a "heuristic" manner. You'll tend to be more interested in slogans and analogies (even inappropriate ones) than you are in facts. This heuristic-systematic dichotomy explains much about how politicians campaign and advertisers persuade people to buy their products.

In graphics, a similar dichotomy was found in a study I conducted that tested how well people recall graphics. The study (see Appendix B for details) found that people who have a personal stake in an issue tend to get more out of a graphic that is highly organized and that features simple, charted data without a lot of clutter—what statistician Edward

Tufte called "chart-junk." On the other hand, people without personal stakes in an issue get more out of a graphic if something visual attracts their attention, even if the visual does not convey data. Simply put, the systematic reader is attracted by the steak (see Figure 3.9); the heuristic reader is attracted by the sizzle (see Figure 3.10). Knowing this can give you a tremendous advantage.

3.9

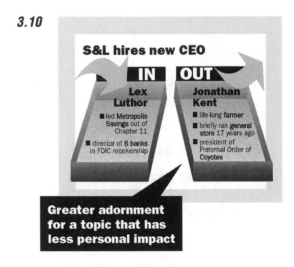

3.10

Borrowers, savers will feel S&L pinch

Troubled Smallville Savings & Loan will tighten its policies in an attempt to avoid a federal takeover.

Borrowers

■ Shorter **grace period** on loan payments

*Rather than wait until the start of the next month, the bank will charge late fees after **five days**.*

■ Higher rates on **credit card** purchases and advances

18% interest will be charged on purchases after 21 days and on all advances from the date of the advance

Savers

■ Increased penalty for **early withdrawal**

CDs cashed before maturity will earn no interest instead of the previous passbook rate.

■ Lower rates, higher fees on **passbook** accounts

4% interest will be paid, with a $5 monthly fee for balances of less than $1,000

S&L hires new CEO

IN | OUT

Lex Luthor | **Jonathan Kent**

■ led Metropolis Savings out of Chapter 11

■ director of 6 banks in FDIC receivership

■ life-long farmer

■ briefly ran **general** store 17 years ago

■ president of Fraternal Order of Coyotes

Greater adornment for a topic that has less personal impact

Readers have a less identifiable stake in executive-level changes. Vivid graphics draw their attention even if it does not present specific information.

Little adornment for a topic that affects readers

Readers have a stake in the bank's changes. Visual elements become an obstacle, so organization is needed instead.

Four Design Strategies of Graphics

Graphics employ four design strategies: vividness, organization, use of visual data metaphor and simplicity of data metaphor, as explained in Figure 3.11. Basically, graphics are used to attract attention (vividness), to rank information hierarchically (organization) and to chart specific information (metaphor) with or without "chart-junk" (simplicity). The more a graphic uses organization and simplicity, the more it appeals to systematic readers. The more a graphic uses vividness and data metaphor, the more it appeals to heuristic readers.

3.11

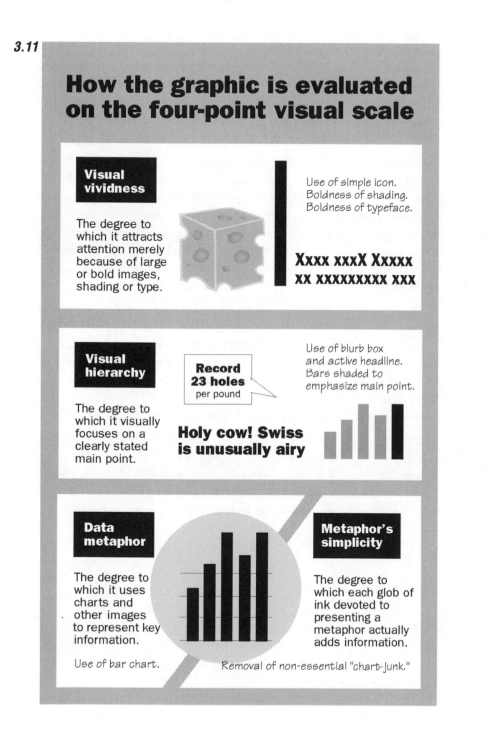

How the graphic is evaluated on the four-point visual scale

Visual vividness

The degree to which it attracts attention merely because of large or bold images, shading or type.

Use of simple icon. Boldness of shading. Boldness of typeface.

Xxxx xxxX Xxxxx xx xxxxxxxxx xxx

Visual hierarchy

The degree to which it visually focuses on a clearly stated main point.

Record 23 holes per pound

Use of blurb box and active headline. Bars shaded to emphasize main point.

Holy cow! Swiss is unusually airy

Data metaphor

The degree to which it uses charts and other images to represent key information.

Use of bar chart.

Metaphor's simplicity

The degree to which each glob of ink devoted to presenting a metaphor actually adds information.

Removal of non-essential "chart-junk."

A graphic about the type of bread members of Congress eat might err on the side of being overly visual and under-organized—the *USA Today* approach. A graphic about how much the members of Congress will be increasing your taxes might err on the side of being under-visual and overorganized—*The New York Times* approach. Each is a effective strategy, but only if it matches the audience profile.

In Figure 3.12, you'll find four sets of graphics. Each set deals with a different topic. Within each set, the graphics are the same size and contain the same information. The only difference is which of the four qualities—vividness, organization, metaphor and simplicity—they stress. None of the graphics is perfect. Each was specifically designed to show extremes, high in one category and low in all others. A real graphic might seek a more middleground approach, like the one used in the graphic dissected in Figures 3.1, 3.2 and 3.11.

Even if you aren't sure how readers will respond, it's useful to analyze how extensively a graphic relies on each of these four design techniques. Typically, every graphic uses some vividness, some organization, some data metaphor and some simplicity of metaphor. Keeping these in balance helps ensure that the graphic appeals to all readers, regardless of whether they have a stake in the topic. Shifting the balance lets you target the graphic at specific audiences.

When you create a graphic, give it a score of 0 to 4 on each of the four quantities. If you find your graphic scoring lower in one area than another, or if you anticipate that its scores won't match the audience's level of interest, the graphic may need revision or further attention. If all the scores are low, chances are your graphic needs major revisions.

3.12

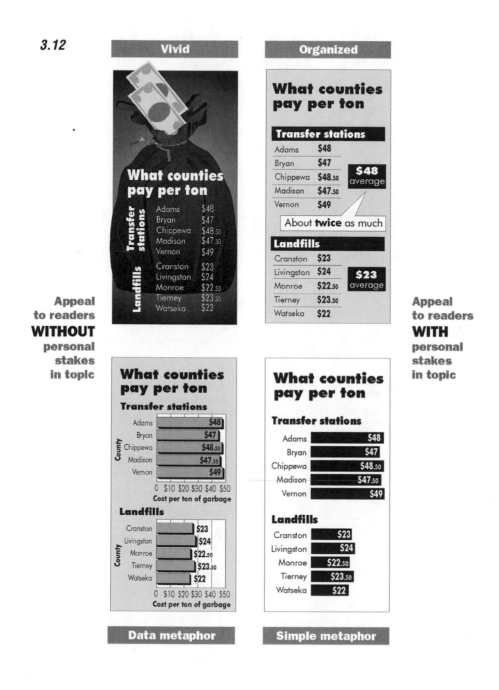

Appeal to readers **WITHOUT** personal stakes in topic

Appeal to readers **WITH** personal stakes in topic

3.13

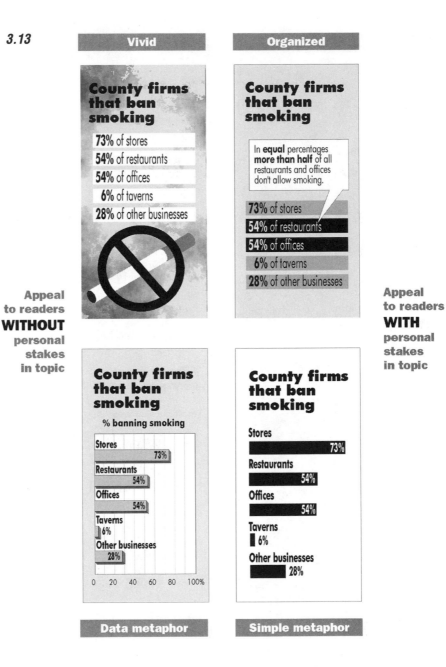

Vivid

Organized

County firms that ban smoking

73% of stores
54% of restaurants
54% of offices
6% of taverns
28% of other businesses

County firms that ban smoking

In **equal** percentages **more than half** of all restaurants and offices don't allow smoking.

73% of stores
54% of restaurants
54% of offices
6% of taverns
28% of other businesses

Appeal
to readers
WITHOUT
personal
stakes
in topic

Appeal
to readers
WITH
personal
stakes
in topic

County firms that ban smoking

% banning smoking

Stores 73%
Restaurants 54%
Offices 54%
Taverns 6%
Other businesses 28%

0   20   40   60   80   100%

County firms that ban smoking

Stores 73%
Restaurants 54%
Offices 54%
Taverns 6%
Other businesses 28%

Data metaphor

Simple metaphor

3.14

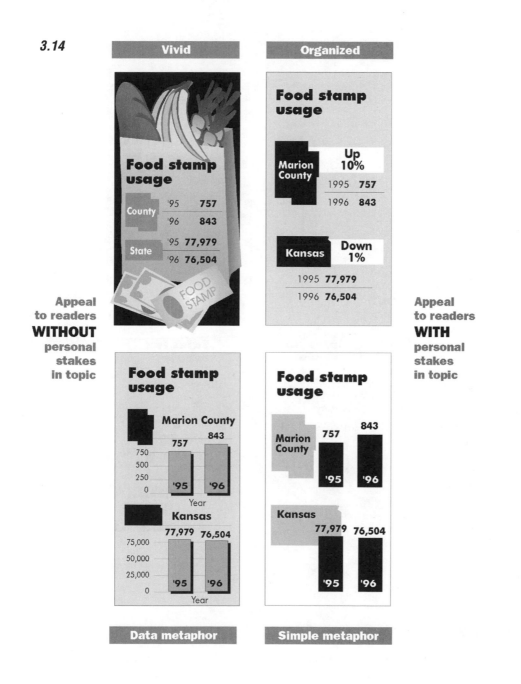

Vivid

Organized

Food stamp usage

County	'95	757
	'96	843
State	'95	77,979
	'96	76,504

Food stamp usage

Marion County	Up 10%
	1995 757
	1996 843
Kansas	Down 1%
	1995 77,979
	1996 76,504

Appeal to readers **WITHOUT** personal stakes in topic

Appeal to readers **WITH** personal stakes in topic

Food stamp usage

Marion County
757 843
750
500
250
0 '95 '96
Year

Kansas
77,979 76,504
75,000
50,000
25,000
0 '95 '96
Year

Food stamp usage

Marion County
757 843
'95 '96

Kansas
77,979 76,504
'95 '96

Data metaphor

Simple metaphor

3.15

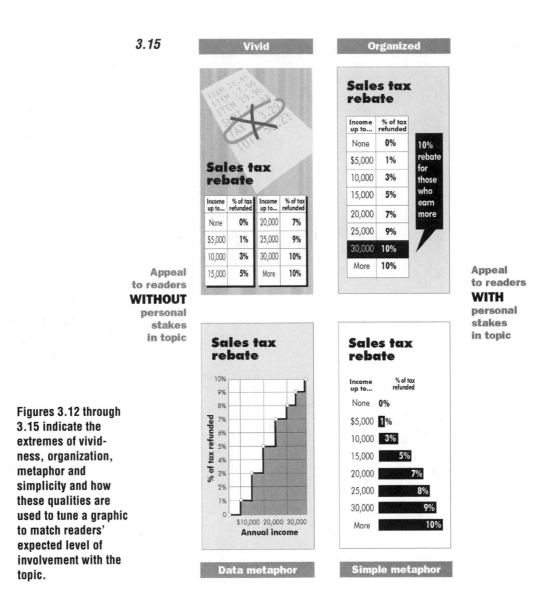

Figures 3.12 through 3.15 indicate the extremes of vividness, organization, metaphor and simplicity and how these qualities are used to tune a graphic to match readers' expected level of involvement with the topic.

Avoid Keys

You can stop any possibility of a graphic ever being read quickly by using keys to explain your important data. Keys are boxes containing explanations of the colors or symbols used in a graphic, like a map legend. In Figure 3.16, the key shows what the black, gray and white bars represent. Keys function well in business presentations and economic texts. In graphics prepared for ordinary readers, they hinder rapid readership.

Think about it. You attract all sorts of visual attention with big, bold bars or slices of a pie, but you don't manage to tell anyone what they mean until they get to the key. Eye-Trac head gear could get dizzy with all the jumping around a reader would have to do just to understand what you're trying to show.

It's much better to put the labels directly on the data. The reader doesn't have to jump back and forth to the key, and you avoid creating overly complex graphics.

If you have to depict multiple bars or slices, necessitating a key, try breaking these into separate sub-parts, explained later in Chapter 12. Organize small slices together in broad categories on the pie, then itemize what's in each category in an accompanying table in much smaller type. This moves the details away from the main points and toward the supporting details section, where they belong. Impact and comprehension are much greater if the reader does not have to struggle to decipher your organization.

3.16

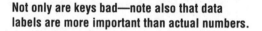

Not only are keys bad—note also that data labels are more important than actual numbers.

Unless the key is visually intuitive—red for hot water, blue for cold in a diagram of a water heater —it should be used only for conveying secondary or supporting details to readers poring over the graphic in search of supplementary information. In such situations, keys can aid organization. When essential and not intuitive, however, they are best avoided.

Labeling Your Graphics

Whenever you chart data, it's good to include a straightforward phrase telling exactly what it is that readers should be seeing. Something like "Prices rose 0.5 percent in June" inside a box pointing to the data item should suffice.

In many graphics, both the "chatter" section and the pointer box can serve this function. Imagine them as being captions for your total visual package. (Graphics never should have traditional captions, the layout of this book notwithstanding.) Keep in mind that graphics that can't be understood without their chatter or pointer boxes are no better than photos that can't be understood without first reading the captions beneath them. Flaws like these are fatal for visual efforts. Meaningless visuals attract attention but are useless in conveying information.

The idea of showing people something, then telling them what they saw, really isn't done for visual and mathematical illiterates, of course. I recently did an experiment with elderly people—20 percent of them high school dropouts—in which I asked them to interpret unlabeled charted data to see whether they could discern the actual numbers and the trends the data suggested. Surprisingly, nearly 90 percent of these people, their average age more than 80, got every answer right.

The value in presenting key points both as charted data and in textual highlights is more theoretical than practical. Researchers tell us that the left and right sides of our brains work differently. One deals with decoding words; the other deals with interpreting images. The "word" half is what we use when we look at a digital clock. It decodes what 7:37 means. The "visual" half is what we use when we look at an analog clock. The little hand is between the 7 and the 8 and the big hand is more than halfway around.

Digital gives us precision, but analog gives the precision meaning. If you get both at the same time, you've done what researcher Allen Paivio calls dual coding. His studies indicate that dual-coded information is by far more memorable than anything presented only visually or only in text.

It works much the same with news stories, an area that researcher Prabu David is only now beginning to explore. Couple a real-world analogy (a vivid metaphor) with a straight factual lead (organized simplicity) and you have a strong piece. The vividness attracts attention, the metaphor makes sure you understand the impact, the organization lets you see what's important, and the simplicity makes sure you don't get confused.

We'll explore how the mind handles images in greater detail in Chapter 6.

Visual inverted pyramid uses the same qualities. Overall vividness attracts attention to the graphic, while use of charts and other visuals provide a data metaphor that helps convey the information with impact. Pointer boxes and other tools organize this presentation, while the removal of extraneous elements provide the simplicity needed to make sure that details don't obscure what's important.

To Help You Think Visually

Return to your favorite daily newspaper or other publication and find five graphics, some good and some not so good. Answer the following questions for each of them:

1. Is it organized in the visual inverted pyramid style?

2. How could the graphic have been better organized?

3. How would you score the graphic for vividness, organization, data metaphor and metaphorical simplicity?

4. Could the balance among these quantities be improved to better target the graphic at its likely audience?

Chapter 4

How to Find Information for Graphics

Now that you know how to use graphics effectively, the next step is learning to find information. The best-designed graphic is useless if it contains less-than-useful information. Finding the facts becomes the single most important challenge an information designer faces.

Much of the material needed for graphics information is a natural by-product of the reporting process. Someone provides information to a writer, or the writer seeks it out. A few ripped-out pages of a notebook and you have information for your graphic.

In the real world, unfortunately, it seldom works that way. Original information sources often fail to provide all the information a graphic needs. Sources, for example, may note that 10 percent of homeowners are complying with new recycling regulations, but the sources fail to account for what the other 90 percent of homeowners are doing. Why should they? In text, the 10 percent figure is all the writer will need. For your graphic, however, after you use that figure to make the main point, you'll have nothing left to make the secondary points or to offer supporting details. The writer may not even realize that he or she needs to help. Colleagues who regard graphics as shallow sops to MTV-addicted illiterates fail to recognize that graphics, although they simplify, approach topics in greater detail than does text alone.

This paradox is something that graphics' most regular users, newspapers, discovered long ago. For nearly a decade, graphic designers at newspapers nationwide have been finding themselves becoming graphic reporters. In fact, some newspapers have hired people specifically as graphic reporters. Four of 11 graphics departments in a 1988 survey by the Society of Newspaper Design reported that graphics staff members did more than 50 percent of the research for the graphics they created. Responses ranged from 95 percent at the *Chicago Tribune* to 10 percent at the *Seattle Times*.

Whatever the percentages, it is clear that those who conduct research for text can't always be counted on to do research for graphics. If major newsrooms, filled with researchers, have this problem, imagine the prognosis in other professional settings. If you find yourself in such a situation, how can you find the information you need?

Interview the Writer

Regardless of his or her visual literacy, the author of the text is the best source to contact. It's also imperative to contact the writer before research is completed, not after. Ask the writer where the project is going and what its key points are, then develop with the writer a strategy for expressing those points both verbally and visually. By making sure the sources are asked the questions you need answers for, you make life easier for you, the writer, and the writer's sources. Otherwise, sources have to be interviewed a second time to get needed information.

Tips for Writers

If the writer is unsure where the story is going, encourage him or her to "think graphic" along the way. Often, that means nothing more than becoming a bit "info-retentive." Everyone has a relative who's never thrown anything away. Somewhere, buried in Aunt Jenny's stacks of mementos, you'll probably find that fifth-grade geography test you proudly got an "A" on. Encourage writers to be just like your aunt:

- **Grab every handout** you can lay your hands on and keep them on file.

- **Get photocopies of complete sets of figures** anytime a source refers to one figure from a particular set.

- **Ask for the names and phone numbers** of people who assembled a report. That way, they can be quickly contacted later.

- **Whenever information is offered for any one month or year, ask to have the same information provided for the past dozen months or years.** If it's too time-consuming to provide the information during an interview, ask that it be faxed to you as background material.

- **Pick up fact-filled booklets, brochures or maps** wherever you go, not just when working on specific stories. All of these things can be kept on hand to provide maps and figures when a need arises. (You'd be amazed how many newspaper air-crash graphics have been created out of seat-back emergency cards pilfered from previous flights.)

You can also follow these tips from Charlotte Fletcher Thibault of New Hampshire's *Concord Monitor:*

- **Take a map** with you when you go to a zoning hearing, developer's office, or crime scene. Get the location pinpointed then and there. Draw the site, area of destruction, proximity of landmarks and so on.

- **Borrow the architect's conceptual view or floor plans.**

- **Get solid numbers** as soon as you can. If not now, whom can we call in the morning?

- **Ask questions** such as: How does it work? What comes next? Is there a photo, diagram, or sketch we can use? Is there a hierarchy? Is there a set of steps involved?

This list is only a beginning. Develop your own list for the specialized topics you deal with most often. Keep track of what information turns out to be the most valuable, add references to that type of material, and periodically distribute the list to your colleagues. I can tell you from personal experience that the best thing I ever did professionally was have a series of informal, brown-bag lunches with colleagues in which I explained some of the subjects within this book, then handed out a list of tips. Your colleagues want to do their jobs professionally; you'll be surprised how cooperative they can be once they understand and appreciate your needs.

The one thing you do *not* want your colleagues to do is to pick up finished graphics for you. All too often, eager colleagues see a stack of handouts, notice that one of them features a finished graphic and discard the others in favor of that one. They are trying to do you a favor; in fact, they are not. Trying to duplicate already-charted data is a perilous proposition. Without the actual underlying numbers, errors can be introduced or exaggerated. You can never know whether the chart actually matches the data it purports to show. Encourage colleagues to get not just the chart but also the information it was based upon. That way, you'll be able to reproduce it easily, accurately, and reliably.

Visit the Library or Bookstore

Chances are, whoever wrote the text won't be able to give you everything you need. The writer may be a busy executive who doesn't have time to track down details, a copywriter who doesn't know where to begin, or a reporter too busy working on a breaking story to help. That's where your bookshelf, your department library or your community's public library can help. Here are just a few of the information sources you can consult:

- **Almanac.** An Almanac is perhaps the greatest treasure-trove for graphic research. If you work at a newspaper, you may be able to get one free from your public service department. Even if the almanac doesn't give you precisely what you are looking for, you may find the name of an organization that keeps records of that sort. A follow-up call can get you what you need.

- **Encyclopedia.** An encyclopedia also can be a treasure-trove of information. It is particularly good for stating complex issues in simple terms. If a kid in your town has built her own nuclear bomb, the encyclopedia probably can be used to produce a graphic explaining how easy her task was.

- **Statistical abstracts.** Available from a variety of sources, statistical abstracts are invaluable. One particularly useful set, issued monthly, keeps track of all economic data issued by the federal government. Other statistical abstracts are issued by foundations, governments, and agencies worldwide. A public library, university library or the business desk, national desk or library at a newspaper should carry these. Ask for help locating the statistics you need. Reference librarians have years of training and experience in locating information. Take advantage of their expertise.

- **The World Wide Web.** Virtually anything you want can be found on the Web. It can take a bit of looking, because the Web extends in countless directions, but tremendous sources are there for the reading.

  If you have an Internet account and Web browser software, ask someone to show you how to use a search engine such as Digital's Alta Vista. (Its URL address is *http://www.altavista. digital.com.*) Using a search engine such as Alta Vista, any techno-nerd should be able to put you in touch with, say, the latest forestry management estimates of fire peril in Idaho or the current trajectory of the Hubble space telescope.

  Nearly every government agency puts its reports online, and indices of these reports can be found throughout the Internet (at *http://www.fedworld.gov,* for example). You can access official street maps of any community in the US, with or without customized data coding, directly from the Census Bureau via its free Tiger data map service (*http://tiger.census. gov*). You can get all manner of data directly from the Bureau of Labor Statistics (*http://www.bls.gov*). Even the White House is online; you can send a message to *president@whitehouse.gov.* I doubt you'll get a personal interview, but you never know until you try.

Finding information on the Internet is worthy of a book in its own right. It's an area you should explore even if you do so only in a limited way by means of Prodigy, America Online, CompuServe or another commercial service. All offer useful information on their own, and most offer convenient windows to the Net itself. If you do visit the Web, be sure to drop by my home page. You can find it at *http://www.newslink.org* or send a message to *meyer@newslink.org*.

● **Specialized books.** Books on the military, anatomy, sports, or any other topic also are invaluable aids. Most large newspaper, college, or public libraries should have a good collection.

In Appendix C, we offer a bibliography, written with the help of information scientists at one of the nation's top research libraries, listing the top books you should be on the lookout for. See how many your business has and press your corporate librarian to complete the collection. He or she will probably love it that you are justifying the library's request for additional funding.

● **Annual reports.** These reports from publicly held companies contain a wealth of information on corporate history, finance and, to some extent, on products. Your broker, business office, business desk or library should keep them on file. If not, you can request copies from the company.

Be careful when reading such reports. It's best to enlist a veteran business reporter, accountant or business manager as your guide, at least in your first attempts. The most important information often comes in footnotes at the bottom of long tabulations of numbers. Learning how to read an annual report is one of those tasks you should put high on your list of things to do.

● **Planning reports.** These reports can contain information related to your main subject. A report on a sewage treatment facility last year could contain the information you are looking for in preparing a graphic on a new industrial park. Planning reports frequently include data about the community in which they are issued. *The Milwaukee Journal,* for example, once used a report on freeway construction to produce graphics on baseball ticket sales. How? A key question was whether the baseball team was drawing equally from all segments of the community. The highway report contained up-to-date population figures necessary for evaluating ticket sales. Save planning reports whenever you see them. You never know when they might come in handy.

Find Your Own Sources

Just because you aren't Bob Woodward of *The Washington Post* doesn't mean you can't make calls, ask questions and get facts the way a text-based journalist does.

If you can avoid it, don't call the same sources your colleague already has interviewed. Although we know all too well that our office is far from being an organized monolith, sources often don't understand that different people do different jobs within an organization. When possible, it's best to let the original writer re-contact any sources already interviewed. Still, a variety of additional sources that the original writer might not have contacted can be used:

- **Regional planning agencies.** These agencies usually branches of state government, keep statistics on topics from population and pollution to employment and transportation. Need to know the estimated number of toilets in some ritzy suburb? Chances are, if anyone has the information, your regional planners will. More important, if they don't have the information, they know who does. Numbers are the lifeblood of any planning agency, and researchers usually are eager to share any insights on which numbers could help tell a story or on where such data could be found.

  Let's say a major factory in your town is closing and you must assess the situation for the Chamber of Commerce newsletter. The company can tell you the number of jobs that will be lost, but you can go a step further by contacting your regional planners. They'll be able to quantify how the addition or loss of a single job affects other jobs. They can list how employment in the factory's economic sector has changed over time. They'll even be able to compare the average wages in the sector with wages in other sectors, or with wages in the same sector in other areas of the country. This can enable you to graphically evaluate the employers' contentions about labor costs playing a role in the decision to close.

- **Federal economic agencies.** Agencies such as the Bureau of Labor Statistics employ helpful analysts who not only have access to statistics, but also are aware of private research that may directly address your issue. The secret, as with the regional planning agencies, is to get past the public relations personnel and talk directly to analysts who specialize in the area in question.

  Suppose, for example, you're trying to find a graphic to accompany a whimsical story about Congress objecting to a pay raise. At first, the bureau tells you that it has no numbers related to that, but if you talk to analysts in its Chicago office, you'll learn about a management consultant who is working on something closely related. Give the consultant a call and suddenly you have definitive numbers to accompany what otherwise would be a no-graphics story. You even get a good quote or two to pass along to the reporter. Score one for the graphics desk.

- **Other specialized agencies.** There are many organizations both public and private, which can be helpful. Build a list of contacts at your state's agriculture and transportation departments, for example. You'll be surprised when they come in handy. They may not be the source of information on Christmas tree prices that you're looking for, but they probably will know the name and telephone number of the National Christmas Tree Growers Association. (It's in Milwaukee.)

Information designers live and die on the quality of their source lists. You don't need to know exactly where every piece of data is kept, but you do need to know the people who know. Develop your source list and guard its contents. Cultivate these sources as if you were a reporter covering them for a beat, which in your case is statistics. If you "cover" your beat well, you'll be amazed how quickly you can uncover data. You may even discover, as Associated Press graphics journalists did during the Persian Gulf war, that one of your best sources may be a toy store. Model airplanes, it seems, frequently come with all manner of performance specifications that the government won't give out.

How did the AP staffers find such a source? By asking questions *before* the need arose. A good information designer regularly reads newspapers, magazines, professional journals, and research reports even when not looking for graphics material. Develop the habit of reading the source line at the bottom of every graphic you see. Make a mental note of where the information came from. You may even want to leaf through almanacs and other reference books so that you can develop a sense for where to obtain information. Most important, do what you should tell your writers to do: become "info-retentive." It's the best career investment you can ever make.

Exercise

Using the research strategies cited, develop a strategy for answering the following questions:

1. How has the US Consumer Price Index for All-Urban Consumers (the version most commonly cited in inflation reports) changed monthly over the past year?

2. Who are the Kurds? Where do they live? What sets them apart from others in the region? What has been the history of Kurdistan, which some seek to re-establish?

Now go back and develop a second and third strategy for getting the same information. If you find a roadblock that prevents you from getting current information in one area, you may have to shift gears. Practice thinking of multiple ways to get the same information. You may need to use all of them to get what you are looking for.

Chapter

A Brief Look at Statistical Ethics

For reasons that have baffled some and been exploited by others, seeing is believing. For information designers, this can be fatal.

Although a reader might challenge a verbal claim, a graphic often is accepted unchallenged—not only by the reader but also by the journalist or information designer who uses it. If it's charted, it must be true. Why else do you suppose that our ersatz hero, Ross Perot, was so eager to present his claims with graphics? And why is it that graphics always seem to pop up in commercials for products such as pain relievers, antacids and long-distance telephone services?

As ethical professionals, we must avoid visual deceptions. Sometimes the deceptions can be subtle, as when *Time* magazine enhanced a booking photo of O.J. Simpson, making him appear more sinister. Had *Newsweek* not used an unenhanced version of the same photo on its cover the same week, the world never would have known. Sometimes the deceptions are more insidious, as when *Newsday* used Photoshop to put Nancy Kerrigan and Tonya Harding close together on the ice during practice for the 1994 Olympics. In fact, the two celebrated rivals practiced far apart.

Everyone agrees that examples such as these are clearly unethical.
Where they disagree, or fail to note problems, is when the deception is
not an alteration of a photo but rather an alteration of data.

When the Truth Isn't the Whole Truth

Often, whether your numbers lie is more a matter of how you present
the number than what the actual numbers are. Failing to account for
inflation, failing to clearly label projected figures as such and failing to
use a consistent scale in charting data are three ways graphics can lie.

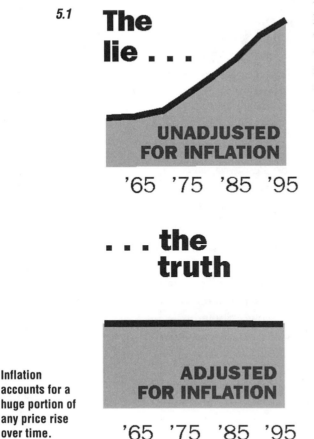

5.1

If you're an unethical public-relations
practitioner, you could make a fine career
out of the list of lies that follows. If, on the
other hand, you are an ethical information
designer, keep this list in mind so you can
spot a lie before you propagate it:

Want to Make a Price Look as If It's Risen Sky-High?

Simply chart it back a few decades, through
the extreme inflation of the mid-'60s to early
'80s. A cup of coffee went from a nickel to
nearly a dollar during that period. The fact
that a postage stamp went from three cents
to 32 cents doesn't seem that unusual in
comparison. But how many times have you
seen respected publications bemoaning the
soaring price of postage, complete with
graphics that do exactly what's suggested
here?

Avoid misinformation like this by charting
prices that cross periods of inflation as
inflation-adjusted amounts, as in Figure
5.1. Your source will do so if price stability
is what she or he wants to show.

Inflation accounts for a huge portion of any price rise over time.

If you're uncertain how to make inflation adjustments, call a regional office of the Bureau of Labor Statistics or the economics department of a nearby college. BLS even has a Web page on the topic at *http:// stats.bls.gov/cpifact3.htm*. Once you get a few numbers entered into a spreadsheet program, you can easily make future adjustments as the need arises.

To get you started, we'll offer you a relatively simple inflation adjuster. After talking to the BLS or your friendly neighborhood economist, you may want to use one that's more complex, but this one should handle most everyday tasks in the meantime.

The first thing you need to do is find where the Consumer Price Index stood in each of the years in question. You can find CPI data on the Internet from the government Web site at *http://stats.bls.gov/cgi-bin/surveymost?cu*.

For our adjuster, we chose the Consumer Price Index for All Urban Consumers (1982-84=100), one of several flavors the index comes in. This is the flavor usually cited in news reports about inflation, but it's not the one commonly used for cost-of-living adjustments in pensions and wages.

Once you get the figures for each year you need, simply move the decimal point two places to the left (as done in the accompanying table) so that 1982-84 is equal to 1, not 100. You then can transform any past amount into what economists call "constant 1982-84 dollars" by dividing that amount by the number corresponding to the year for which the amount was recorded.

Inflation Divisors

1980	0.824	1988	1.183
1981	0.926	1989	1.240
1982	0.965	1990	1.307
1983	0.996	1991	1.362
1984	1.039	1992	1.403
1985	1.076	1993	1.445
1986	1.096	1994	1.482
1987	1.136	1995	1.524

Suppose a cup of coffee cost five cents in 1953. Take five cents and divide it by 0.267, the inflation divisor in 1953. In 1953, coffee cost 19 cents in constant 1982-84 dollars. If the same cup of coffee (which by then probably would have been mighty cold) cost 95 cents in 1995, take 95 cents and divide it by 1.524 to find that coffee that year cost 62 cents in constant 1982-84 dollars.

You can get fancy with the numbers by converting everything to "current dollars" instead of 1982-84 dollars. To do so, you must find out where the CPI for All Urban Consumers currently stands. A quick surf over to the Internet address *http://stats.bls.gov/cgibin/surveymost?cu* should give you exactly what you need. Move the decimal point two places to the left and divide each number in the table by the new number you obtained. Then simply repeat the procedure we used before.

Suppose the current CPI-U, as it is known, stands at 153.1. Divide 1995's 1.524 by the current 1.531 to produce an inflation divisor for 1995 of 0.995. The 1953 divisor similarly becomes 0.174. Doing the math, we learn that a nickel cup of coffee in 1953 would have cost 29 cents today, while a 95 cent cup of coffee from 1995 would have cost somewhere between 95 and 96 cents today.

Yes, it's tricky, and you probably got into this field because you hated math. What's clear is that you don't need a Ph.D. to convert price data into constant dollar amounts. You just need a calculator and a bit of patience.

Want to Make a Company's Future Look Bright?

Go easy on the actual data, providing only a year or two's worth, then tack on lots of the company's guesses as to how well it will do in years to come.

Projections are only as valid as the credentials of the people doing the projecting, yet in a graphic those credentials show up in type the size of a footnote. Trade associations are notorious for projecting that the products they sell will take off in years to come.

Make sure if you chart such projections that you ask for plenty of actual data from years prior. It's highly important to clearly show which data is actual and which is projected, as in Figure 5.2. Putting disclaimers in small type may work for lawyers; for information designers, it's unethical. Yet it's the most frequent error in graphics on most newspaper business pages and in the supposedly graphically revered *USA Today*.

Want to Exaggerate a Trend?

Break the scale of the charted data, as done in Figure 5.3. If, for example, the number of murders in a town has dropped from 200 to 195 to 190, chart the numbers starting at 180 instead of zero. Suddenly, a five percent drop looks like a 50 percent drop. The mayor is happy. The police chief is happy. You, meanwhile, can hang your head in shame.

Government agencies love this trick. They use it to show how many more clients they have to provide services for, or how well they've done in reducing a problem. You'll also see it whenever private firms brag about their growth or try to pass along rising costs they pay.

They won't actually lie. As in Figure 5.3, they'll put a tiny hash mark over on the left side of the chart's scale to show that it has been broken. Again the reader is forced to examine the fine print to find the truth. All the while the powerful tools of visual journalism pass along a lie.

Breaking scales isn't always bad, of course. You can ethically break a scale if the numbers measured by it are not intrinsically meaningful. Fifty degrees is not twice as hot as 25 degrees, so it doesn't matter where you put the zero point. (Don't believe me? How would you compare −25 and +25 degrees? Is −25 or +25 negative one times as hot as the other? It makes no sense.)

You also can break a scale ethically if the amount being measured always exists within a narrow range. The classic example for both of these is in measuring body temperature. You can ethically start a fever chart at 97 or 98 degrees. You should be careful, however, when making assumptions about other things that "always" exist in a narrow range. It's a sad assumption indeed if we assume that several hundred murders will take place each year or that the federal budget deficit will always be in the several billions.

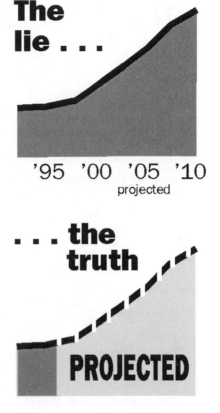

5.2

The lie . . .

'95 '00 '05 '10
projected

. . . the truth

PROJECTED

'95 '00 '05 '10

Projected data must be clearly labeled.

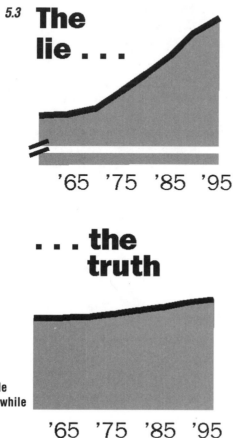

5.3 **The lie . . .**

'65 '75 '85 '95

. . . the truth

'65 '75 '85 '95

Breaking a scale often deceives while the full scale reveals.

A data analyst might argue that you must break a scale in order to see the actual month-to-month or year-to-year movement in the data. This is commonly cited as the reason for breaking the scale when charting readings on the Consumer Price Index. Unfortunately, it is false. What we are interested in when we chart the CPI is not prices but inflation—a measure of the *change* in prices, just like acceleration is a measure of the change in speed. Inflation can be positive or negative (deflation), just as acceleration can be positive or negative (deceleration). If, as the analyst says, what's important is the change in prices, we should be charting inflation or change in the size of the debt, not prices or the debt itself. Examples of how to do so are explored more fully in Chapter 12, when we examine the differences between line and bar charts.

When the Truth Isn't the Truth at All

Mixing apples and oranges may make for a great fruit salad but it makes for lousy information design.

Failure to make certain there's a valid, common point of reference is essential in ethical information design. Otherwise, you've left making up answers to questions like these:

Want to Make Something Routine Sound Superlative?

Compare it to the absurd. The mayor brags that she got so many letters of support for her new proposal that if she placed them end to end, they'd reach from City Hall to the edge of town. Comparisons are valid only if you have a common frame of reference. Did the mayor get as many letters of support as she got complaints when she vetoed a previous plan? That's an apples-and-apples situation.

The most common problem journalists run into in this area is with weather stories. Associated Press writers and some law enforcement officials love to spout figures about the number of deaths, fender-benders or other tragedies related to inclement weather. An ethical journalist makes sure she or he knows what **normally** would happen during the same time. The "raft" of 25 rush-hour fender-benders during a snowstorm might be a lower total than would have occurred during a normal day. The five hunting deaths due to heart attacks might have been the same number as would have been expected had these people not been hunting at the time.

Want to Create a Trend That Doesn't Exist?

Use another of the apples-and-oranges tricks: comparing the incomparable. Last year your store did $1 million in business. Through the first half of this year, it's done only $250,000 in business. It must really need that tax break you're looking for, right? Everybody deserves a tax break, but not because of data like this. Compare your current business with how well the store did in the same months of the previous year. The average retail firm does half its annual business in the months before Christmas. Ethical graphics compare only equivalent periods or use that famous government phrase, "seasonally adjusted," to alert readers that data from different periods have been altered to make the two periods comparable.

Be warned that seasonally adjusted data, just like projected data, are only as reliable as the credentials and ethics of the people doing the adjusting. If such adjustments are questionable, don't try to get around the problem with a legal-sounding footnote.

Is There No Truth in Surveys?

The best way to lie with information design is to invoke a four-letter word: poll. Surveys are perhaps the best way to lie. In fact, surveys have so many ways to lie, it's hard to account for them all. We'll only begin to scratch the surface here. If you're really interested, pick up a copy of a book such as Philip Meyer's (no relation) *Precision Journalism.*

5.4 **The lie . . .**

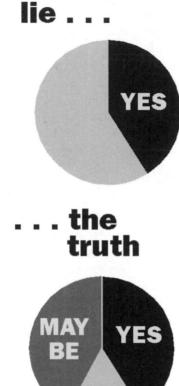

. . . the truth

Poll graphics often commit sins of omission.

Incomplete data, loaded questions, bad methodology and overstatement of results are just a few of the ways you can lie by answering these questions:

Want to Put Your Own Spin on Something's Popularity?

Do your best imitation of *Family Feud*'s Richard Dawson and bellow: "Survey says...."

Want to show how offering cut rates to student moviegoers has failed? Report that only 10 percent of students say they go to movies more often now than they did before the new rates were imposed. Don't bother to tell anyone about the 65 percent who say they go "somewhat more often" now; they don't help make the point. Just draw up a graphic with the 10 percent number, send it to the newspaper and watch a graphic artist publish it unchallenged.

Researchers are good at coming up with distortions like this. That's particularly true of marketing department researchers and others who conduct research aimed at making a specific point. They can combine categories of answers or ask questions in certain ways to prove almost anything.

Avoid lies such as this by insisting on getting—and reporting—the actual survey questions asked and the actual percentages recorded for each possible response. If you end up having to paraphrase or simplify, you can still tell an honest story, as shown in Figure 5.4.

Make sure you don't introduce bias into poll results. Be wary of questions which can be interpreted in multiple ways. Is "excellent, OK, or poor" a full spectrum? Does the respondent mean "it was just OK," or does he or she mean, "yeah, it was really OK"? When in doubt, leave the graphic out.

Want to Panic Someone into Action?

In this example, the contention is that three-fourths of all middle school pupils that were surveyed fear for their safety in class every day. Let's ignore that the survey was taken only in schools where firearms had been seized. Chances are, a graphic artist won't pick up on the survey's inherent bias.

Avoid this kind of lie by checking how a survey was conducted. Was it a scientifically selected, random sample? When were the questions asked? Is it possible that bias might have crept in because of the methodology or timing? People might be more concerned about financial arrangements, for example, around income-tax time than at any other time of the year. Don't be like the newspaper that insists on conducting its political surveys by telephone on Friday evenings. Do you suppose it's possible that people who go out on Friday evenings, and thus aren't surveyed, are somehow different from those who stay at home? It's worth considering, and not just in footnote fashion.

Graphics are journalism that cannot be hedged. Although you often can soften the impact of text by inserting "claims" or "asserts," putting notations into the source line of a graphic doesn't reduce its impact. If you don't trust a statistic, don't use it, regardless of how strongly worded your disclaimer might be.

Want to Create Demographic Differences?

In a scientifically selected, random sampling of 600 adults, with a margin of error of five percentage points, 55 percent of whites said they preferred the new *Star Trek* to the old, while only 40 percent of African Americans did. In contrast, a whopping 75 percent of Asian-Americans said they preferred the new series.

What's wrong? Chances are none of these contentions is statistically significant.

First, the whites: Fifty-five percent preferred the new; 45 percent, the old. The margin of error is five points. That means anywhere from 50 percent to 60 percent preferred the new while anywhere from 40 percent to 50 percent preferred the old. In short, it could be tied at 50-50, with no preference.

5.5

The lie . . .

. . . the truth

ERROR MARGIN

Poll graphics should take care to tell the whole truth.

How about the blacks and Asians? One of the seldom-explained facts of survey data is that when you break data down by subgroups, the error margin goes up. While the pollsters reached 400 people total, perhaps only 80 of them were black and only four of them were Asian. The error margins for these subgroups become astronomical.

If the person who conducted the survey is reputable, she or he should be eager to provide the correct margins for each subgroup. When you chart such data, be sure to indicate, not just in a source line, how accurate the numbers truly are. One way to do this is to show the range of the error margin as part of the bars in a bar chart or slices in a pie chart, as done in Figure 5.5. The reader sees the whole truth and can interpret it as she or he sees fit.

There's No Margin for Error

Remember: Contrary to what "opinion researchers" say, surveys cannot prove or show anything. They merely indicate. A reputable survey never pretends to represent what all of society believes.

Survey error margins are statistical constructs based on the infamous bell curve (or "standard distribution") that everyone seems to be cursing these days. No one went out and asked every person on the planet what he or she believed, then compared this to survey results to come up with reported error margins. Rather, error margins, when properly stated, are stated this way:

If this survey were conducted 20 times, statistical theories indicate that in 19 out of 20 times the results for an equally divided question should vary by no more than five percentage points in either direction.

In other words, there's a 95 percent chance (technically called a "confidence interval") that the results would be within five percentage points of a second survey's results. There also is a five percent chance that the results of a repeated survey would vary more than that.

If we are talking about a simple yes-no proposition, with equal likelihood for people to answer yes or no, the spread between yes and no must be more than 10 points for the difference in survey results to be valid. If yes comes back as 55 percent and no as 45 percent, the race between yes and no remains a statistical dead heat. This is because yes could be anywhere between 50 percent and 60 percent and no could be anywhere between 40 percent and 50 percent. At best, the survey indicates one might be leading over the other. At worst, it could be a 50-50 tie or a 60-40 landslide.

Even then, these numbers are valid only 19 out of 20 times. The results you base your graphic on could be from the one time in 20 in which the survey results vary by a greater margin. The greater margin should be only slightly greater, but such quibbling points are lost on someone who sees only the main point of the graphic you produce.

How do they figure all this stuff out? Unless you really want to take a mini-course in statistics, it's based on the idea that if you flip a coin 300 or 400 times, you'll come up with approximately equal numbers of heads and tails 95 percent of the time (no more than five percentage points variance between them). That's how error margins and confidence intervals are computed.

Technically speaking, if you accept a 95 percent confidence interval, which is standard for most research, you determine the error margin on the basis of the number of people you survey:

Error margin	People surveyed
3 points	1,067
4 points	600
5 points	384
6 points	268

If you need other error margins for yes-no type questions, divide 0.9605 by the square of the margin you want and you'll have the number of people you need to survey. To compute the number of people you would have to survey for seven-point error margin, for example, divide 0.9605 by the quantity 0.07 times 0.07 to come up with the number needed: 196.

Contrary to popular belief, it does not matter how big a population you are surveying. To get a five percentage point margin nationwide or in your hometown, you have to survey the same number of people, even though the population you are projecting the survey results to varies considerably. The margins cited here are for populations of 500,000 or more. To get a five-point margin of error in a population one-tenth that size, you need only three fewer interviews. To get the same error margin in a population one-fiftieth that size, you need only 14 fewer interviews. The number of interviews needed never gets below 278, and that's for a population of only 1,000.

Not Guilty? Maybe You Were Errantly Sample-Framed?

After resolving questions of error margins, you still have the task of figuring out whether your survey really says anything.

To be valid, a survey must make certain that every individual in the population being surveyed (the "sample frame," as it is known) has exactly the same chance of being selected. This is hard to guarantee. If you conduct a survey by telephone, you automatically violate the standard. I, for example, have two phone lines in my home. My next-door neighbor, with three adults and two children in the household, has only one. My chances of being picked in a phone survey are much greater than the chances of my neighbors. Moreover, some people don't have phones at all. In fact, the Census Bureau says, only 92 percent of the population has telephone service at home. Any survey taken by telephone automatically misses all of those without phones while giving others with more than one phone more than one chance of being surveyed. And that doesn't begin to account for the potential of being called at work as well as at home.

Reputable surveyors try to get around problems like this by dialing random digits from a database of that lists only one number for each residence that has phone service. Such techniques can miss college students, people in nursing homes and residents in various institutions, but it gets around the fact that in some communities up to 50 percent of all residential phone numbers are unlisted.

Some Surveys Don't Tell the Complete Truth

Reputable pollsters also worry about such things as who is most likely to answer a phone in a residence in which more than one adult resides. Call during the day, for example, and you'll be likely to skew your results toward the view of child-care providers. One trick they use to get around this is to ask for the adult who most recently celebrated his or her birthday. Complicated, huh? There's more.

For a survey to be valid, once an individual is picked in the randomizing process, that specific individual must be the one the pollsters talk to. Otherwise, the sample is no longer random. Who's in the sample and who's out begins depending on something other than the luck of the draw. So, if you get an answering machine or if the person who most recently had a birthday isn't home, you must keep trying until that specific person is reached. You can't just go looking for someone else. If you did, people would no longer have equal chances of being selected.

Obviously, poll-takers often fail to reach everyone selected and do have to look for someone else. When they do, the "completion rate" of the survey begins to suffer.

For a survey to be considered valid, pollsters shoot for a completion rate of at least 80 percent—meaning that 80 percent of those selected at random were actually reached. There's no easy way to figure how a completion rate of less than 100 percent affects the statistical error margin, but it's a fact that even an acceptable 80 percent completion rate greatly reduces the accuracy of a survey.

To be truly accurate in expressing results from a survey with an 80 percent completion rate you would have to list 20 percent as having unknown opinions in response to every question. No pollster actually does this because it renders almost all results meaningless. What might have been a statistically significant 56/44 split without the unknowns becomes a statistically insignificant 45/35 split with 20 unknown. Moreover, if all of the 20 sided with the 35 and there was a five point error margin, the actual results could have been as high as 55/45 the other way!

Not only do most reputable firms ignore this fact. Many publish survey results even if their completion rates slide to as low as 60 percent. Should you immediately throw out all such surveys? Probably not. But

if low completion rates are coupled with sample frame problems or
other concerns, you should become increasingly leery of the results.

It's Not the Answers, It's the Questions

All of these concerns are for naught if the survey questions—the items
included in the "survey instrument," in the langauge of pollsters—aren't
asked in a special way. Obviously, they should be clear and unbiased,
and they should present enough options so that a respondent is
comfortable with his or her answer. Answers also have to mean the
same thing to all people.

On top of that, something as simple as the apparent race, gender or
competence of the polltaker may affect the outcome. Book after book,
scholarly report after scholarly report, has been devoted to the topic of
explaining where surveys go wrong.

Can You Trust Your Survey?

When all is said and done, how do you decide whether to trust a
survey enough to use its results in graphical form? If you were a
statistician, you would have to consider such things as:

- The error margin
- The sample frame
- The completion rate
- The survey instrument
- The interview procedure

As someone who's not a statistician, how much you trust any survey's
results depends not only on the methodology but also on the track
record of the survey firm. A reputable organization with a proven track
record is probably worth a graphic; the Fly-By-Night Aluminum
Company's survey results probably are not. They might be worth a
story, where all the disclaimers can be put in perspective, but information design makes disclaimers ineffective.

The fact that disclaimers are ineffective in graphics is a good reason
why you should never use graphics to report the results of mail-in or
phone-in surveys. These are not scientific surveys, as their results tend

to be skewed in favor of intensely held opinions. (People with strong opinions are more likely to take the time to respond.) While you might think you can get away with putting a disclaimer to that effect in your graphic, keep in mind that the average reader will focus on the findings, not your disclaimer.

Ultimately, it's your credibility that's on the line, not the survey firm's. If you have a chance, talk to whoever organized the survey. If that person can't give you straight answers about completion rates, sample frames, question bias and the like, you'll know where to put the results—in the wastebasket. If you are uncomfortable with having to stand behind your graphic's information, don't use it. Exercise every bit of care and prudence you can. Graphics are such powerful communicators that they require even more care and prudence than do verbal accounts of the same events.

To Help You Think Visually

Scan your favorite daily newspaper or other publication until you find a graphic that you think somehow misrepresents reality at first glance:

1. How could the misrepresentation be eliminated?

2. Why do you suppose the publication did not correct this graphic?

Develop a habit of questioning everything you see. As a revered professor once taught his students, "If your mother says she loves you, check it out." For our purposes, if charted statistics seem to be saying something, check them out. By regularly challenging what you see, you'll begin developing a sixth sense that helps you effectively evaluate graphical data.

Beginning to Think Visually

Many of us look at information graphics as tools that help us do our jobs. With them, we can make newsletters more effective, breathe life into annual reports, issue compelling brochures and releases, report research results efficiently and make our cases to juries, boards of directors or consumers more convincing.

In the specialized field of newspaper and magazine publishing, information graphics carry with them even greater responsibilities. Deemed by many to be essential to a publication's success, graphics provide livelihood to entire departments of professionals, give rise to big-stakes consulting and even have led to the creation of a new name for the field: "visual journalism." It's a name worth considering even if your line of work isn't journalism.

The gurus of graphics would like to have America's publishers think otherwise, but there's no mystery to practicing good information design—or good "visual journalism," if you will. The secrets are blurted out in the newly coined name for the field:

- Do your work visually.
- Judge its merits journalistically.

The Medium

The Techniques

The Forms

The Profession

Unfortunately, the training for journalists and other professionals usually is exactly the reverse. From day one they typically are told to do their work verbally—to write stories, present scripts or otherwise communicate with words. And all too often the work they produce is judged more on its aesthetic merits—the style of writing or delivery— than it is on its information. Colleagues may be more interested in the techniques, but the audience is more concerned with the message.

The transition from verbal thinking to visual thinking can be a difficult one. It takes a bit of practice and, perhaps, a bit of un-learning. But almost anyone can begin to think and work visually. It is, after all, how the human mind works on its most fundamental level.

Thinking with Your Mind's Eye

"To envision information," writes statistician Edward R. Tufte, "is to work at the intersection of image, word, number, art."

Galileo, he notes, effortlessly merged words and drawings in his 1613 observations of Saturn. But Galileo was a genius. How do less gifted mortals master information design? It may be as simple as remembering.

Remember your last birthday. Did you do something special? Get a special gift? The thought summons up memories, right? And the memories come in the form of pictures. You see the sweater that your sister sent you. You remember the look on a loved one's face as you unwrapped his or her present. You recall the ambiance of the restaurant you visited. You have a clear picture in your mind of how flat your car's tire was when you tried to leave for home. And you'll never forget that creepy guy who wandered by while you were trying to change it.

If you had a less traumatic celebration, perhaps you remember how pretty and thoughtful were the cards you received, or how increasingly shaky an elderly relative's signature seemed on one of them. But do you remember the exact words imprinted on the cards without first seeing the cards in your mind?

Unless your system of recall differs radically from the average person's, the vast majority of your memories are sensory, and a large number of those sensory memories are visual.

Science is only beginning to understand exactly how the human mind operates, but one thing for sure is that different parts of the brain perform different tasks. One half is the logical half. It sees the letters of an unfamiliar word, deciphers what they say, then consults the other half—the analog half—to check whether the word represents something it might have seen and cataloged in the past. One half thinks abstractly. The other half remembers with images. Put the two together, as in Figure 6.1, and you get meaning.

That's an overly simplistic explanation, of course. In reality, both halves can and do arrive at complete meanings independently. A simple word like "cat," for example, might be seen initially by the analog half not as separate letters but as a complete token standing for a feline memory. The logical half would hardly need to be involved. The more you involve both halves in a single thought process, however, the more impact that thought process is likely to have.

6.1

A picture, as the saying goes, is worth a thousand words. In fact, Kodak engineers calculate it's worth more like eight million. It takes, they say, 34 megabytes—more words than the full text of the Bible—to store digitally all the data captured on a single 35 mm color negative, scanned at maximum resolution. Mental pictures are even more detailed, capable of discerning nuances that film cannot record.

Reading involves one half of the brain processing text and the other half summoning up memories that give the text meaning.

With minds naturally equipped to store such huge amounts of data visually, is it any wonder humans seem more likely to recall the color of a friend's hair by summoning up a mental image of the person than recalling the simple word "brown"? The word is a verbal token for a complete thought stored visually.

Such memories rely upon sensory input, but the senses aren't the only things that cause visual thinking.

Memories Aren't All That's Visual

When do you plan to eat this evening? Think about it for a moment. When you encourage the thought to cross your mind, do you see the time indicated on an imagined clock face? Or, perhaps do you see the quarter pounder with cheese that awaits you? Maybe you see a task you must complete, or an environment in which you must complete it, before you can enjoy your meal. What you probably don't see are the digits that make up the time at which you plan to eat.

How much money do you have in your pocket or purse right now? Do you see something between the crisp $20 bills you got on your last payday and the six assorted coins you will have the day before your next payday? Chances are you see the currency, not a dollar sign and decimal point.

What's today's date? When will your next birthday be? Don't count the months or days, but create an image in your mind of how far apart the two days are. Does your mind's eye see some form of calendar or list, however abstract it might be? Compare your image of time with other people's. You'll be amazed at how differently people envision weeks, months, seasons and years.

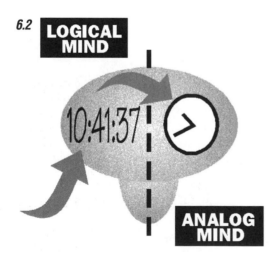

6.2 LOGICAL MIND

ANALOG MIND

Images give thoughts meaning. Remember your old digital wristwatch? Why did you trade it in for an analog? Sure the digital watch was more precise. But with your new analog watch, as Figure 6.2 shows, you can just glance at the clockface and instantly know what time it was without having to think. The logical mind sees the trees; the analog mind sees the forest.

The logical mind deals in precision whereas the analog mind deals in less precise but more meaningful data.

What impression is created by a person who replies, "It's 10:41:37," to your question, "What time is it?" Wouldn't it have been more useful—and less anal-retentive—if he or she had simply said, "It's almost quarter to 11"?

To understand simple concepts like this, you don't need years of art training. Chances are good you don't need to learn how to think visually. You just need to un-learn what you have been taught to do all your professional life—translate visual memories into verbalizations. The best writing paints a verbal picture. In graphics, the visuals stand on their own.

If you're having trouble getting this, don't worry. Learning how to express ideas without words is somewhat akin to learning how to read without moving your lips. Practice never hurts. Now might be a good time to put down this book and do just that. Ponder how you keep track of time and dates in your mind, how you organize lists of things to do in your head, how you balance positives and negatives in weighing a decision. The visualizations you subconsciously use are perfect grist for graphic treatments. Getting in touch with them is the key.

Conveying Thoughts without Words

Remember NASA's deep space probes—the ones with the universal greetings of peace inscribed on them? They communicated fairly well, if you consider that the likely audience, if any, wouldn't understand any other human language. (All extraterrestrials don't speak English the way they do on *Star Trek*.)

6.3

How about the "NO RIGHT TURN" sign a few blocks down the street? The universal symbol of a circle and a slash covering a right arrow (see Figure 6.3) gets its point across a lot more quickly than do the words "NO RIGHT TURN." Simple symbols like this work. They're quickly understandable, even on a subconscious level, and thus are very easy to comprehend on a conscious one.

By the time you would have read and decoded the words "NO RIGHT TURN," you might have been halfway into the intersection.

Other symbols, of course, are not so communicative. How many times have we wondered whether the blinking bowling-pin pattern of lights on a photocopier (see Figure 6.4) means that the machine is warming up, out of toner, has too much toner, is jammed, out of paper, or operating only for native speakers of some foreign language? The more abstract an image becomes, the more difficult it is to understand. In the process, the less memorable it becomes as an image, the less quickly that image may be understood.

6.4

If you've ever worked a photocopier, chances are you've seen this icon. But what does it mean? Overly abstract icons don't communicate.

As any observer of the Mona Lisa knows, art is in the eye of the beholder. Its meaning is personal and subject to interpretation. But communication is not art. Aristotle rated poetry as a much higher form of art than narrative. Poetry's message requires introspection to understand. It takes on different nuances with each different reader. If poetry is so wonderful, why don't journalists write in verse instead of narrative? To be sure, journalists appreciate style. But they are in a communication business, not an art business. They must make certain that each message they communicate can be understood clearly and universally. They thus choose the narrative over the poetic.

Likewise, information designers choose the visually informative over the visually decorative and try at all times to avoid the most common error aspiring designers make: decorating everything with clip-art icons, ignoring the chance to truly inform with images.

The results can be more than just wasteful. Often, in selecting icons, they ignore the fact that cultural and experiential differences abound. Not only is space lost, meaning is lost as well. Does a check mark, for example, mean that something has been selected and verified as having been done? Does it mean that the information offered is correct or incorrect? The message an aspiring information designer imparts by creating a check-mark icon for a list of civic proposals is mixed indeed.

Information, not Icons

Even veteran visual journalists make the mistake of substituting decorative icons for informative visuals. In his primer on newspaper layout, *The Newspaper Designer's Handbook,* Tim Harrower offers a collection of how-to graphics. A classic example of missed visual opportunities is his offered "bio box" on the Black Rhinoceros (see Figure 6.5).

The text within the bio box offers much grist for visual comparison: The rhino weighs 2,000 to 3,000 pounds at maturity. A newborn weighs 55 to 90 pounds. An adult stretches 10 to 12 feet in length and lives about 60 years.

6.5

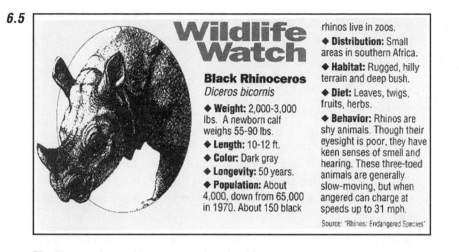

Wildlife Watch

Black Rhinoceros
Diceros bicornis

◆ **Weight:** 2,000-3,000 lbs. A newborn calf weighs 55-90 lbs.
◆ **Length:** 10-12 ft.
◆ **Color:** Dark gray
◆ **Longevity:** 50 years.
◆ **Population:** About 4,000, down from 65,000 in 1970. About 150 black rhinos live in zoos.
◆ **Distribution:** Small areas in southern Africa.
◆ **Habitat:** Rugged, hilly terrain and deep bush.
◆ **Diet:** Leaves, twigs, fruits, herbs.
◆ **Behavior:** Rhinos are shy animals. Though their eyesight is poor, they have keen senses of smell and hearing. These three-toed animals are generally slow-moving, but when angered can charge at speeds up to 31 mph.

Source: "Rhinos: Endangered Species"

Tim Harrower's graphic stresses what the rhino looks like.

What's interesting about these facts? Probably how the rhino compares to a human or to other animals in the world (see Figure 6.6). A sketch showing a rhino and a human, sized to scale, graphically makes the point about how long the beast is. Showing a rhino matching in weight an elevator full of 25 adult humans or a couple of compact cars tells you more than a data list ever could. Comparing the rhino's life span to that of a human, a dog, a cat or other familiar animal by way of a bar chart would be more informative than simply listing the number of years a rhino lives.

Rather than choosing any of these informative facts as the thrust for his visual, Harrower chooses instead to decorate his graphic with an icon. His sketch indicates that we're talking about a rhinoceros, but that's all it says. It tells you no more than you learned at your first visit to the zoo or when you first picked up an animal picture book.

6.6

Wildlife Watch

BLACK RHINOCEROS

Diceros bicornis
Length:
10 to 12 feet

Weight:
2,000 to 3,000 pounds

Longevity:
60 years

Not all would be needed, but here are several examples of how to tell the rhino's vital statistics.

This alternative, although much less visually appealing, tells the rhino's story better.

Moreover, by sketching rather than photographing the rhino, Harrower violates one of the basic tenets of effective visual communication:

- If it's tangible, photograph it.
- If it's intangible, illustrate it.

Ask anyone who has riled a rhino while on safari. There's absolutely nothing intangible about a ton and a half of horned beast bearing down on a Jeep. Rather than have an artist spend several hours laboriously decorating, why not instead put the time into reporting information visually?

Photojournalists know only too well how to avoid the pitfall of decoration. Telling a story visually doesn't mean telling what the subject looks like. It means telling what he or she does, what makes him or her worthy of being photographed. A verbal journalist would never write a feature story about someone for whom there was no news peg. A photojournalist would never settle for an environmental portrait when story-telling photographs were possible. Similarly, a graphics journalist should not settle for an icon when more informative material is available. And the same holds true for those practicing information design in non-newspaper settings.

Charles Dickens told compelling stories. Was he a reporter?

Ansel Adams photographed beautiful landscapes. Was he a photojournalist?

To be sure, a good reporter must have some technical skills as a writer. A good photojournalist must likewise have some technical skills as a photographer. But just as writing skills do not make a good reporter and technical photo skills do not make a good photojournalist, technical art skills do not make a good information designer. The ability to communicate informative facts—clearly, effectively, powerfully—is the goal of all communications, either verbal or visual.

The goal is not to make things pretty but to use visuals as a way to enhance communication. If you can't use it to be informative, lose it for being merely decorative.

What Research Says about Graphics

A thorough review of scientific research on how graphics are perceived is located in Appendix B. Rather than bore you with details right now, here are some of the key findings:

Text-and-graphic combinations transfer meaning better than two pieces of text or a single piece of text alone. Graphics are superior to text in speed of information processing. Elaborate cartoon-like graphics limit comprehension. Readers may focus more on the illustration than on the data and miss the point. Overall, graphics are generally more memorable, more quickly processed and more believable than text.

Part of graphics' value appears to relate to the separately motivated left and right brains. While one half of the brain is busy processing text, the other half can almost subconsciously absorb the analog images of a graphic. Without the need for elaborate processing, these images come in quickly and are hard for the seeing-is-believing half of the mind to challenge.

Put a message in both the visual channel and the textual channel, and you get both sides of the brain working on it at once, resulting in what researcher Allen Paivio calls dual-coding phenomenon—an additive method of very efficiently imprinting information onto memory. It's a message that educators and business executives have been getting for years. Why else do you think that Microsoft has been selling so many copies of presentation programs such as PowerPoint and that every classroom in the world seems to have a chalkboard, dry-erase board or overhead projector?

In an era in which information is often regarded as being less personally relevant to readers than it might one day have been, graphics have emerged as a tool that is particularly important not only for attracting attention but also for getting messages across to audiences that may not be inclined to systematically read. Whether graphics are capable of luring people into reading things that they otherwise would not have read is subject to much debate. It is clear, however, that they cause information to be conveyed that otherwise would not get across. Graphics can, therefore, be very powerful tools.

The best way to take advantage of this power is to think visually, not artistically. Even "cartoon" artist Nigel Holmes is beginning to agree. In 1994, *Design* magazine quoted him as saying:

It was quite telling that in [H. Ross] Perot's programs before the last election, this man who has more money than anybody and who could have had the slickest animated presentation, actually sat at a desk and pointed to a hand-drawn chart. This means something. It means you may not trust all this slick stuff… So I think the future of information graphics will be a backlash against overproduced things. They'll get simpler. They will start to play more of the…explaining role they ought to do.

To Help You Think Visually

Imagine how you spend a typical day: waking up, going to school or work, having lunch, maybe dropping by a health club or cocktail lounge, then going home for dinner, TV and bed.

1. Using only your doodling skills, sketch out a schematic of your day, including a map showing where you go and the times at which you do these things—all without using any words. (For a particularly inspired exercise, try to figure out how to sign your name to it without using letters or resorting to Pictionary-style pictures that sound like your name.)

2. Write up the exact same information in text and compare the two.

3. Give each summary to a friend. Question your two friends afterward. See which summary produced the greatest recall—overall and in specific areas.

Chapter 7

An Overview of Graphics Software

If you think this book is going to teach you all the mysteries of the Macintosh or PC, magically transforming you into an information designer, close the cover right now, take a quick hike over to the bookstore and demand your money back.

Teaching someone to type does not make him or her a writer. Teaching someone how to use a camera does not make him or her a photographer. Teaching someone the intricacies of graphics software does not make him or her an information designer.

Technical skills are important, but technical training no more imbues a person with the ability to be an information designer than does teaching an engineer how to draft or teaching a chef how to use a food processor. The secret is not in learning to use the tools but in learning what you can do with the tools.

Later chapters show you a few of the techniques. But for the most part, purely technical training is best left to technical schools and to the manuals that come with graphics programs. It's amazing how much you can learn by simply reading the instructions. You'll quickly find that there's no magic command labeled "Create Graphic." In fact, the bulk of the work that goes into a graphic takes place far away from the computer, where the creature doing the stirring is you, not the mouse.

Still, there is some truth to the saying that a craftsman is only as good as her tools. Pick your favorite one. More often than not it will be chosen for you on the basis of what's available where you work or go to school. Subsequent chapters outline common ways each of the programs can be used. Keep in mind, however, that regardless of the tools, you should be able to accomplish anything this book undertakes. To make sure that's true, only the most rudimentary tools were used in creating all the sample graphics.

Macromedia (Aldus) FreeHand

Available for the Mac and for IBM-compatible computers that run Microsoft Windows, FreeHand™ is the program of choice for most small- to medium-sized newspapers and at many smaller organizations. For many years, Associated Press graphics were supplied in Version 3 of the program. A new interchangeable format, in which graphics supplied by AP can be read by enhanced versions of FreeHand and its chief rival, Adobe Illustrator, now has taken over. But huge archives of graphics created in FreeHand 3 mean that it and advanced versions of FreeHand will be around for some time to come.

Aldus FreeHand 3, still in use at many offices and computer labs, is a relatively simple program, with few bells and whistles. It has superior tools for aligning and equally spacing separate elements, but suffers from one serious flaw: an antiquated system for entering text. Rather than simply clicking on an area where you want to position text and writing it on the spot, you must open up a text "window" (see Figure 7.1) and type your text inside this box. Worse yet, if you later want to revise the text, you cannot simply highlight and change the text the way you do in most other programs, by using the I-beam Text tool. You must first reopen the text window by selecting the text with the "arrow" object-movement cursor and double-clicking or invoking Command-I.

Version 4 of FreeHand solved this problem and added many occasionally useful bells and whistles. In doing so, however, it created a whole host of other shortcomings, not the least of which is a user interface that was wholly unintuitive. It quickly was replaced by a new version.

7.1

FreeHand 3 is plagued by cumbersome text-editing tools.

FreeHand 5, marketed under the Macromedia name for both Mac and Windows, corrects some of the version 4 problems but retains a few quirks. The most puzzling is a dialog box called Inspector, which is designed to make it easy for so-called power users to interface to the program. Unfortunately, unless you are an all-day power user, you likely will find that Inspector is more of a Clouseau-like nuisance than it is an aid. If, for example, you want to change the point size of type, you may go to either a normal pull-down menu or to a special floating menu. But if you also want to change leading (the space between lines), you find it somewhere else entirely—in Inspector. Failing to provide one consistent home for commands that are frequently used together is the single greatest failing of Version 5's Inspector.

Macromedia takes Inspector (see Figure 7.2) several steps further, and does make some improvements in it, in its new, highly touted version 7, which features several different Inspectors. Early reaction to the cloned Clouseaus is mixed, however.

7.2
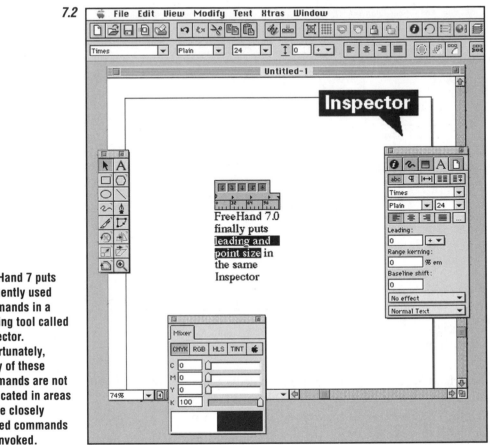

FreeHand 7 puts frequently used commands in a floating tool called Inspector. Unfortunately, many of these commands are not duplicated in areas where closely related commands are invoked.

Like all programs, FreeHand 3 and 4 have their devoted followers, but those most devoted to these programs tend to be the same people who insist that Betamax and eight-track tapes are superior technology. They may be right, but they aren't keeping up with the times.

Better than both is FreeHand 5. It has the same basic functionality of FreeHand 4 but with a few of the rough edges polished off. Many smaller newspapers that started with FreeHand 3 now have upgraded to FreeHand 5, which because of its simplicity vis à vis other graphics programs also is commonly taught in college graphics courses.

FreeHand 7 (whatever happened to FreeHand 6 is as much a mystery as why Windows 95 was sold in 1996) was being billed as a "killer app"—a program that opens up completely new areas of functionality. In fact, FreeHand 7, released late in 1996, does have some fine new features, accompanied by a corresponding reduction in the program's speed. But most of the new features merely catch FreeHand up with its chief competitor, Adobe Illustrator, and try needlessly to make FreeHand an all-encompassing solution that includes somewhat rudimentary versions of layout tools found in QuarkXPress and Adobe PageMaker.

Adobe Illustrator

Long a favorite of serious artists, Illustrator has emerged as the likely program of choice for graphics journalists at large newspapers and magazines and for information designers in dedicated design depart-ments of other businesses. The latest Macintosh release, version 6, has virtually every bell and whistle imaginable and is somewhat intuitive in its design.

A big hit in Illustrator's repertoire is its built-in charting tools (see Figure 7.3). Just enter the data, and Illustrator roughs out the bar, pie or fever charts for you.

At times the complexity of Illustrator can overwhelm non-artists. (How many different variants of a cursor, a few of them shown in Figure 7.4, do you really need?) For this reason, many colleges and smaller professional organizations have avoided it. Still Illustrator is operable on a simpler level, and its use of standard encapsulated PostScript files (as in FreeHand 5 and above) makes it easy to use in combination with other programs.

7.3

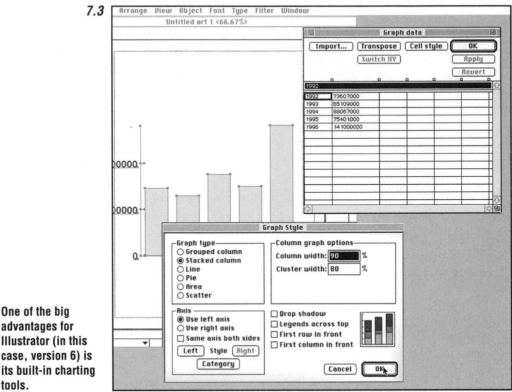

One of the big advantages for Illustrator (in this case, version 6) is its built-in charting tools.

7.4

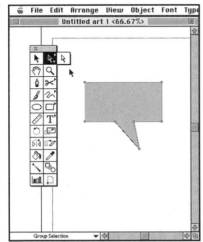

A big drawback to Illustrator is its complexity, particularly its uses of pointing tools.

Seldom will you find anyone who professes to be a master of this rather sophisticated software. Unlike the program's earlier versions, however, seldom will you find anyone who professes to be completely befuddled by it either. The earliest usable versions of Illustrator—1.1 and 88—are rarely found in use anymore. A few still cling to version 3, although it continued an early Illustrator tradition for not allowing users to work in Preview mode. Only confusing keylines could be seen when an image was being edited. Version 4, a brief-lived phenomenon like version 4 of FreeHand, corrected this but retained another early Illustrator quirk—the need to create multiple separate shapes, rather than simply invoke radial or graduated files, in creating tonal blends. (More on such shading techniques in

Chapter 10.) Version 6 is a nice improvement over version 5 of the program. However, both remain in substantial use.

The program is available in both Mac and Windows versions. Typically, new versions are available first on Mac and several months later on Windows.

A special note for *Star Trek* fans: Illustrator is used by the series' and movies' artists and designers to create many of the special effects, including all the instrument panels.

QuarkXPress and PageMaker

Graphics programs? These are really page-design packages, aren't they?

True, but Quark in particular also has emerged as a powerful tool for creation of information graphics that don't rely on extensive illustration or that use photographs or photo-editing programs to create their visual images.

Like PageMaker, Quark, available for both Mac and Windows, excels at handling type. It lacks the alignment tools of FreeHand and later versions of Illustrator, but it makes up for them with superior grids, a simple and familiar user interface (see Figure 7.5), and superior commands both for tabulating material and for intermingling graphic elements and text. (Its step-and-repeat function is even a value-added workaround for lack of alignment tools.)

7.5

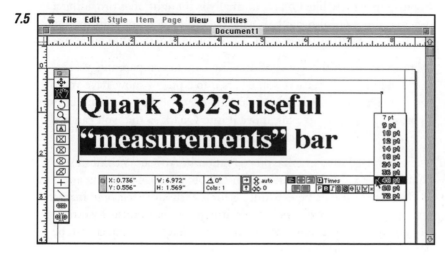

The "measurements" bar in XPress 3.32 is what Inspector fails to be in FreeHand—a useful compendium of frequently used settings that does not replace the ability to change the same settings elsewhere.

Although its drawing tools are extremely limited, Quark is able to import images from other programs quickly and easily. As a result, it is becoming a good choice for everything from small entry-point graphics to heavily text-based tabulations. Quark also is the program of choice for creating mega-graphic pages that integrate elements created in other programs. AP frequently uses Quark to supply full-page features packages.

PageMaker, at one time marketed under the Aldus name, is a very similar program. For reasons known mostly to marketing experts, it has failed to make much of an impact on the communications industry except in very small markets. The merger of PageMaker into the Adobe product line might change that. PageMaker and Quark work much the same. PageMaker tends to be used in non-communications industries, whereas Quark is used in communications industries.

One clear advantage in learning either of these is that they have changed much less over the years than have drawing programs. Version 3 of Quark, for example, has been concurrent with Illustrator 1.1, 88, 4, 5 and 6 and with FreeHand 3, 4, 5 and 7. Quark tends to change its basic program very seldom, making most of its modifications via add-on elements that you can choose to install or not install, thereby controlling your own need for retraining.

Adobe Photoshop

Photoshop, which, like Quark, normally is thought of as providing a different function, also can be a valuable tool in creating information graphics, particularly when used in conjunction with other programs.

Want to be creative? Instead of drawing bars to compare this year's snowfall to last year's, carve some bars into a pile of snow, have your bar chart photographed and import the image by way of a scanner into Photoshop. Dress it up a bit, move it into Quark so that you can add type, and you have an interesting graphic.

Want an image for a graphic on starvation in Africa? Why not use a photo of the real-life human tragedy? Photoshop can help you tweak it. Don't try to use its type-handling tools without specialized instruction; fonts may come out as jagged bitmaps or with unusually erratic spacing between the letters if you do. Still, many other things can be done quite well in Photoshop.

All those simplistic old icons stored away on your hard drive (see Figure 7.6) can take on new life if imported into Photoshop and enhanced with the program's air-brushing tools, texturing and feathering tools (see Figure 7.7). As artistic trends stray from the flat, paint-by-number look of computerized graphics, Photoshop has emerged as a tool of choice for softening lines and smoothing textures of flat images, transforming two-dimensional doodles into three-dimensional artwork.

7.6

A simple icon like this can be dressed up...

7.7

...to look like this. Photoshop lets you soften lines and add textures in ways that most drawing programs, particularly in their early versions, cannot.

Moreover, with a scanner, Photoshop enables you to "borrow" images created by someone else and alter and enhance them until they become your own. Be wary of plagiarism of copyright material, however. There's more on legal concerns in Chapter 18.

Like the other programs, Photoshop is available for both Mac and Windows environments. And contrary to what many people might claim, all of these programs work pretty much the same on either platform. An out-of-the-box Mac might be better configured to run some of them, but if you spend as much money on a Windows machine as you do on a Mac, chances are the programs will perform equally on either platform, particularly if the program is designed for 32-bit Windows NT 4.0 or Windows 95.

CorelDRAW!

Virtually no one in the communications industry except a handful of workers at weeklies and small dailies use this program for serious information design. And that's a shame. It is relatively inexpensive, comes with its own bundled charting and photo-editing programs, links to its own equivalent of Quark (Ventura Publishing) as well as the WordPerfect 7 word processor, has a huge array of pre-drawn clip art and is capable of doing almost anything the other programs can.

Why is it so seldom used? Unlike the others, CorelDRAW! tradition-ally is a Windows-only program, and information design generally is thought of as a Mac-only club. But with all the other programs clamoring to be available for Windows, this someday might change.

The biggest advantage CorelDRAW! has is that it provides a way to do graphics at almost any size of organization. While a small organization might have no Mac and be unwilling to pay $500 or $600 for any of the more popular graphics programs, chances are it already has the $150 version 3 of CorelDRAW!, CorelCHART! and CorelPHOTO-PAINT!. Ask around. CorelDRAW! probably is being used to create ads, signs or other things, and you undoubtedly can use it whenever you want.

Does it work? You be the judge. Many of the graphic elements in this book were created in CorelDRAW! 3 (see Figure 7.8) to demonstrate how useful it can be.

Particularly in its early versions, CorelDRAW! was not quite as smooth as the other programs. But, if you are patient, it is extremely intuitive and can accomplish almost anything the more popular programs can. Corel concurrently markets versions 3, 4, 5 and 6 of its DRAW! package and soon will be issuing version 7, a true 32-bit application that takes advantage of Windows 95 and NT speed.

7.8

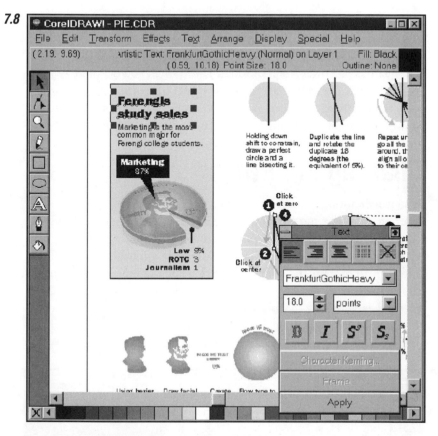

Even an outdated version of a Windows-only program such as CorelDRAW! 3 can be used to create sophisticated images.

Claris MacDraw

At one time, this in-house Apple product had it all. With a facile user interface and superior text and alignment functions, it stood far ahead of Illustrator and the little-known FreeHand in the early years of electronic graphics journalism. It was, in fact, one of the badges of honor for graphics journalists to brag that they preferred MacDraw to the more artist-inspired Illustrator.

But MacDraw lost its market share when an ill-fated version of the program, called MacDraw Pro, hit the market. It was slow, cumbersome and under-powered compared to the competition.

Somewhere in the recesses of a hard drive you inherit may be some old graphics created in the original MacDraw or MacDraw II program, probably done on a Mac that looked more like a boom box than it does the Quadras or Power Macs of today. Pause when you do and pay your respects to the difficulties someone overcame in creating graphics with tools not nearly so advanced as are those available today, and marvel at how far infographic technology has come in less than 10 years.

Charting Programs

Also worth noting are several programs designed specifically for charting data. The most popular is DeltaGraph (see Figure 7.9), but others abound. While none replaces a drawing program—in fact, anything they produce usually is so clunky that it must be imported into such a program and completely redone before use—some graphic journalists swear by them. Others merely swear at them. In Chapter 12, we'll explore how to work with such programs, which often clutter their graphics with so many irrelevant, distracting accouterments that veteran information designers prefer not to use them.

7.9

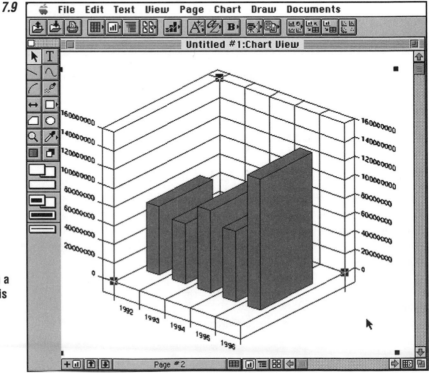

Spotting DeltaGraph's distinctive 3-D accouterments in a finished graphic is one of the first clues that an information designer is a neophyte.

Charting programs are basically spreadsheets and work much the same as other spreadsheet programs do. A standard office suite package, such as Microsoft Office with its Excel speadsheet program, can be used to accomplish most of the same tasks.

To Help You Think Visually

Determine which program is right for you, locate its manual and find out:

1. If you draw a rectangle, how do you un-group, un-join or release the points so you can select one of them and delete it to form a triangle?

2. How can you change how condensed or expanded a typeface will be?

Finding how to do these simple tasks will help you in coming sections and will familiarize you with how the program operates and how to find information in the manual.

How to Draw on a Computer

Drawing on a computer is a lot like doodling on children's placemats at family restaurants: If you can tell a circle from a square and can figure out how to complete a dot-to-dot puzzle, you, too, can draw. How well you draw depends more on your visual insight than on your technical prowess.

In essence, electronic drawings are nothing more than overlapping collections of rectangles, ovals and dot-to-dot polygons. Shaded or not, they are little more than sets of mathematically defined points joined by straight or curved lines. The only thing that counts is what shows when it's printed.

If you've ever drawn a cube, you know the routine. One square is the front wall. Another square, offset, is the back wall. Connect them by drawing side walls, and you have a three-dimensional drawing (see Figure 8.1).

8.1

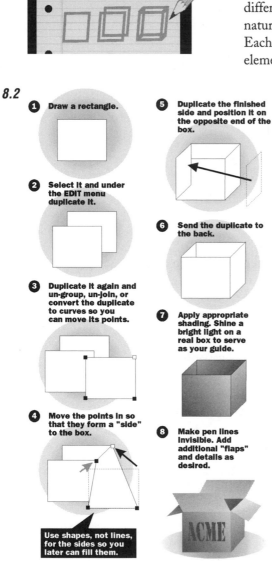

8.2

❶ Draw a rectangle.

❷ Select it and under the EDIT menu duplicate it.

❸ Duplicate it again and un-group, un-join, or convert the duplicate to curves so you can move its points.

❹ Move the points in so that they form a "side" to the box.

Use shapes, not lines, for the sides so you later can fill them.

❺ Duplicate the finished side and position it on the opposite end of the box.

❻ Send the duplicate to the back.

❼ Apply appropriate shading. Shine a bright light on a real box to serve as your guide.

❽ Make pen lines invisible. Add additional "flaps" and details as desired.

ACME

Drawing programs enable information designers to make realistic-looking shapes out of what essentially are doodles.

Electronic drawing takes this a step further, as shown in Figure 8.2. By filling each shape with a different shading, you can eliminate the see-through nature of your doodle and make it look realistic. Each separate element is shaded appropriately, elements belonging in the back are sent behind elements in the front, and suddenly you're an artist. Just remember to use the tools as they are intended. In most programs, this means avoiding the freehand and straight-line tools. Instead, stick with the polygon tools for most tasks.

The Send to Back and Bring to Front commands of drawing programs are among their most important features and can be used to hide a multitude of sins. If there's an imperfection in something hidden by something else in the foreground, only you will know it.

Other features of digital drawing make it superior to traditional drawing for those of us whose last art class was in how to make turkeys out of paper plates to hang on refrigerators:

● Zooming in on a section of a drawing, or creating it at a large size and then shrinking it to fit, masks minor imperfections.

● Tools that automatically draw straight lines, perfect rectangles and properly proportioned ovals don't require steady hands, although taking advantage of certain features may require using polygon tools instead.

- Grouping commands enable you to put separate elements into singular groups for re-sizing, shading or other use. With borders eliminated, groups of simple shapes, filled with the same shading, can be used to create complex shapes that no longer are seen as merely collections of circles and squares. With compounding or joining, they can take on the entire complex shape as a single unit.

- Copy, cut, paste and duplicate enable you to duplicate shapes perfectly, making it unnecessary to draw both the front and back of your 3-D cubes. Simply draw one and make a copy of it.

- Polygon tools enable you to create dot-to-dot shapes and relocate individual dots within them so that portions of the shape can be altered without having to re-draw them.

- Bézier curves change straight lines between sets of dots into flowing curves. Jagged drawings can be smoothed into sleek shapes, looking as if they were drawn with singular, unhesitating strokes of a pen.

- The Shift key, in many programs, constrains whatever shape you create so that the path from one point to the next is at a pre-selected angle, or so that your rectangles are perfect squares and the ellipses you draw are perfect circles.

Most of you probably are familiar with QuarkXPress, PageMaker or a similar page-design program. Mastery of such a program at a basic level is becoming as common a requirement in communications schools as the 25-word-per-minute typing test was in years gone by. The most common of these programs, Quark, enables access to all but the Bézier curve and joining features of the more advanced drawing programs.

Drawing a shape, filling it with shading, grouping it with another shape, and enlarging or reducing it is old hat to many of you. Chances are, you may have tried Quark's Polygon tool and its Reshape Polygon command, allowing certain points to be repositioned without disturbing the rest.

If, however, you're like those of us who managed to get by a typing test without really knowing how to type, perhaps now is a good time to refresh your memory on the basic drawing commands in Quark, PageMaker, Microsoft Word or whatever other program you might know that features rudimentary drawing capabilities. Try drawing, for example, a profile of your face. You can start with an oval, add a polygon for the nose and other features, then group and re-size the elements until you get something resembling you.

Be sure to print your work. It'll make a handsome addition to your refrigerator door and will be of use in the next section. Don't be alarmed that your drawing isn't very pretty (or, more to the point, that it doesn't look much like you). Avoid the temptation to give up at the thought of never being able to draw with a Macintosh. Drawing on a Mac is like "tracing with a brick," as one critic put it, but your draw-ing—and the critic's lament—comes from an era gone by, before the smoothing effects of Bézier curves.

Don't Let Béziers Throw You a Curve

Each major drawing program has access to a version of the powerful Bézier tool. Each does so differently and each refers to it with a different set of nomenclature, but each lets you use the basic tenets of curving and smoothing to one extent or another. The theory, basically, is this: Between two points exists a line. Absent any other influences, the line is straight, but within the two points at either end of the line lies the potential for additional points that would specify a curvature of the line. Right now, these additional points are retracted. In other words, they occupy the same space as the basic point itself. But by unlocking the additional points, you can alter the flow of the line.

How you unlock them varies from program to program. Typically you must double-click, hold down the Option key, choose a different cursor or invoke a get-information command. Consult your pro-gram's manual for specifics. Suffice it to say you must transform what

otherwise is a line or connector point, with its additional handles **8.3**
retracted, into a curve or cusp point, which consists of the main
point and two lever points attached to it. (Different types of points
all work differently. In most cases, you want the one designated as
a "curve" point, not a "connector" or "corner" point.)

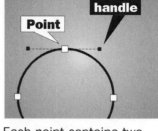

Each point contains two
hidden handles that
determine curvature.

The easiest way to see lever points, or "handles," is to draw a circle.
Although most of us would construct a circle the way a compass
would, most drawing programs construct circles as objects consisting of four points, each with Bézier levers extended.

Draw a circle in your chosen drawing program, then un-group or
un-join the points. Select one of the points making up the circle.
There should be a point at the top, one at the bottom, and one on
either side, as in Figure 8.3. Note that when you select an individual point (again, how to do so varies) an imaginary teeter-totter
appears, with points extending to either side of the main point.
These are the Bézier handles.

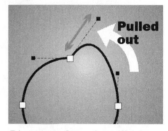

Distance from handle to
point determines severity
of curvature.

Select the point at one end of the teeter-totter lever and move it
around. Note how the original circular shape is affected. It gets flat
if you move the lever toward either the main point or the center of
the circle. It gets bulbous as you move the lever point away from
the main point or from the center of the circle.

You won't often need to alter the smoothness of a circle, but you
will frequently need to alter the smoothness of polygons. Remove
your Quark self-portrait from its place of honor on your refrigerator door. Using your drawing program's Polygon (or Pen) tool, re-
create your fabulous artwork. After you've finished re-creating the
jagged image, edit the individual points on your drawing and
activate their Bézier handles. Instead of giving yourself a chiseled
nose, use the handles to smooth your nose into a natural appearance. Don't forget: You can zoom in or create your drawing at
huge scale, then reduce it, letting you mask minor imperfections.

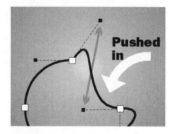

Relationship between
adjoining handles
determines direction.

**Notice how handle positions
affect curvature of the line.**

The curvature of each segment of the drawing is affected by the
handles on both its beginning point and its ending point. Adjust
the right handle of the left point and the left handle of the right point

8.4

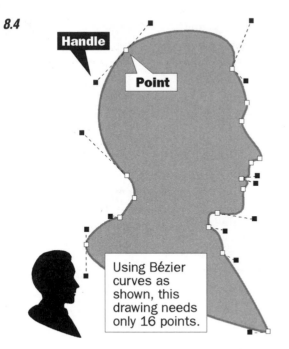

Handle

Point

Using Bézier curves as shown, this drawing needs only 16 points.

Using Béziers, try to duplicate this image.

until you get the curvature you want for each segment. A finished portrait, requiring only 16 points, is shown in Figure 8.4. But don't just look at it. The only way you'll learn how to draw with Béziers is to practice.

Keep in mind when drawing with Bézier curves that less is more. The fewer main points you have, the more free-flowing your drawing will seem. Eliminate unneeded points and let the curve handles do the work for you. (A couple of high-end drawing programs even offer a special command that reduces the number of points to the minimum needed.)

A good way to practice using Bézier curves is to scan an image and import it into your program. (You might want to try by scanning and tracing Figure 8.4. It should be relatively easy, because the points needed already are located on it.) Trace the object with your Polygon tool, creating as few points as possible. Leave the scanned image underneath your drawing as a guide, then use Bézier curves to match the contours of your tracing to those of the original you scanned. Repeat the task several times, each time starting with fewer points. Save all your drawings and print them at the same size. Chances are, the one you used the fewest points to draw will look most like the original.

For years, artists at a major newspaper have staged a contest to determine who can draw the same object with the fewest points. It's a worthwhile exercise and good practice for someone getting used to Bézier features. Not only do your drawings look better, they also take less time and memory to print.

Many drawing programs make drawing an even simpler task by providing a "draw over" or "automatic tracing" feature. Select an image you have scanned, and the program automatically traces a polygon in the shape of the image. You then can fine-tune it with Bézier curves. Unfortunately, most programs create far too many points when they "automatically trace," and many users find that it's easier to trace by hand. Explore how your program handles this and decide whether you agree.

That's How...but Why?

Good question. While you continue to ponder drawing your face, here are a few facts about drawing programs and Bézier curves:

Drawing programs, which computer scientists call "object-oriented," store everything you draw as mathematical representations. Lines, shadings, and letters are nothing more than sets of geometric points and formulas stating the relationships between them. A box begins at coordinate X,Y, ends at coordinate X',Y', is bounded by a line of W width, and filled with a screen of S percent.

8.5

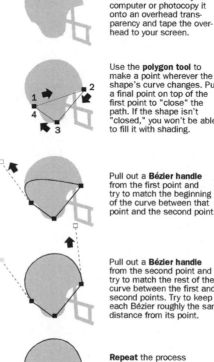

Select a shape you want to draw. **Scan it** into your computer or photocopy it onto an overhead transparency and tape the overhead to your screen.

Use the **polygon tool** to make a point wherever the shape's curve changes. Put a final point on top of the first point to "close" the path. If the shape isn't "closed," you won't be able to fill it with shading.

Pull out a **Bézier handle** from the first point and try to match the beginning of the curve between that point and the second point.

Pull out a **Bézier handle** from the second point and try to match the rest of the curve between the first and second points. Try to keep each Bézier roughly the same distance from its point.

Repeat the process between points 2 and 3 and between points 3 and 4.

Why is this important? If, instead, the program "drew" images the way Photoshop or another "bitmap" painting program such as MacPaint does—as specific white, black, color or shaded dots—it would retain information only at the resolution shown. Blow it up or print it on a higher-resolution printer and it looks jagged.

Object-oriented drawings, on the other hand, can be enlarged infinitely. A line, specified geometrically, is composed of an infinite number of points, not a finite number of bitmaps. The only limitation on resolution is imposed by the printer.

To Help You Think Visually

Using Bézier curves, draw several sports icons or team logos of your choosing.

1. Use as few points as possible. A football helmet, sans face guard, can be drawn with as a few as three points.

2. Assemble your finished logo/icons into a master form for a "week ahead" graphic that lists each of the team's upcoming games. Check out the Sunday sports section of most newspapers for examples.

Advanced Drawing Techniques

About the only thing modern drawing programs won't do is clap on and clap off. So, without any applause, please, switch yours on, bring up that great self-portrait you drew last chapter and we'll continue our voyage into drawing techniques.

Now that you've mastered Bézier drawing, you're ready to move on to the next advancement: the ability to select specific points on a Bézier or polygon image.

In programs that allow this, activate the mode that can select an individual point on a shape. Then, using the Shift key or your area-selection tool, add to your selection the points that comprise the tip of your nose in your self-portrait. The points can be pulled out to make you look like Pinocchio or shoved in to make you look like Rocky Balboa.

It's fun, but the ability to select specific points also has a serious side. Such procedures can make one part of a drawing bigger, and thus seem closer, enabling you to add perspective. Still, any good drawing program already has perspective, skew and distortion commands. So why have this procedure, too?

The Parts are Greater than the Whole

Techniques vary, but a good drawing program enables you to separate selected points from a polygon or to join them to a polygon. Images can be assembled one segment at a time to create perfectly symmetrical drawings, as in Figure 9.1, or portions of one drawing can be reused in another, eliminating the need for redrawing, as in Figure 9.2.

9.1

 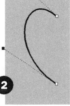 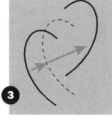 

Try drawing a valentine for a special friend. It'll make your friend happy and give you valuable practice in joining paths.

1 Draw a **straight line** and activate the handles at either end.

2 Adjust the **Bézier handles** to form half a heart.

3 **Duplicate** the half-heart then **mirror or reflect** the duplicate along its vertical axis.

4 **Align** the two halves and **join** them to form a perfectly symmetrical heart.

To separate part of a drawing from another, you must use a variant of a knife or break command at both ends of the segment. Such a tool can, in essence, cut off your nose to spite your face. More important, you can duplicate your original image, select only a segment of the duplicate, re-size it as a group and use it as a perfect outline for an area of shading within the original.

Remember those old paint-by-number sets? They achieved a 3-D image by making use of shading. A gun barrel, for instance, had a lighter glint below its top, indicating light from above. It also had a darker shadow below its bottom, giving testament to its three-dimensional nature. The ability to select a portion of a polygon lets you create such highlights and shadow areas, without having to re-draw them.

This ability also lets you reuse previously drawn images in different ways. You can, for instance, cut off the foot of a fully drawn image and use it in a graphic about podiatrists. By using the join or compound command (the exact reverse of the knife command), you can combine two separate polygons into one, grafting the foot onto a previously drawn leg.

9.2

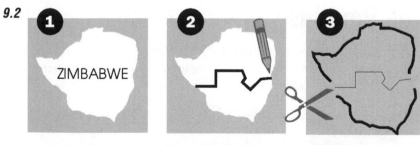

1 Start with a standard map of the **whole** area.

2 Draw the **line** that will divide one half from the other.

3 Break the polygon apart where the line intersects it.

4 Copy the line and **join** one copy to each polygon half.

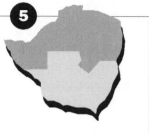

5 You may now shade and move the two halves **independently**, to create whatever effect you desire.

Software should help you do your job, not make it more difficult. Why retrace something you've already drawn when knife commands let you create an exact duplicate?

Veteran graphic artists make repeated use of previously drawn material, stealing segments and adding them to other segments. Even if you can't draw, you can combine pieces of separate icons to create new images.

This form of polygon slicing and grafting can also create tight-scale, detailed maps out of looser-scale, larger ones. You can also copy a boundary from one map in exact detail and combine it with another boundary you've drawn.

Toe the Line

These fundamental tools serve as a reminder that what you're working on is not just a drawing machine; it's a computer. And as a computer, it can automate tedious tasks for you.

9.3

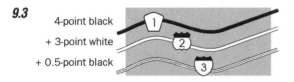

4-point black
+ 3-point white
+ 0.5-point black

Imagine that you want to create a divided highway symbol from the Rand McNally road atlas: three lines, equidistant apart, symbolizing the inbound and outbound lanes, with an area of white between them, as in Figure 9.3. Rather than drawing each line separately, try this instead:

Draw one line representing the road. Set the "stroke," "line" or "pen" of the line at four points and the color at black. Copy the line, setting the stroke of the copy at three points and the color of the copy at white. Copy the line again, this time setting the stroke at 0.5 points and the color at black. Select all three lines and align them left-to-right and top-to-bottom at the center. You now have a perfect divided highway.

At the risk of making this sound like SimCity, you also can create straight sections of railroad (see Figure 9.4). Begin by drawing a perpendicular tie at one end of the railroad. Then use the Duplicate command to make dozens of ties, enough to reach the end of the line. Position only the first tie and the last tie where they belong. Select all the ties, align them up-and-down and distribute them equally left-and-right. Group the ties, add the rails, align the rails and the ties, group the railroad and rotate it until it fits your map perfectly.

9.4

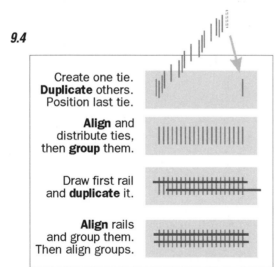

Create one tie.
Duplicate others.
Position last tie.

Align and
distribute ties,
then **group** them.

Draw first rail
and **duplicate** it.

Align rails
and group them.
Then align groups.

In Illustrator and FreeHand, if you carefully position the first duplicate, final alignment and distribution may not be necessary.

Charting a New Course

With such powerful tools as alignment and distribution, a bar chart should never have its bars out of alignment or unequally spaced left to right. Using alignment and the ability to re-size, you have a quick and easy method to chart bars semi-automatically:

1. Create a master bar half an inch wide by 100 units (or some other round number) high.

2. Duplicate it until you have as many bars are you need.

3. Re-size their height only (hold down Shift to do this in some programs) and make each bar, in order, conform to what its particular reading should be, as done in Figure 9.5. If you are charting the numbers 25, 50, 75, 100 and 150, for example, make each length match those numbers or some factor of them. The actual units and multiplication favor you use in charting makes no difference, as long as it's used consistently for all bars in the chart.

4. Select all the bars, bottom-align them and distribute their widths.

5. Group the bars and re-size them as a group until they fit your graphic's design.

You now have an accurate and perfectly spaced bar chart, drawn without a charting program and in a fraction of the time a charting program would take.

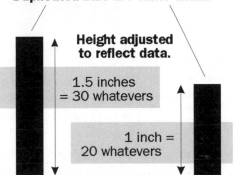

9.5 **Duplicated bars are same width.**

Height adjusted to reflect data.

1.5 inches = 30 whatevers

1 inch = 20 whatevers

Both aligned to bottom.

Align and distribute help you make bar charts without the need for a charting program.

Filling Shapes

Along with solid fills of white, black and all manner of grays (not to mention colors), most drawing programs enable you to fill a shape with specialty fills. Procedures vary, as does the effectiveness of each program. This tool is so useful, however, that it should not be ignored just because it is difficult to use in some programs (notably, early versions of Adobe Illustrator).

As shown in Figure 9.6, a graduated fill starts with one shade and gradually moves to another. A rainbow-like spectrum of color or shading is created across the width or height of the object. In most programs, you can control the angle at which the blend progresses. A radial fill works much the same way, except its gradients move from center to edge rather than from side to side.

9.6

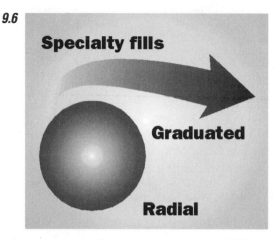

Radial and graduated fills can be used to give objects three-dimensional shading.

Draw a circle in your favorite drawing program. Remove the line from it by making it invisible or clear, then fill the shape with a radial fill that goes from a medium gray on the edges to white or a very light gray in the middle. If your program allows it, change the center of the fill's effect to somewhere above and to one side of the circle's center. You now have what appears to be a three-dimensional globe, not merely a flat circle.

Some monitors and printers are better than others at rendering such fills. Before going too far with your artwork, check what your printout looks like. If several printers are available, try all of them. Also consult your program's manual on how to best configure your fills for the printer and monitor you plan to use. Unlike anything else, radial and graduated fills tend to look better on printouts than they do onscreen. A typical monitor may have only eight shades between black and white. These noticeably "band" onscreen when using radial or graduated files. A printer, particularly a new 600-or-more dot-per-inch unit, is much better equipped to display seamless shifting from one shade to the next.

Radial and graduated fills are important now that graphic artwork has swung away from the "computer look" of pen lines around each shape and consistent fills throughout. The more you can make your images look as if they were created by hand with airbrush or water color, not pen and ink, the more en-vogue your work will be. (This, incidentally, is one of the true legacies of *USA Today*, which insisted from the start on a soft, hand-drawn appearance for its graphics.)

Adding delicate shading, which radial and graduated fills allow, and then removing pen lines is one of the best ways to achieve this soft appearance. Artwork created this way looks more sophisticated, professional and, more important, more realistic. Only you know that it was created on a computer by someone whose last art class involved tracing hands on paper plates and decorating them as Thanksgiving turkeys.

To use shading tools properly, you must always keep in mind where the light source is in your drawing. If it helps, draw in a representation of the sun. Remove it, of course, after you have adjusted the shading. If you can't envision shading this way, grab an actual object that looks like what you're drawing, hold it next to a very bright light and watch where the light falls.

9.7

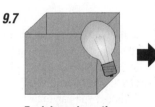

Envision where the light source is for an object.

Shade the drawing accordingly, and eventually remove the imaginary light source you drew in.

It's important that you pause and take time to experiment with these features. Draw a Bézier shape and use the knife tool to create highlights and shadow segments within it. Then fill both the basic shape, the highlight and shadow segments with various combinations of radial fills until you have created an illustration that looks three-dimensional. Remember: You can further enhance the dimensional image of an object by exporting it to Photoshop and using its tools, which include an airbrush tool and a shading blend tool, to create the desired effects.

To Help You Think Visually

Using the tools mentioned, try your hand at duplicating the cardboard box, all four of its flaps open. Once you're comfortable with that, move on to drawing an open carton of eggs, as viewed from slightly above and slightly to one side or the other.

1. Create one egg by altering an oval after activating its Bézier points. Duplicate it several times. Make the duplicates smaller and smaller to account for perspective, then position them using align and distribute.

2. Draw one section of the carton to fit around the original egg. Duplicate it and join the duplicates together to form the carton's bottom. Follow the same strategy regarding perspective.

3. Shade the eggs and the carton to accurately reflect the lighting as you envision it. You may or may not have to create special shapes inside the eggs to account for different shading strategies. Make sure you remove all pen lines, then print it out.

Don't expect perfection, but keep in mind that what doesn't show doesn't count and what's important here is the practice you're getting, not your ability to draw with realistic accuracy. Create the drawing as if it were to fill a sheet of letter-size paper, but after printing it once, reduce it to three inches wide. Surprise! You can draw better than expected.

C h a p t e r

The Specialized Vocabulary of Graphics

Graphology. Typography. It matters not whether you're finding hidden meaning in handwriting or making the meaning of printed material come out loud and clear. You first need to learn the terms. As a budding information designer and would-be typographer, the first terms you need to learn involve type, screens and color. We'll look at them in order, followed by how they combine in graphic form.

Type, in its infinite diversity, used to be pure, with its own family values. As shown in Figure 10.1, letters of a specific design and size were a "font." Identical fonts of various sizes were a "face." Similarly designed faces of various weights and widths were a "family." Each family belonged to a "race."

The Medium

The Techniques

The Forms

The Profession

10.1

"Helvetica" is a family. Different weights create different faces. Different sizes create different fonts.

A font's values were literally stereotyped at birth. A face was designed with calligraphic brushes, its fonts were engraved letter-by-letter into dies and each letter's final fate was cast in lead—rendering it unalterable without going back to the drawing board.

Today, computers have rendered such values obsolete. Faces, fonts, families and races routinely are bastardized by computer manipulation. Even the terms have changed. Font now means what face used to, and whole families can be cloned from a single font. Type still has its family names: the Bodonis, the Cheltenhams, even the Grotesques. Families still belong to races: the Romans, the Gothics, the Scripts, the Squares. But with TrueType and PostScript fonts easily altered in size, width and weight, and new fonts easily created with Bézier tools, the names and faces have become confused. What used to be Helvetica may be

Helios or Arial on your computer. What used to be Condensed or Black (or both) may be only a manipulation of normal letters. What used to be a long-term commitment to Helvetica over Futura may be changed on a moment's notice. Only one of the original concerns remains: race.

These Serifs Don't Have Deputies

The most pervasive of the races is the Romans, whose text type empire extends to nearly every newspaper in the world. Roman type takes its characteristics from the way it originally was drawn—with a flat-edged calligraphic brush held horizontal, making up-and-down strokes thicker and side-to-side strokes thinner, as shown in Figure 10.2. Added to each painstakingly created letter were finishing touches called "serifs."

10.2

Bodoni, a Modern Roman, was the first to use sharply chiseled serifs.

Varying stroke widths and serifs are characteristics of Roman type.

Perhaps because we are accustomed to such stroke variances and to the subtle visual "hooks" provided by serifs, Roman type is seen as the most readable for large masses of text. Books, magazines and newspapers all use Roman typefaces for the bulk of their text, or what is known in the trade as "body copy."

Legibility—the ability to distinguish one letter from another, particularly when comparatively few letters are displayed—is another matter. The serifs and the varying strokes of Roman faces clutter up basic letter forms, making them unsuitable for eye charts and highway signs. In those cases, stark block letters are used instead.

Nowadays, these frighteningly dull letter forms, known as Monotone Gothics (shown in Figure 10.3), are lumped together with slightly less inelegant Monotone relatives under the generic label of unserifed or "sans serif" type. Roman, meanwhile, has become known simply as "serifed" type.

10.3

Franklin Gothic has neither serifs nor varying strokes, but will "pinch" a stroke slightly to avoid monotony.

Nearly uniform strokes, only occasionally "pinched," characterize Gothics.

Although such labels are technically incorrect, far be it for us to take up the mantel of defending type family values (Egyptian, for example, has a Monotone body with serifs, making it technically a member of the Squares race).

For graphics purposes, type can be broken into three categories: the serifs, the sans serifs and everything else, as shown in Figure 10.4. The serifs are the most readable, the sans serifs the most legible and the rest—well, they mostly are reserved for special purposes.

10.4

Serifs	Sans serifs	Others
Bookman	Bauhaus	*Brush*
Century	Eras	**Chancery**
Garamond	Franklin	Courier
Goudy	Futura	**Dom Casual**
Times	Helvetica	*Mystic*

Serifs include such familiar fonts as Century, Goudy, New York and Times. Sans serifs include Geneva, Franklin Gothic, Helvetica and Univers. Special purpose fonts include the ones that look like handwriting, labelmaker tape, scoreboard digits and the like. A list such as this could go on ad nauseam. Any given computer can house hundreds of faces and new ones—mostly variants of existing faces—are created daily.

Putting on a Proper Face

Choosing which face to use is an aesthetic decision. Choosing which race to use requires determining how the type will be read. Although newspapers use serifs for body type, headlines can go either way. Traditionally, papers that emphasize newsstand sales choose sans serifs, while papers that emphasize home delivery choose serifs. Sans serifs are legible at a distance, making headlines easy to recognize, even from a newsstand. Serifs stand out less but ease reading and improve comprehension. In advertising, public relations and other applications, the choice is more a matter of taste than functional design.

In graphics, however, there is a function to consider. Think of a graphic as a miniature front page, crying out to be heard from a cluttered newsstand. People seldom look for graphics; graphics must look for them. Sans serifs faces are thus a logical choice. Because graphics are seldom laden with large masses of text, any decline in readability is negligible.

Newspapers have remarkably consistent style specifications for graphics while other publications' styles may vary radically. Most newspapers specify a bold, condensed version of a sans serif for graphics headlines and a lighter, less condensed version of the same sans serif for graphics text. As shown in Figure 10.5, many use Franklin Gothic or Helvetica Bold Condensed for heads and the unbolded, uncondensed version of those faces for text.

10.5

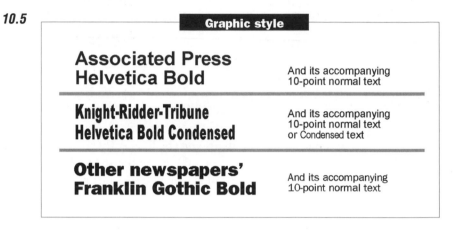

While other publications' styles may vary, almost all newspapers' graphics look similar.

What's your favorite? Now's the time to pick one. Just make sure that it contrasts with standard headlines and, perhaps, matches standard photo captions. Matching graphics typefaces to typefaces already in use elsewhere creates an impression of unity and coordination.

When selecting fonts, avoid the temptation to create your own computer-condensed versions. It's easy to play Dr. Frankenstein on a Mac, but doing so ignores niceties that designers insert into fonts they create specifically for condensed use.

In Figure 10.6, compare a font that is designed to be "condensed" to what can be done with a non-condensed font to reduce its horizontal scale. Note how strokes look inelegant and indiscriminate in the computer version (thinner vertically, thicker horizontally) but graceful and purposeful in the custom condensed font. Only a few old-time typographers will know if you electronically "cheat" with a font. But so too will only a few know if you fudge a quote here or there. It's a matter of professionalism.

10.6

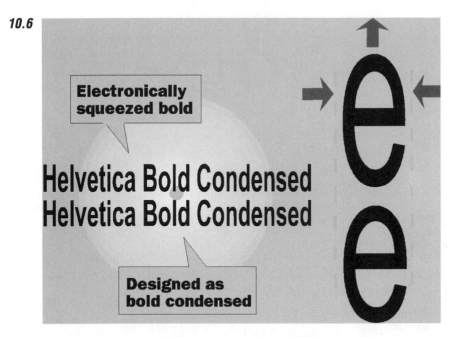

Condensing type electronically distorts the elegance of the original's strokes.

Also to be avoided is the temptation to use slanted type, as is done for effect in this paragraph. For Roman faces, slanted letters are called Italics. For others, despite what computers might say, they technically are known as Obliques. Whatever the terminology, both readability and legibility suffer when type is slanted. And that's ironic. A person calling for slanted type usually does so to add emphasis. In fact, Italics and Obliques obscure more than emphasize. Punching a word into bold sans serif accomplishes what slanted type does not.

Type sizes are measured in units called points. Each point is 1/12th of a pica, or 1/72nd of an inch. Officially, the measurements are taken from the top of a capital letter to the bottom of a lower case letter that extends below the baseline. In reality, how big a letter seems to be is more a factor of its "x-height," the distance from the baseline to the top of a lower case letter, as shown in Figure 10.7.

10. 7

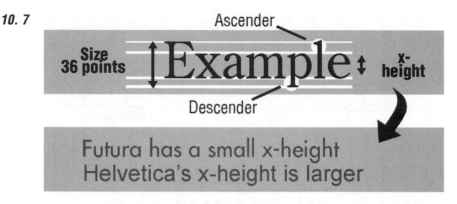

Type of the same point size may appear bigger or smaller, depending on its x-height.

Don't worry whether your type's point size is numerically bigger or smaller than someone else's. That's just point-size envy. Worry instead that it looks right. Graphics text should appear to be at least as big as, if not bigger than, the type used for non-graphics text. It doesn't matter whether it accomplishes this at nine point, 10 point, 11 point or 12 point.

Setting a Screen

Today's Pulitzer Prize winner may be tomorrow's bird cage liner, and you should keep that in mind when designing graphics. It's not that your work is transitory; rather, it's that the material it is printed on tends to be among the cheapest and most disposable. Yes, da Vinci painted some of his greatest works on old boards, but he never had to paint on toilet paper, which has close to the same properties as newsprint.

The first thing to be wary of is shading. Although your computer and laser printer are more than up to the task of showing a full spectrum of grays, from five percent to 95 percent black, you should consider yourself lucky if your newspaper's presses are able to reproduce more than two shadings between solid black and solid white. A graphic containing a spectrum that looks like this:

10.8 **What you print . . .**

10% 20% 30% 40% 50% 60% 70% 80% 90%

is likely to reproduce like this, in clumps of white, gray and black:

10.9 **. . . and what your readers are likely to see**

White   15%   35%   Black

Small dots used in light screens of less than 15 percent tend to "drop out," and larger dots of 50 percent, 60 percent or more tend to smear (or "gain") into solid black.

If your production department is very careful and your presses very good (and very slow), you may do better, but don't count on it. If possible, find a way to sneak a spectrum bar like the one in Figure 10.8 onto a press run. If you can't, keep track of how your graphics reproduce various shades and develop a gray palette based on that.

Until then, stick with the suggestions that Figure 10.9 dictates: solid white, something around 15 percent black, something around 35 percent black, perhaps something around 50 percent black and solid black.

The Not-So-Wonderful World of Color

Developing a good color palette is far trickier. The first thing to remember is that colors look subtle, almost translucent onscreen. This is illusion. Computers render colors by projecting red, green and blue light. Printed pages render colors by reflecting light off cyan, magenta, yellow and black inks. The more red, green and blue a computer screen projects, the lighter the image becomes; pure white is 100 percent red, 100 percent green and 100 percent blue. The more cyan, magenta and yellow a press prints, the darker the image becomes; pure black, if you chose to reproduce it that way, would be 100 percent cyan, 100 percent magenta and 100 percent yellow.

Obviously, the computer and the press don't speak the same language. With adjustment, computers can come close to showing what you'll get. Without fail, however, a crucial color selection will look nothing like its onscreen color when printed.

To prevent such problems, create a thorough color test, generated on the equipment you normally use and including all the color combinations you want. If your publication is willing to pay for color presswork, it ought to be willing to accept the minor additional expense of producing a color test. Once that's done, you'll know how to adjust. Until then, try these other tips:

- Limit your percentages of **cyan** and **magenta** to roughly what you would do with black—15 percent, 35 percent and 100 percent, possibly adding 50 percent as a fourth gradation.

- Use **yellow** only at 30 percent and 100 percent. Yellow tends to come out either solid or nonexistent. You could try adding 10 percent magenta to 30 percent yellow to make sure a light yellow doesn't fade away.

- To darken a color, add **black** rather than another color. A little black (10 or 20 percent) darkens cyan into blue without running the risk of turning the blue into purple by adding magenta. The same holds true with adding black to magenta instead of risking turning red into orange by adding yellow to magenta.

- Avoid **browns** and most other three- and four-color mixes. What you set up as a medium brown, the old burnt sienna from your Crayola box, might end up being green at the start of a press run and purple at the end. The one who'll get burnt in the process is you.

Selecting colors for objects other than those occurring in the real world is another matter. Obviously, oceans are blue (even though they aren't), grass is green (even though mine isn't) and the traffic light you ignored on your way here today was red. But what about blurb boxes and bars in charts? What color should they be?

Nanette Bisher, creative director of the *Orange Country Register*, offers these tips:

- Colors relate to **emotions**. Reds and yellows tend to be evocative; greens and blues, calming. A graphic warning that public tap water is contaminated might well feature reds and yellows. One dispassionately conveying less urgent information about interest rates falling might veer toward blues and greens.

- Color preferences have close ties to **age**, **ethnicity** and **geography**. Study the dominant natural colors of your publication's circulation area. Is your home in the brilliant Southwest, with bright skies, sand and Native American colors of turquoise and orange? Or is your home in the gray, wintry confines of the Northeast, where the gray-blues and browns of business suits prevail? Try to adopt a basic color scheme that somehow matches the personality of your readers and the environment in which they live. Vary the scheme by seasons if appropriate.

- Within production limits, avoid the comic-book look of having too many plain reds, blues and yellows. Experiment with new shades. The Color Marketing Group says that red-oranges, blue-greens and red-blues are "in."

Knowing What to Call Things

As languages go, French is magnifiqué. Before words may be added to the lexicon, they are subjected to careful review and scrutiny. Information design speaks a much more guttural language that, at times, seems nonsensical. There's no genitive or subjunctive to master, but it does feature an assortment of oddball terms worth learning, as itemized in Figure 10.10.

10.10

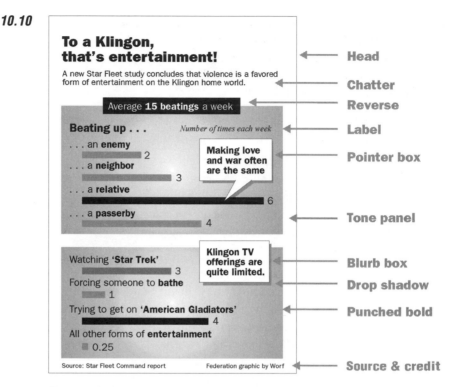

**To a Klingon,
that's entertainment!**   ← **Head**

A new Star Fleet study concludes that violence is a favored
form of entertainment on the Klingon home world.   ← **Chatter**

Average **15 beatings** a week   ← **Reverse**

Beating up . . .   *Number of times each week*   ← **Label**

. . . an **enemy**
                    2
. . . a **neighbor**   **Making love   ← **Pointer box**
                         3   and war often
                                     are the same**
. . . a **relative**
                              6
. . . a **passerby**   ← **Tone panel**
                    4

Watching '**Star Trek**'   **Klingon TV   ← **Blurb box**
                    3   offerings are
Forcing someone to **bathe**   quite limited.**   ← **Drop shadow**
          1
Trying to get on '**American Gladiators**'   ← **Punched bold**
                         4
All other forms of **entertainment**
        0.25

Source: Star Fleet Command report   Federation graphic by Worf ← **Source & credit**

Here are the names we use to describe various parts of a graphic.

By no means should you expect every graphic, other than one created
with that specific purpose in mind, to contain all of these elements.
Here are some guidelines on when each element is needed:

The Musts

Every graphic must have an active **head**, a complete **source** and an
honest **credit**. (We don't always use sources and credits in this book,
but that's only because most of the sample data was made up.)

Write the head as you would a headline for a news story. Use it to
convey the main point of the graphic in a bright, fact-filled way, telling
what the graphic says, not just what it is about.

The source should list in order of importance where the data came
from, including any intermediate stops data took along the way. If you
are using Commerce Department data you received from the Associated Press, both Commerce and AP should be listed.

The credit is where your name and your organization's name go. This is more than just an ego trip. Creating a graphic involves interpreting data. Readers have a right to know whose **interpretation they are reading**.

Almost Always

Rarely will you find all three, but a singular **pointer box, blurb box** or **reverse** is a handy tool for driving home a graphic's main point or for offering the "why" behind a set of data. Remember that these callouts are among the first things a reader sees. Don't waste them on dull footnotes. Use them to explain important points. Particularly common is the dual coding in textual form of what a chart says in visual form.

Likewise, **punched bold** is a powerful tool for guiding a reader's eye through a graphic. Used well, it makes key information stand out.

Usually

Unless a graphic is extremely simple, **chatter** is an important element. It describes the background of the graphic in a way that even non-visual readers can understand, often giving specific clues about the graphic's secondary points.

Chatter should follow up on what the head says and summarize what the rest of the graphic shows. It's fine to restate what a visual shows, but try to avoid duplicating another element's function in the package.

Chatter frequently is used to dually code a graphic's most significant secondary point, as explained in Chapter 3.

As Needed

Drop shadows, tone boxes and **labels** help organize information hierarchically.

Data labels, incidentally, often are done in slanted type to diminish their visual power. This is one way in which an information designer can force a dull-but-necessary item to the bottom of the visual inverted pyramid.

None of these elements should ever be used just because they look nice. In Figure 10.10, for example, a tone panel is used only to give greater emphasis to the blurb and pointer boxes by increasing their contrast against the background.

To Help You Think Visually

Create a style guide for the graphics you will undertake in Part 3. Make this guide in the form of an actual graphic, as in Figure 10.10, with specifications for each technique cited in the margins. Make sure you address these steps:

1. What typefaces and sizes will be used for heads, chatter, labels, blurb and pointer boxes, reverses, punched bold, sources and credits?

2. What screens will be used for tone boxes, drop shadows and data bars?

3. What standards will you establish for spacing, line weights and so on?

4. Don't forget to address the acceptable widths of completed graphics. For most publications, you will have standard sizes and grids, so these are essential. Standard newspaper column widths vary slightly from newspaper to newspaper but generally are close to two inches for one-column graphics, 4.2 inches for two-column graphics, 6.4 for three-column, 8.6 for four-column, 10.8 for five-column and 13 for six-column. Graphics produced in widths other than these typically run the risk of not being usable because appropriate space for them is hard to create.

Chapter 11

Glances

You've explored the strategies. You've explored the tools. Now it's time to put them into practice as you learn specific techniques to create specific types of information graphics. In the next six chapters, you'll examine each major type of graphic, starting in this chapter with glances.

Applying a label to a type of graphic is, of course, artificial. To many, glances fall within the realm of typography. Graphs, maps and diagrams (Chapters 12, 13 and 14) are charts. Sequence graphics (Chapter 15) are hybrids of the two. Illustrations (Chapter 16) are more art than information design. The labels used here are designed to help you focus on meta-skills, not to pigeonhole graphics into artificial typologies.

The first meta-skill you will work on is visual organization, and there's no better place to begin than with glances.

For a glance to succeed, it must live up to its name. Glances provide essential information—not at a long stare, not at a quick read—but at a glance. Key words and phrases should pop out, catch the reader's eye and convey the material in a split second. Properly designed, glances enable readers to decide instantly, on the basis of a few words, whether to examine the graphic and text in greater detail.

Just because you have no data to chart or no image to create does not mean that information design is impossible. Organizing text, even without images, is one of the most important challenges an information designer faces.

Glances come in several varieties:

- **Bio boxes** stress a person's accomplishments.
- **Breakouts** stress the key points of a lengthy text.
- **Rankings** stress relative strengths of items ordinally.
- **Ratings** stress relative strengths cardinally.
- **Tables** stress specific data combinations.

We'll explore each in detail, but first we'll offer a few tips for glances in general.

Compared to other graphics, glances are more difficult to "tune" to specific audiences using the techniques discussed in Chapter 3. With no data to chart, they possess few visual data metaphors and little opportunity for metaphorical simplicity. How you "tune" a glance so it reaches readers who do or don't have personal stakes in the information being presented becomes a question of how hierarchically organized or visually vivid you make each graphic. With practice, it's possible to do both, as shown in this chapter's graphics. The key, as you will see in each example, is not just in using visually vivid icons but also in making certain that they reside in the background, where they do not interfere with the information.

Glances are effective at attracting attention from readers browsing for information. Casual information browsers, who form the majority of readers, skim material in search of interesting facts. Only when they find such eye-catching facts do they examine the material in greater detail, the way someone looking for specific information would. This pattern of reading suggests that most material should be organized in hierarchical, not categorical, fashion (see Figure 11.1).

What's the difference? Imagine a glance to be like your resume. When you're looking for a job, you want recruiters to see at a glance what makes you different. Your resume therefore hierarchically stresses such things as "supervised 28 professionals," "won six awards" and "developed staff training program." Once you have your job, however, the personnel department may want to consult your records to find specific information. Your human resources file thus is organized by category, with "seniority," "salary" and "insurance options" leading the way.

11.1

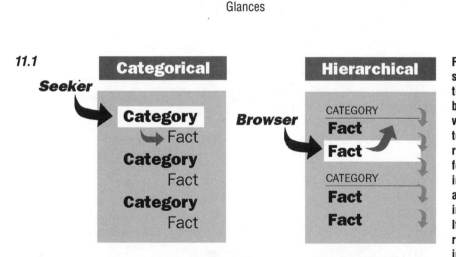

Readers seeking specific information are attracted by categories, which they follow to find facts. The reader browsing for interesting information is attracted by information itself. If the browsing reader finds it interesting, he or she will seek out further information.

Recruiters, casually browsing for information, are attracted by facts, not categories. Personnel workers, systematically consulting records for specific information, seek out categories first, then find the facts.

Understanding the difference between information seeking and information browsing is essential in understanding how to organize glances. Only 1.5 percent of the information we learn in any given day is the result of specific information seeking, communications researcher W. Russell Neuman estimates. Most of the time, we benefit from organization that stresses what the information **is**, not what the information is **about**.

Glances, like graphics as a whole, are designed for casual information browsers. If you can make a case that the material in your glance appeals exclusively to information seekers—that is, that the information is highly desired and that readers would be motivated to use categorical rather than hierarchical organization—there's another place where such material could effectively go: in "agate," the tiny type used for listing stock prices and sports box scores in the back of newspapers. If someone is desperate to read it, a reader will look until he or she finds it.

Glances aren't designed to convey details. They're designed to convey the big picture and to do so at a glance.

GLANCES BOXES *at a glance*

Best suited for:	**Highlighting** essential information Expressing **qualitative** relationships
Least suited for:	**Summarizing** statistical data Expressing **qualitative** relationships
Answer the questions:	**Who, what** and **why**
Often used as:	**Entry points** within text (see Figure 11.2) Occasionally, secondary visual elements
Typical size:	**1 to 3 inches** wide Occasionally, somewhat wider
Key challenges:	**Simplifying** information (Chapter 3 and this chapter) **Recognizing** the need for them (Chapter 2)
Key techniques:	Evaluative typography, particularly **punched bold** (Chapters 3 and 10) Occasionally, **icons** (Chapters 6, 8 and 9 and this chapter)
Temptation to avoid:	**Categorical** instead of hierarchical organization

11.2

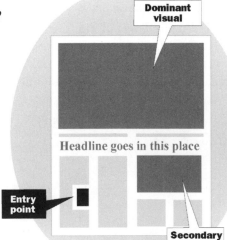

All visuals serve as entry points. Larger ones also are classified as dominant or secondary visuals. Glances tend to be among the smallest of visuals.

Bio Boxes

The accomplishments of an individual or an entire group are typically told in a bio box like the one in Figure 11.3.

11.3

This bio box uses a standard, almost cliché dossier backdrop to increase its visual vividness. Notice that it presents key information rather than rote bio-graphical facts. Figure 11.5 at the end of this section demonstrates step-by-step how this graphic was constructed.

Bio boxes are less "Who's Who" and more "Why Him or Her?" Details of when someone was born, where she went to school and what her hobbies are might be interesting to the person's parents, children and significant other. But such facts don't tell the story of why we are bothering to present a graphic about her. A bio box should stress key points that paint a big picture, not minor details that would best be told in "agate."

Remember our example of Smallville Savings & Loan in Chapter 2? Figure 11.4 demonstrates how categorical information is transformed into a hierarchical graphic. Begin with basic biographical information about birth, family status and education—the stuff of "Who's Who." Evaluate that information in terms of why the person is of current interest. In the case of Figure 11.4, it becomes apparent that family information is irrelevant, but that the education and career information tell an interesting story.

Once recast, this information is transformed into the type of hierarchical organization pattern needed for the finished graphic, which explains as its main point why the two men are being profiled. (Remember: People usually read graphics before, not after, they read accompanying text.) Categories are downplayed, often so much so that they are only implied. Key facts are highlighted in punched bold and the true story emerges: A popular, local man with no training or experience has been replaced by an outsider with top educational credentials and a track record of work in the involved area. In a categorical graphic, you **might** glean such information but only after studying it carefully. In a hierarchical graphic, you get it at a glance.

11.4

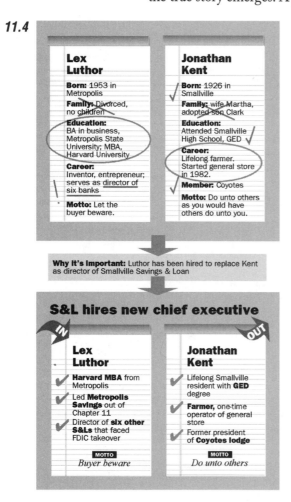

A categorically organized graphic is marked up to be recast as a hierarchically organized one.

Also note in Figure 11.4 how a single oddball category can breathe life and, in some cases, greater understanding into a dry litany of facts. When gathering information for a bio box, never hesitate to ask "boxers or briefs?" or some other offbeat question like those from a Dewars profile. You'll be surprised how often answers to unusual questions about favorite books, favorite TV shows or favorite sayings shed tremendous light on a subject's personality. (My personal favorite is: "In the Great Book of Life your name is listed and next to your name 25 words or less. What do the words say?")

Bio boxes need not contain backdrops such as the file folder in Figure 11.3 or the legal pad in Figure 11.4. These do, however, add an element of visual vividness to what would otherwise be non-alluring displays of type. Photographs of the subject can accomplish the same, as can informative icons, such as Figure 11.4's "IN" and "OUT" arrows, which provide a minimal amount of visual data metaphor.

The legal pad motif in Figure 11.4 is accomplished with a collection of aligned and distributed lines and rectangles. The file folder motif in Figure 11.3 requires a bit more work. However, as explained in Figures 11.5 and 11.6, it is easily created, even by a novice information designer.

How Figure 11.3 Was Constructed

The dossier backdrop in Figure 11.3 was created as a series of rectangles. A normal rectangle is drawn with a modest corner radius. In some programs, this involves use of a rounded-rectangle tool or of corner-radius command that is activated after the rectangle is drawn. The rounded original is then duplicated. The duplicate is resized and sliced in half with a knife command. The original is duplicated again. Each of the sliced halves is aligned with the top edge of one of the full-size versions. Using the pen tool, points are added where the smaller sliced halves meet the full-size versions. The knife tool is again used to slice out the portion of the full-size version between the added points. The halves are then grafted onto the larger shapes at those points with a join command. Perspectives are adjusted slightly by rotation commands. The front and back are shaded separately, the two are grouped and the grouped item is rotated as needed. Details such as a screened "PROFILE" label in a typewriter font such as Courier are added. Type for the bio box is then placed in position. After all type is added, the finished graphic and the type are grouped, then skewed slightly to produce an illusion of depth.

11.5

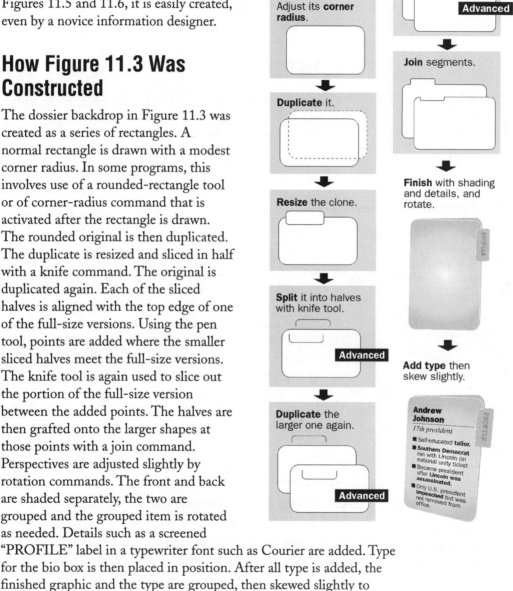

Draw a **rectangle**

Adjust its **corner radius**.

Duplicate it.

Resize the clone.

Split it into halves with knife tool.
Advanced

Duplicate the larger one again.
Advanced

Create points on the larger ones and slice away areas for grafting.
Advanced

Join segments.

Finish with shading and details, and rotate.

Add type then skew slightly.

Andrew Johnson
17th president
■ Self-educated **tailor.**
■ **Southern Democrat** ran with Lincoln on national unity ticket
■ Became president after **Lincoln was assassinated.**
■ Only U.S. president **impeached** but was not removed from office.

11.6

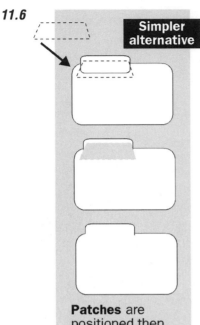

Patches are positioned then shaded to match the overall shape. Pen lines are then removed.

Instead of using knife and join commands, a similar though less elegant effect may be created with simple polygons. A "patch" with no pen line and a fill the same as the other objects' is positioned so that it eliminates extraneous lines. The key point to remember is that, when drawing on a computer, it's what shows in the end, not how you did it, that counts.

Breakouts

Half-headline, half-graphic, a breakout sits firmly atop the invisible fence that all too often separates story design from page design.

Breakouts, like the one in Figure 11.7, highlight the key components of a plan, the key points of an article or the key features of a product. They are, in many regards, bio boxes without the bio. In fact, many call breakouts "fact boxes" to stress their similarity to bio boxes.

The challenges posed by breakouts and bio boxes are much the same: Avoid categorical organization and use hierarchical structures instead. Above all, make certain your graphic remains a glance box, not a "stare" box. The goal of reducing information to its absolute minimum, while not oversimplifying it, is a far greater challenge than designing logos or other icons to accompany the material. Keep in mind that people who read your graphic may read none of the text it accompanies. Make sure the graphic you create can be understood fully and accurately without the complete text.

DO

● **Highlight key facts** with punched bold.

● **Eliminate non-essential information.** Whatever is included should be vital, not merely the person's "vital statistics."

● **Include offbeat questions** in your interviews, but use them in your graphic only if they shed light on the subject's personality.

● **Include background images or photos** to increase visual vividness, but don't let these get in the way of the bio box's main points.

DON'T

- **Organize by category.** Stress the facts, not the categories where the facts may be found.

- **Allow your glance to become a gaze.** Deal in short phrases or bulleted lists, not long sentences or paragraphs.

- **Use bio boxes as a substitute for small-type agate lists.**

At times, particularly with breakouts, a case can be made for using categorical organization instead of hierarchical organization. Such cases are rare but do occur. If a headline is so compelling that it turns all readers into instant information seekers—a headline like, "Most qualify for huge tax rebate"—readers could appreciate a graphic that organizes its information categorically, along the lines of "who qualifies," "how much do you get" and "how do you claim the refund." For categorical organization to be viable, however, the breakout must be designed in lockstep with the overall package, using the headline and other visuals to convert browsing readers into information seekers before they reach the breakout portion of the layout.

The role of the rest of the layout is also important in determining how visually vivid a breakout or other graphic needs to be. Breakouts, like bio boxes, are often the least "graphic" of graphics. Many consist of organized text, while others use shading, bullets, icons and other visually vivid adornments, as in Figure 11.8. Several factors determine how vivid a graphic is, not the least of which is the

11.7

New starship set to launch

Its five-year mission:

✓ To **explore** strange new worlds

✓ To seek out **new life** and new civilization

✓ To boldly go **where no one has gone** before

This breakout uses a standard, clipboard backdrop to increase its visual vividness. Notice how punched bold is used to accentuate its hierarchical organization. Figure 11.9 at the end of this section demonstrates step-by-step how key elements of this graphic were constructed.

general style of the publication. The graphic at left in Figure 11.8 might not be graphic enough for *USA Today*, while the one at right might be too graphic for the front page of *The New York Times*. Style, however, isn't the sole determining factor. Both content and context also play a role.

11.8

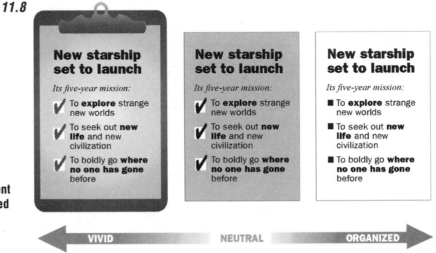

The same content can be expressed with or without added visual vividness.

Content's role is related to the question of how to "tune" the graphic to match what you expect will be the readers' personal involvement with the topic. As explained in Chapter 3, the less a reader is expected to be personally affected by a topic, the more visual the graphic should be. However, even in cases in which content dictates vividness, a graphic can intentionally be designed in less vivid fashion. That's where context plays a role. If a graphic is to be used as a minor entry point in a layout already featuring a dominant visual element, an equally vivid secondary element or both, turning up the visual "volume" on the graphic could cause it to be as much an "exit point" as an entry point for readers. The principles of integrated design, detailed in Chapter 17, make it vital for graphic designers to consider the whole package, not just the graphic. And this is never more important than with breakouts, which frequently cut across the boundary between graphics and headlines.

If, for example, the text accompanying one of the graphics in Figure 11.8 was accompanied by other, larger visuals, an overly vivid graphic might do little more than distract from the visual impact of the larger images. The sparsely vivid graphic at right in Figure 11.8 might perform better because readers lured by the larger visuals could quickly gain information from it. Designers must not only judge the readers' expected level of personal involvement, but also at what point in the reading process the graphic will be encountered. If that point is likely to be after browsers have decided to check out the information, less vividness and greater organization—even categorical organization—is in order.

Visual vividness is not solely a function of icons and images, either. Simple things such as background shading and bullets also add to visual vividness, particularly when color is used. The middle graphic in Figure 11.8 is only modestly vivid. It features a gray background, white boxes and black checkmarks. Convert the background to a pale blue and the checkmarks to a bright red and the graphic's vividness increases considerably—although, as Mario Garcia and Pegie Stark point out in *Eyes on the News*, not by as much as you might expect. In their study, black-and-white photos attract as much attention as color photos. Color's true value, according to other research, seems more related to getting readers to pick up a page than it does to getting them to read individual items contained on it. By the same token, color has been shown to divert attention from non-color elements on a page. The most prudent course, pending further research, is to use color in soft, non-jarring shades so that it does not detract from the vividness of other visuals. In the case of this graphic, medium to dark blue checkmarks on a pale blue background would be less jarring but still a vivid alternative.

How Figure 11.7 Was Constructed

11.9

The only trick to designing the visually vivid version of the graphic in Figures 11.7 and 11.8 is construction of the clipboard clip. Unlike the previous dossier example, where items may be joined or grouped, this drawing requires use of join commands.

Draw half of of the clip- board "clip" with **Bézier tool.**

Reflect a duplicate of the half horizontally and **align** it vertically with the other half.

Don't group. Rather, **join** the halves. Add a circle and join it to the joined halves as well.

Add **graduated shading.** Note how joining gave the clip a see-through "hole."

DO

● **Trim mercilessly** but intelligently. Think of each line of text in a breakout as being more like a headline than an element in an itemized list.

● **Highlight key words** within each point using punched bold.

● **Make the graphic work with other elements** in the overall layout, including other visuals and headlines.

● **Include background images** to increase visual vividness, but only if the topic is one of lower reader involvement and the vividness does not compete with other elements in the layout.

DON'T

● **Organize by category** unless other elements in the package are expected to convert browsers into information seekers before they reach the breakout.

● **Allow your glance to become a gaze.** Deal in short phrases or bulleted lists, not long sentences or paragraphs.

● **Use breakouts to convey details.** Use them more like secondary "decks" on a headline.

Rankings

If breakouts sit atop a fence dividing headlines from graphics, rankings sit atop another fence, one that divides graphics from agate. Breakouts ride their fence with ease, but rankings often ride theirs in a way that creates more than a minor pain in the derrière.

Whether information belongs in a ranking, like that in Figure 11.10, or in an agate list, like that in Figure 11.11, is determined by the reason for publishing the information. Agate reports the overall contents of a list; rankings stress the relative strengths or movements of list members.

If your publication serves fans of the University of Kansas basketball team, or if the primary purpose for publishing the Top 10 teams is to show how Kansas has moved up in the ranking, Figure 11.10 is appropriate. If, on the other hand, your goal is to tell readers which teams placed where in the new Top 10 list and you could care less about any specific team (save, perhaps, for a general interest in which team is Number One), agate or a variation like Figure 11.11 would be a more appropriate medium.

Examine Figure 11.10 in terms of the visual inverted pyramid approach explained in Chapter 3: The main point is that Kansas is No. 2. The secondary point is that it recently moved up to that slot. The supporting details are the other teams that comprise the Top 10. Both the main and the secondary points are hierarchical in nature. They deal with relationships and movements that could catch the eye of someone who isn't looking for the type of material offered in the supporting details. The supporting details, like the list in Figure 11.11, are categorically organized; readers must seek this information. Hierarchical arrangements catch the eye. Categorical arrangements wait for the eye to come.

Will a list dominated by bold numerals 1 through 10 catch the eye? Not likely. When was the last time you thought, gee, I wonder who's No. 6? More likely, you might wonder where a specific team you follow is ranked or how its ranking might have changed. Even more likely, you don't really care about the rankings at all but suddenly realize that a familiar team has joined the list or moved up. People who make it a habit to look at lists don't need hierarchical arrangements to

11.10

Kansas soars to No. 2 in poll

1. North Carolina
2. Kansas
3. Duke
4. Kentucky
5. Indiana
6. Marquette
7. Illinois

8. Oklahoma
9. Kansas State
10. Ohio State

Rankings don't simply report the contents of a list. They show movement or relative position of particular items of interest. This one is designed with a seemingly elaborate hoop-and-ball icon that could easily be eliminated if vividness were not needed. How to create the icon is explained in Figure 11.13 at the end of this section.

11.11

Basketball's
Top 10

1. North Carolina

2. Kansas

3. Duke

4. Kentucky

5. Indiana

6. Marquette

7. Illinois

8. Oklahoma

9. Kansas State

10. Ohio State

To the uninitiated, this may look like a graphic. In reality, it acts like agate and would be just as effective if presented in the tiny type that gives agate its name.

persuade them to look. The browsers who don't make it a habit **do** need them. They want to know more than what the information is **about**, which is all that Figure 11.11 tells us. They want to know what the information **is**—Figure 11.10's goal.

Graphics like the one in Figure 11.10 tell them what the information is and more. Note how subtle visual data metaphors are employed to relate the main and secondary points. You see even without the numbers that Kansas ranks somewhere near the top of the list. An arrow leading from the team's former position makes the upward mobility of the Jayhawks easy to spot. Such eye-catching vividness and data metaphor, coupled with hierarchical organization, are what gives a graphic its power. Without such benefits, a graphic is just agate, blown up to a bigger point size.

Not only should the list not take a prominent role. At times, the list can be so trivial in relation to the main points that it can be omitted. Figure 11.12 offers a perfect case in point. Imagine this graphic accompanies a news story about the factors that limit life expectancy in Illinois. Listing where each individual state stands is at best a minor supporting detail. The main points deal with where Illinois stands and the secondary points deal with which states are the best or worst in each category. Although it might be nice to offer data for all 50 states in each of the four categories, there isn't enough space to do this on Page 1 and even if there were, it would detract from the main and secondary points. Instead, the list of states is omitted and Illinois' position on each list is charted in a visual metaphor that quickly explains where Illinois ranks. The full list can run in agate inside.

To be sure, you can create a ranking graphic that is nothing more than an agate list set in a bigger type size and adorned with a compelling icon. You'll see such graphics, if they can be called that, in sports pages every time a new basketball or football poll comes out. A case can be made that the list itself is a newsworthy fact and that listing its members in bigger type attracts more attention than agate would and, therefore, serves as a valuable tool of information design. But is it? In reality, bigger type attracts attention solely because it is bigger, just as a particular passage of text might attract attention if typeset in 14 point type instead of 10 point. Such a change brings in people who forgot their reading glasses and maybe those who see a particularly interesting word that otherwise might have been missed, but that's about it. The other benefits that a non-inverted pyramid ranking graphic could offer—tabulation of the data, rather than presenting it in text—are just as available in agate as they are in graphics.

11.12

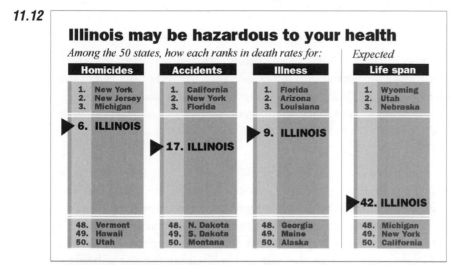

Illinois may be hazardous to your health

Among the 50 states, how each ranks in death rates for: *Expected*

Homicides	Accidents	Illness	Life span
1. New York	1. California	1. Florida	1. Wyoming
2. New Jersey	2. New York	2. Arizona	2. Utah
3. Michigan	3. Florida	3. Louisiana	3. Nebraska
▶ 6. ILLINOIS	▶ 17. ILLINOIS	▶ 9. ILLINOIS	▶ 42. ILLINOIS
48. Vermont	48. N. Dakota	48. Georgia	48. Michigan
49. Hawaii	49. S. Dakota	49. Maine	49. New York
50. Utah	50. Montana	50. Alaska	50. California

When the full list is of relatively trifling significance, rankings may be reported only in terms of a visual data metaphor. The complete list, if needed at all, might run in agate at end of the accompanying text. This technique poses some challenges for accuracy of charting. How to meet these challenges is explained in Figure 11.14 at the end of this section.

At the risk of sounding a bit risqué, in information design it's not the size that counts but how you use it. With non-inverted pyramid "graphics," the reverse is true. Size is all that matters and it matters only for a short time.

Eventually, big type starts losing its influence. You get used to the fact that everything is bigger, just as you get used to listening to a person who always shouts. Soon there becomes no value in shouting. When the wolf really does come, no one recognizes the cries for help as being any different from ordinary conversation.

Suppose you're the principal of a high school and are publishing the semester honor roll. You can tabulate the list in small type, in normal-size type or in headline-size type. If you wanted to make parents particularly proud a particular semester, you might choose to do it in headline style. But that's a tool best reserved for occasional use. If such techniques are routinely used, readers get so used to the screaming that whispers become more noteworthy and you will have conditioned them to expect exactly the reverse of your system of importance.

See how it works? The "whispers become more noteworthy" ends up being more memorable and compelling than the rest of the text in the previous paragraph. In fact, the paragraph you're reading right now probably attracted as much attention as the previous one merely because of the contrast. Size didn't tell the words any better. In fact, it may not have told them as well.

The same type of thing happens if you consistently use non-hierarchical graphics instead of agate. People get so used to the technique that you begin weakening the value of all graphics. This is particularly true if you are producing graphics for an ongoing publication. Readership habits are based in large part on how predictably efficient a publication is. Graphics play a significant role in this by easing the task of browsing for information. If, however, graphics constantly shout without purpose, failing to make it easier to find what is interesting, the predictability and efficiency of your publication suffers. So, too, does its readership and ultimately your paycheck.

If a graphic doesn't have a main point, why put the information in graphic form? Just because something isn't text doesn't mean it should be a graphic. A reader looking for specific information is likely to seek it with or without visual vividness or data metaphor. Organization and metaphorical simplicity play a greater role for such readers, but agate is just as organized and as metaphorically simple as a non-inverted pyramid graphic is.

At times, it may be appropriate to present information in non-inverted pyramid graphics. The case of the categorical graphic about tax cuts in the previous section comes to mind. Realize, however, when you use such techniques you are shouting; make sure the wolf really is there before you begin crying out.

How Figure 11.10 Was Constructed

11.13

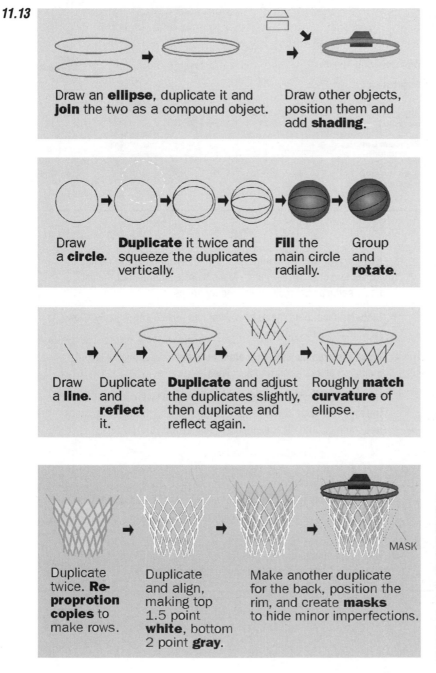

Draw an **ellipse**, duplicate it and **join** the two as a compound object.

Draw other objects, position them and add **shading**.

Draw a **circle**.

Duplicate it twice and squeeze the duplicates vertically.

Fill the main circle radially.

Group and **rotate**.

Draw a **line**.

Duplicate and **reflect** it.

Duplicate and adjust the duplicates slightly, then duplicate and reflect again.

Roughly **match curvature** of ellipse.

Duplicate twice. **Reproprotion copies** to make rows.

Duplicate and align, making top 1.5 point **white**, bottom 2 point **gray**.

Make another duplicate for the back, position the rim, and create **masks** to hide minor imperfections.

MASK

Circles and lines do most of the work in creating the hoop and ball in Figure 11.10. The rim is created much as the see-through clipboard hole was in Figure 11.9. The ball is simply a set of shaded ellipses. The backboard is a series of shaded round- and square-corner rectangles. The net is created much as highways were in Chapter 9's Figure 9.3.

How Figure 11.12 Was Constructed

11.14

One of the easiest ways to chart data is to create graph-like grid lines, then delete them. To create grid lines, simply draw a rectangle, duplicate it, carefully align the copies and use the equidistant lines they create as your guides.

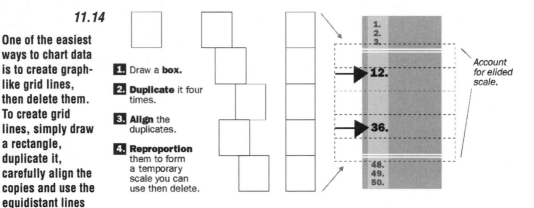

1. Draw a **box.**

2. Duplicate it four times.

3. Align the duplicates.

4. Reproportion them to form a temporary scale you can use then delete.

1.
2.
3.

12.

36.

48.
49.
50.

Account for elided scale.

DO

- **Explain why the list is important** by highlighting relative position, movement or other key items. Make these elements, not the list itself, serve as the main or secondary points.

- **Include visual data metaphors** wherever possible to visually show relative position or movement.

- **Make the graphic work with other elements** in the overall layout, including other visuals and headlines.

- **Include background images** to increase visual vividness, but only if the topic is one of lower reader involvement and the vividness does not compete with other elements in the layout.

DON'T

- **Simply display the list** unless certain elements could convert information browsers into information seekers before they reach the ranking.

- **Use breakouts to convey details.** If the entire list conveys only supporting details, feel free to cut it off as necessary.

Ratings

While rankings stress relative strengths of items ordinally, ratings stress relative strengths cardinally, like Figure 11.15 does. That is, they evaluate items by grading them—either with a letter grade, as in a report card, or with a "star" grade, as in an entertainment review.

Ratings are among the most categorical of graphics. Readers scan a list to find a particular item and its rating. As a result, ratings are primarily for information seekers, concerned more about organization and simplicity than about vividness and data metaphor. Unfortunately, that is typically the reverse of how most ratings graphics, including Figure 11.15, are constructed.

Let's simultaneously examine Figure 11.15 and an alternative method of presenting ratings information by creating a non-visual graphic that rates Figure 11.15 on Chapter 3's qualities of vividness, organization, data metaphor and metaphorical simplicity. Figure 11.16 is the result. Its ratings give high marks to Figure 11.15's vividness, mediocre marks for its use of data metaphor and low marks for its organization and metaphorical simplicity. It shows these grades in a graphic that itself uses very little vividness and a simple data metaphor—a simplistic drawing of a mouse as a ratings "star."

What does our analysis show? For one, it reveals Figure 11.15 to be like a ranking that fails to make a point. Quick, what's the best film? Is the original *Miracle on 34th Street* a classic or just pretty good? How does *Christmas Story* compare with the Richard Attenborough remake of *Miracle*? Yes, they

11.15

With a film backdrop, a Christmas tree icon and a greeting card typeface, this ranking stresses vividness. But it also uses data metaphor by pictographically showing each rating as an instantly visual number of ornaments. An improved version of this graphic is shown in Figure 11.18. Techniques used to make it are detailed in Figure 11.19.

11.16

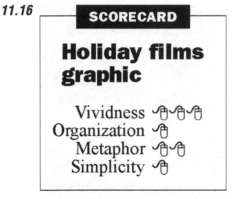

This rating, which critiques Figure 11.15, stresses simplicity of data metaphor.

11.17

Keys typically are to be avoided, but in the case of ratings graphics they often are appropriate. Iconic ratings can be read intuitively at first glance. The additional information offered in a key tends to be information from somewhere beneath the main point, farther down into the visual inverted pyramid.

are questions you can answer by referring back to the graphic, but the answers didn't come to you at a glance. They come at a long stare. The main point of Figure 11.16—that Figure 11.15 has some weaknesses—is a lot easier get at a glance.

What would help our poor, low-rated graphic in Figure 11.15? For one thing, anytime a rating is used, it's useful to know what the rating scale is. If your high school grade point average was 2.95, it makes a world of difference to know whether your school graded on a three-, four- or five-point scale. Adding a key like the one in Figure 11.17 could make Figure 11.15 a better graphic. It's not a classic key. You don't need to consult it to understand main-point differences between items. Rather, it's a secondary or supporting key, offering additional details, and, unlike classic keys, is valid to include.

What else would help make Figure 11.15 be a better ratings graphic? How about putting the films in order? This could be alphabetical order, which would further the categorical appeal. Better yet would be to organize the films hierarchically, with the best ones first and the worst ones last. Now we are doing more than just decorating a list with vivid images; we're making the list instantly understandable. In addition to the "star" rankings, we've created hierarchical organization as well. This organization and the accompanying key make it a lot easier to answer whether the original *Miracle* is rated as a classic or how *Christmas Story* compares with the Attenborough *Miracle* remake.

But we need not stop there. Remember from Chapter 3 our discussion of how a graphic should have a beginning, a middle and an end, and that a failed graphic contains nothing beyond what can be gleaned at a glance? Here's a perfect opportunity to prove that point. In addition to the ratings themselves, how about adding a key reason for each rating, as is done in the remade version of the graphic in Figure 11.18?

Now the graphic has a raison d'être. It doesn't just report the ratings the way agate would. It organizes them and explains them the way a graphic should. In the process, the graphic justifies the visual "shouting" that accompanies use of a large graphic instead of a small, agate-like entry point, such as our simple Figure 11.16 scorecard. Only if a rating offers the additional value present in Figure 11.18 should it be considered appropriate to "dress it up." Otherwise, it's just as effective if done in the manner of Figure 11.16. Ratings tend to be very categorical to begin with. Only if a hierarchical mission also can be served do they justify exposure greater than that accorded to glorified agate.

Once you've solved the content question with a ratings graphic, execution should be easy, involving nothing more than standard type, image and alignment techniques. In the case of Figures 11.16 and 11.18, a single sprocket is created as a square and is duplicated repeatedly. The duplicates are then aligned horizontally and distributed vertically. The sprockets from one side are grouped and then duplicated to create the sprockets for the other side. Individual frames within the film are created the same way and icons are created using simple combinations of circles, rectangles and polygons. Only in the case of the Christmas tree is the slightest of Bézier curvature involved. All these techniques have been explored in previous sections, but, for the record, a quick overview of them is offered in Figure 11.19. By now they should be as familiar to you as this book's bad puns.

11.18

This improved version of Figure 11.15 substantially increases the original's organization by ranking the films in order and offering brief reasons for each ranking.

No crops given

11.19

What should by now be familiar drawing techniques are the only things needed to create images like those in Figures 11.16 and 11.18.

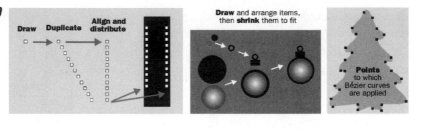

DO

● **Organize** the information hierarchically so that it is more than just a table of raw scores.

● **Explain briefly** why each item is rated as it is and what each rating means.

● **Use simple icons** to function as pictograms for each rating "star" awarded.

DON'T

● **Use undue vividness** unless your graphic includes more than categorical information.

● **Assume** that readers will have read the accompanying text. Make sure you include enough background to make the graphic stand on its own.

● **Pad the graphic with details** that might better be told in text or agate.

Tables

Tables may be the most used and abused type of graphic. A table is a set of numbers presented in tabulated, columnar form. Its value is that it presents large amounts of data with precision. Its weakness is that it does so less memorably, less quickly, less believably and less meaningfully than its principle alternative, the graph. Tables are good for identifying particular trees within an informational forest—if readers are willing to take the time to find them. Graphs, the subject of the next chapter, are better for showing the forest as a whole—for quickly presenting the overall picture that statistical data have to offer.

Tables are valuable only when the key information involves a limited number of specific data combinations: How big your tax bill is depends on where the column representing your income intersections with the column representing your number of dependents. Everyone has a different intersection. Most will be motivated, like it or not, to find this information, and the government will want them to find it with precision. Such material is, therefore, best presented as columnar agate. Readers don't need the data metaphor and vividness that an alternative treatment in graphic form would offer.

If, on the other hand, a universal intersection exists and the value created by that intersection is one that people might not bother to look up for themselves, a graphic might be in order.

Figure 11.20, presenting wind-chill information, is a perfect case in point. Its purpose is to explain how dangerously cold the weather has been. The tabular data within it serves as merely a supporting detail in this quest. The main and secondary points are that yesterday's wind-chill reading was a dangerously cold 74 below, caused by winds of 20 mph coupled with an actual temperature of 25 below. The graphic makes this point at a glance by showing how the specific combination of data came together and how it ranked within the danger zone.

11.20

Wind chill at danger level

	5	10	15	20	25	30	35 mph
35°	33	22	16	12	8	6	4
30	27	16	9	4	1	-2	-4
25	21	10	2	-3	-7	-10	-12
20	16	3	-5	-10	-15	-18	-20
15	12	-3	-11	-17	-22	-25	-27
10	7	-9	-18	-24	-29	-33	-35
5	0	-15	-25	-31	-36	-41	-43
0	-5	-22	-31	-39	-44	-49	-52
-5	-10	-27	-38	-46	-51	-56	-58
-10	-15	-34	-45	-53	-59	-64	-67
-15	-21	-40	-51	-60	-66	-71	-74
-20	-26	-46	-58	-67	-74	-79	-82
-25	-31	-52	-65	**-74**	-81	-86	-89
-30	-36	-58	-72	-81	-88	-93	-97
-35	-42	-64	-78	-88	-96	-101	-105

SEVERE DANGER

Yesterday's worst

The thermometer at left isn't what makes this table a graphic. It's a graphic because it explains main and secondary points that arise from the tabular data. The columns of numbers serve only as supporting details. Without the other points, it would better be told as agate.

Without the labeled danger zone, the blurb pointing to yesterday's reading and the lines indicating how that reading was created, Figure 11.20 wouldn't be a graphic at all. It would be decorated agate, shouting that it was important without offering a clue as to why. It would have no main or secondary points, no inverted pyramid to follow, no data metaphor, no hooks to snag browsing readers—in short, no elements that give graphics their power. There would, in fact, be nothing graphic about it. Yet chances are, this winter, if you're unfortunate enough to live in an area where wind chills matter, you'll probably run across a "graphic" like that—and a puzzled artist who can't understand why most readers don't get anything out of it. If you do, consider sending the artist a copy this book as a late Christmas present.

Even when a table is organized well and presented in visual inverted pyramid fashion, it still doesn't inform nearly as completely as a graph. Compare Figure 11.21 to Figure 11.20. Figure 11.21 doesn't give you the pleasure of being able to say it felt like exactly 74 below outside, but you can come away with a better understanding of how wind chills work and when you need to pay attention to them.

11.21

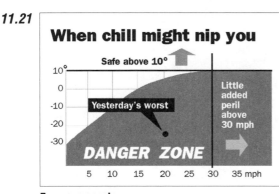

Even a properly organized table like the one in Figure 11.20 might better as a graph. Note how the graph stresses the big picture while the table is mired in details.

Table graphics are best only when the primary goal is to teach how to read tabular agate, when the supporting details are as important as the main point or when charting methods are inadequate to the task.

Suppose you are comparing scores across different categories and different scales. High scores could indicate strength on certain scales, while low scores indicate strength on others. Figure 11.22 offers a good example. To be considered better, a football team must have a high efficiency on third down while holding its opponents to a low efficiency in the same category. Charting the raw numbers without a visual clue to show this inverse relationship would be confusing, so the data items are instead presented in tabular form.

Using table graphics does not mean that hierarchical organization is abandoned. Note in Figure 11.22 how the statistic indicating greater strength in each category is shown in reverse. Readers can instantly determine which team has the edge. More important, a pattern of how many times a team has the edge emerges. This organization and its ability to be read at a glance are what differentiate Figure 11.22 from just another piece of agate.

11.22

How NFC rivals compare

	Packers	Cowboys
3rd down efficiency	38%	31%
3rd down efficiency allowed	21%	29%
Red-zone scoring	92%	84%
Red-zone scoring allowed	54%	52%
Takeways minus giveaways	+19	+11
Current winning **streak**	6	4

Table graphics are most appropriate when conveying information that charting might misstate, in this case because larger numbers are better in some cases while smaller numbers are better in others. Note how the better score is highlighted in each case to give the graphic its main and secondary points.

DO

- **Highlight key data,** particularly how it is read from the table or what it means in relation to other data.

- **Use tables only as a last resort** when supporting details are important, when you need to explain how to read columns of data or when charting data might visually misstate what it shows.

- **Eliminate non-essential information.** Tables are confusing enough without being overburdened by details that aren't vital.

DON'T

- **Use tables as a substitute for graphs** unless it is imperative to prevent misstating the data.

- **Assume** that reader interest translates into a need for "dressing up" a table. Overwhelming interest may in fact mitigate in favor of not decorating the material.

- **Let tables become decorated agate.** Make sure a table graphic always has a main point. If not, convert the information into a tabular agate and run it at the end of the text, rather than as an entry point.

Graphs

True to their name, graphs are the most commonly recognized information graphic. Using them requires some knowledge of that dreaded four-letter word "math," but their power to inform, first articulated by William Playfair, makes them worthwhile.

Every major study involving graphs has found them to be more quickly interpreted, more easily remembered and more likely to be believed than less-visual alternatives for presenting the same information.

Graphs don't convey information with the same precision that tables do, particularly if the information is to be used immediately. Readers of graphs, however, are more likely to come away with memories of the forest, even if they fail to remember specific trees.

To represent quantities visually, graphs present information in analog form, the natural language of the brain. They accomplish this by charting data the way a statistician would or by graphing it with visual analogies the way an artist would. Either method creates what researchers call visual data metaphor. A reader who doesn't have a personal stake in the information is more likely to remember data presented this way. Moreover, if accompanied by minimal charting accoutrements like grids, data labels and axes, graphs can possess the type of metaphorical simplicity that readers who do have personal stakes in the information appreciate. Graphs, therefore, are the rare form of graphic that simultaneously appeals to both major categories of reader.

A graph's principal alternative, the data table, discussed in Chapter 11, appeals to readers who have personal stakes in the information being presented. A table's appeal to other readers is heightened by adding elements of visual vividness, such as an icon. Visually vivid elements, however, can get in the way of the visually hierarchical organization that more systematic readers appreciate. Such tradeoffs can be avoided with graphs.

The only case in which a graph might be considered weaker than a table is when all of the following conditions are true:

- All readers are personally affected by the information.

- All readers are most concerned with how they are affected by specific elements, rather than the overall picture.

- All readers will act on the information immediately.

If, for instance, you are showing your debtors a list of who owes how much and are expecting payment from each of them on the spot, use a table. Otherwise, a graph is in order.

The most common graphs, itemized on the next few pages, reflect both statistical and artistic approaches. The bar (or column) chart, a hybrid of these two approaches, presents interval or categorical data and encompasses such statistical forms as the histogram and the scatter chart. Fever (or line) charts, which fall more on the statistical side, present continuous data. Pie (or circle) charts, which fall on the artistic side, present data in relation to a whole. Area charts, partly like pies and partly like fevers, and pictograms, a mixture of bar and pie techniques, complete the arsenal.

Many information designers manually chart information contained in their graphs whereas others use charting programs such as DeltaGraph, CricketGraph and CORELGraph. Most modern spreadsheet programs, particularly those bundled into an office suite, like Microsoft Excel, are more than adequate substitutes. Some drawing programs, notably Adobe Illustrator, also offer charting tools. After we explore each major type of chart, you'll learn the process of using a charting program and transforming its output into proper graphic form.

Whatever visual weapon is chosen, the rules for safe use of graphs are the same: To achieve maximum potential, graphs must be presented in organized, hierarchical fashion, using the visual inverted pyramid approach. Extraneous material should be eliminated and the main point should be highlighted and restated for dual-coding purposes with a pointer box.

GRAPHS *at a glance*

Best suited for:	Summarizing statistical data
	Expressing quantitative relationships
Least suited for:	Listing specific data for immediate use
	Expressing qualitative relationships
Answers the question:	How much
	Occasionally, what, why and how
Often used as:	Secondary visual elements
	Occasionally, small entry points or visual centerpieces
Typical size:	2 to 4 inches wide
	Occasionally, somewhat narrower or wider
Key challenges:	Accuracy and integrity (See Chapter 5)
	Finding information (Chapter 4)
Key techniques:	Visual data metaphors (Chapter 6 and this chapter)
	Evaluative typography, particularly pointer boxes (Chapters 3 and 10)
Temptation to avoid:	Failing to focus on a single main point

Bar Charts

Whether they are vertical or horizontal, bars represent data readings across intervals of time: college enrollment by decade, your bank balance on the first day of each month or, as in Figure 12.1, annual sales of a product for each of the past five years. The utility of bar charts doesn't stop there, however. Bars also are used to report data totals within specific categories: the enrollment total at each of the 11 Big Ten universities (you'd think those college folks could add), the

12.1

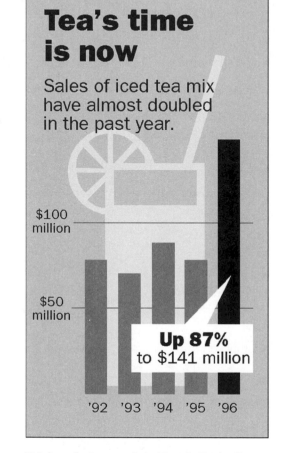

Tea's time is now

Sales of iced tea mix have almost doubled in the past year.

$100 million

$50 million

Up 87%
to $141 million

'92 '93 '94 '95 '96

This bar chart uses a faded icon in the background for vividness, a blurb box and shade-highlighting of a key bar for organization, bars for data metaphor and grid lines for metaphorical simplicity. How the icon was constructed is explained in Figure 12.11 at the end of this section.

balance in each of your several different bank accounts (we didn't say the bars were big) or annual sales for each of several different products within the same general category.

Bar charts are, in short, among the most versatile of graphics. Almost any type of data can be told with a bar chart, even if another chart could tell it better. Other charts are far more restrictive in types of data they can be used to represent. If in doubt, stick with bars. They may not be the best solution, but rarely are they wrong to use.

With such versatility come only a few rules. Usually, no more than a dozen bars and no fewer than four bars are included in any one chart. More bars tend to make a chart confusing; fewer bars tend to make its comparisons meaningless.

Usually, each bar is about twice as wide as the space between it and its neighboring bar (see Figure 12.2). The bars themselves and the space should only consume a minimal space. Challenge yourself to make your bars as compact and efficient as possible, as if you were editing text. Keeping bar width as narrow as possible—just wide enough to allow '97 as a data label, for example—is a goal worth pursuing. Yet it typically is one of the most common problems with the work of inexperienced information designers.

The width of the bars and the space between them are important, but so too is the relationship between the width and height of the largest bar. Look at the three sets of data charted in Figure 12.3. The one labeled "Minimal" features slowly rising data. "Maximal" seems to feature rapidly rising data. "Moderate" falls in-between.

In fact, all three sets of data are exactly the same. The only difference is the ratio of the height of the largest bar to the width of all the bars. For the "Minimal" chart, the largest bar is six units tall and two units wide—a ratio of 6:2 (or 3:1). For the "Maximal" chart, the largest bar is 38 units tall while remaining only two units wide—a ratio of 38:2 (or 19:1).

Clearly, height-to-width ratios can put radically different spins on the same data. Which spin is the right spin? One way to tell is to do exactly what Figure 12.3 does. Chart the data, group it and duplicate it a few times. Stretch some of the duplicates and reduce others. Reduce one set until it makes the change look minimal; stretch another until it makes the change look dramatic. The set of data you will end up using is the one whose spin seems to fall midway between the extremes—unless you're working for a politician and your goal is to skew the data (and do something that sounds like skew to the voting public).

The height-to-width ratio that seems moderate typically falls somewhere between 20:2 and 25:2. In other words, when the biggest bar is somewhere between 10 and 12.5 times as tall as it is wide, as shown in Figure 12.4, data relationships tend to look neither minimal nor maximal. The exact ratio may vary depending on the relationship. A ratio of between 20:2 and 25:2 is, however, a good place to start.

12.2 **Bar proportions**

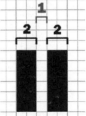

Each bar in a chart should be the same width. The space between bars should be roughly equal to half that width.

12.3

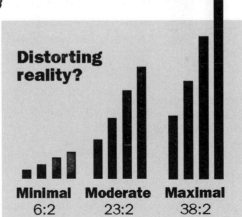

These bars seem to represent different rates of increase, yet the data of each set is identical. The apparent difference is an optical illusion caused by different height-to-width ratios for the largest bar.

12.4

Ideal ratio

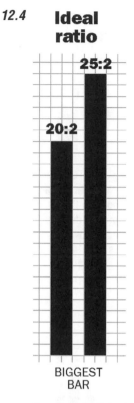

BIGGEST
BAR

Bars tend to distort data the least when the height of the largest bar is 20 to 25 times the space between each bar.

A good charting program, such as DeltaGraph or CricketGraph, makes creating bar charts simple. Even a spreadsheet program like Microsoft Excel can help. Most experienced information designers, however, create bar charts manually. The charting programs' "chartjunk," the non-essential accoutrements that clutter up the data, take more time to eliminate than it does to draw a half-dozen bars manually. And often, charting programs pay no attention to the ethics of height-to-width ratios.

If you manually draw bars, be careful to keep them in proportion to the data they represent. One way to do this is to draw them on top of a reusable "graph paper" backdrop you can create in your drawing program. A grid like the one in Figure 12.5 can be used not only in charting bars, but also in charting fever lines and in duplicating images that, for one reason or another, you cannot scan into your computer. (See Chapter 13 for how this applies with maps.)

Once you have your grid, it's simple to create the bars, as shown in Figure 12.6. Make each bar two grid squares wide, with one square between them. Invent a simple factor that lets you multiply or divide the data in your head so that it can easily be charted. If the data are 50, 100 and 200, for example, you might divide by 10 and chart the data as 5, 10 and 20. In truth, it matters not what factor you use. The bigger the bars, the more accurately you can draw them. It's the relative size, not the actual size, that matters at this point.

Draw a grid line at a known point above zero, then move your "graph paper" backdrop away. Double-check the spacing and alignment of the bars with align and distribute, and use the same align-and-distribute technique to create additional grid lines as needed. Draw in a zero line, which you should align to the base of the bars. Duplicate it as many times as needed to create lines between it and the line you drew when the "graph paper" was present. Align and distribute them to form an equally spaced, perfectly aligned grid. Group the bars and the grid lines, then reproportion the group so that the height-to-width ratio of the largest bar falls within the ideal range.

12.5

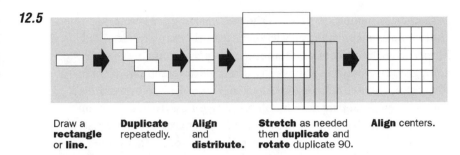

Draw a **rectangle** or **line.**   **Duplicate** repeatedly.   **Align** and **distribute.**   **Stretch** as needed then **duplicate** and **rotate** duplicate 90.   **Align** centers.

A grid like this can aid in charting and drawing. It can be expanded by duplicating it and aligning the duplicates with the original.

12.6

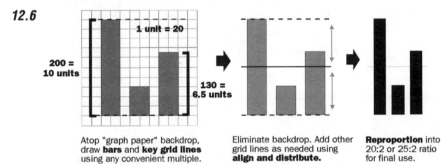

Atop "graph paper" backdrop, draw **bars** and **key grid lines** using any convenient multiple.   Eliminate backdrop. Add other grid lines as needed using **align and distribute.**   **Reproportion** into 20:2 or 25:2 ratio for final use.

Firing up a charting program to handle a handful of bars wastes more time than it saves. With most data, you can easily chart it manually this way.

Many veteran information designers use a faster variation of this trick. Rather than save a "graph paper" grid, they save a set of already aligned and spaced bars, each of which is one inch, 10 picas, 100 points or some other easily remembered (and divided) height. They resize the bars in one dimension only (in many programs, holding down the Shift key constrains the resizing) and watch as the height of each bar changes in the message area of their drawing program's menu bar. When the height reaches whatever value their factor requires, they move to the next bar. At the end, they draw one more bar to specify the height of the key grid line, draw the grid line and delete the bar. The rest of the charting process occurs similarly to the other method.

It can be very tempting, particularly with charting programs, to continue playing with the charted bars after they are proportioned properly. The most common temptation is playing the 3-D game—adding sides, tops and shadows to make the bars stand out as three-dimensional. It's easy to do, as shown in Figure 12.7. However, three-dimensional bars pose problems in two regards. Most obvious, the added depth is not meaningful. It's another accoutrement that, as Tufte puts it, lowers the data-to-ink ratio of the graphic. In other words, it takes ink to create the sides and top of the bars, but doing so does not convey any additional data. Adornments of this nature lower the graphic's simplicity of visual data metaphor (which is important for readers with personal stakes in the information) while only slightly increasing the graphic's visual vividness (important for readers without personal stakes). Adornments can thus helps "tune" the graphic to best reach its audience, but a significant loss of simplicity may not balance a slight gain in vividness.

12.7 **Eight steps to three dimensions**

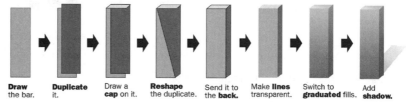

Making bars appear three-dimensional is a quick exercise.

Draw the bar. **Duplicate** it. Draw a **cap** on it. **Reshape** the duplicate. Send it to the **back.** Make **lines** transparent. Switch to **graduated** fills. Add **shadow.**

Moreover, three-dimensional bars also create a different, less theoretical problem. Where exactly does the bar intersect a grid line? In the front? At the rear? As Figure 12.8 shows, whether the grid line cuts across the bar, sits behind it or wraps around it makes a difference, but the difference is such a subtle one that a browsing reader, the type who likes three-dimensional bars, might become confused. If you use three-dimensional bars, it's better to forget grid lines and label each bar with its actual value, a strategy discussed in greater detail later in the chapter.

Grid lines are more likely to be used in vertical bar charts than in horizontal ones, where individual value labels are used instead. Whether bars are vertical (technically known as column charts) or horizontal (the true definition of a bar chart) is not a matter of artistic whim. It depends on exactly what is being measured (see Figure 12.9).

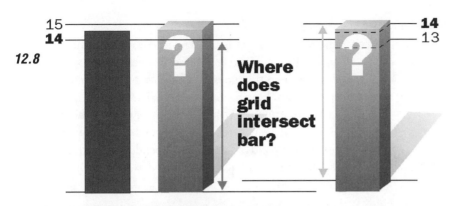

12.8

Where does grid intersect bar?

The value of the left bar clearly is about 14.6, but what are the values of the other two bars? Three-dimensional bars are difficult to place on a grid.

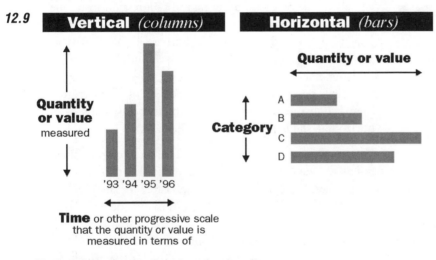

12.9

Vertical *(columns)*

Horizontal *(bars)*

Quantity or value
measured

'93 '94 '95 '96

Time or other progressive scale that the quantity or value is measured in terms of

Quantity or value

Category

A
B
C
D

Vertical bars measure the value of a given item over time or across another scale of activity. Horizontal bars present different quantities or values assigned to different items within a category.

Remember your high school geometry. A vertical bar chart has an independent X axis that is horizontal and a dependent Y axis that is vertical. Both axes measure a progressive variable. The value on the Y axis depends on where along the X axis you are. If you are charting the results of your weight-reduction program, the various weights you have

12.10

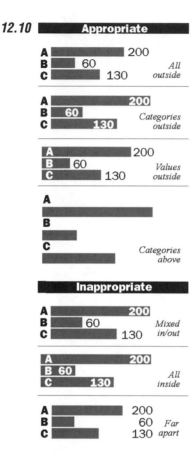

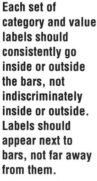

Each set of category and value labels should consistently go inside or outside the bars, not indiscriminately inside or outside. Labels should appear next to bars, not far away from them.

recorded depend on where you are in the plan: Week 1, Week 2 and so on. Weight is the dependent variable that goes along the *Y* axis. Time, measured in weeks, is the independent variable that goes along the *X* axis. You have no ability to control how time passes. That's why it is classified as independent. Although many of us may think otherwise, we do have control over our weight. That's why it is classified as dependent. Its value depends on the time (and, presumably, how diligently you've been avoiding donuts with coffee).

Suppose, on the other hand, that you are charting the total weight loss for each person who has finished participating in your office weight-reduction program. Adam, Barbara, Charlie, Dawn and Edith have names that progress in the alphabet, but there's no other logical progression from one to the next. Charlie isn't twice the person who Adam is. Dawn isn't twice the person that Barbara is. (Well, maybe so, but that's another matter.) Each is an individual—a category, not a scalar variable like time. The only scalar variable is how much weight each person lost. Therefore, there is only one axis and because the first axis is always horizontal, the bar chart becomes horizontal.

When applying labels indicating a bar's category or value, follow the general style explained in last chapter's Figure 11.24 regarding tables. For consistency, keep all category labels either inside or outside the bars and all value labels either outside or inside the bars. It's best not to put both inside because they can interfere with each other, and it is never appropriate to put some from one group inside and some from the same group outside. This has the effect of making differences look less pronounced. Likewise, if labels are outside, make sure that all category labels are either to the left or above each bar and that all value labels are either immediately to the right of horizontal bars or immediately above vertical bars. Figure 12.10 demonstrates several appropriate and inappropriate placement techniques.

How Figure 12.1 Was Constructed

12.11

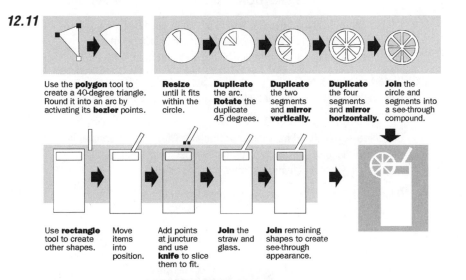

Use the **polygon** tool to create a 40-degree triangle. Round it into an arc by activating its **bezier** points.

Resize until it fits within the circle.

Duplicate the arc. **Rotate** the duplicate 45 degrees.

Duplicate the two segments and **mirror vertically.**

Duplicate the four segments and **mirror horizontally.**

Join the circle and segments into a see-through compound.

Use **rectangle** tool to create other shapes.

Move items into position.

Add points at juncture and use **knife** to slice them to fit.

Join the straw and glass.

Join remaining shapes to create see-through appearance.

When creating an icon for iced tea, it's important to first identify what visual elements "say" iced tea—a tall glass, a slice of lemon and a spoon or straw. Worry about these items first and look for repetitious shapes that enable you to use your computer to help in drawing them. In this case, duplication, rotation and the knife tool are most helpful.

DO

- **Highlight one key bar** in a darker or brighter shade than the others (refer to Chapter 3).

- **Use a pointer box** aimed at that bar (again, refer to Chapter 3) to reiterate the main point verbally.

- **Include icons,** but only if they help identify the subject matter and do not overwhelm the main point.

- **Be consistent.** Make sure bars are precisely aligned at zero and equally separated by one-half the bars' width. Put all data and value labels consistently inside or immediately outside bars.

DON'T

- **Let bar charts become obese.** A typical bar chart need be no more than two inches wide. As a general rule, the smaller the bar the better, provided it maintains an appropriate height-to-width ratio.

- **Distort relationships** Do this by "cutting" scales (refer to Chapter 5) or by using a height-to-width ratio other than a moderate one, typically between 20:2 to 25:2 for the largest bar.

- **Use three-dimensional bars indiscriminately.** They are appropriate only when the topic is likely to be of minimal personal significance to readers and when problems with grids can be solved.

- **Over-label.** Use either value labels or a grid, but not both (see next section.)

12.12

College costs soar

Expense now exceeds many graduates' salaries.

In reporting on college costs, this chart uses a simple icon to generate modest vividness. Alternative designs for this graphic are explored in Figures 12.17 and 12.18 farther along in this section. How to create the data portion of the graphic is explained in Figure 12.19.

Fever Charts

Be careful when using illness as an excuse in graphics class or on the job as a graphic designer. You might escape having to bring in a note from your doctor, but you might have to produce a fever chart to document your illness.

Fever charts like the one in Figure 12.12 report a specific reading's progress across a continuous range such as time. A nurse charts the temperature of his patient every four hours. An economist charts the costs associated with her company's assembly line at various levels of output.

Fevers differ from bars in that the progression of data in a fever is assumed to be along a continuous scale, even if data are supplied only at intervals along that scale. As Figure 12.13 demonstrates, the implicit assumption behind a fever is that, while only a few points are charted (only one point per year, for example), if more points had been provided (one for every month, perhaps) they would fall along a line connecting the original points. Bar charts make no such implications.

12.13

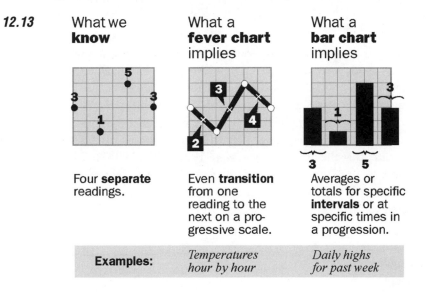

What we **know**	What a **fever chart** implies	What a **bar chart** implies
Four **separate** readings.	Even **transition** from one reading to the next on a progressive scale.	Averages or totals for specific **intervals** or at specific times in a progression.
Examples:	*Temperatures hour by hour*	*Daily highs for past week*

Fever charts measure data on continuous scales. Vertical bar charts measure data on interval scales.

In most cases, there's no question whether a fever or a bar is appropriate. If at 9 a.m. the temperature was 70 degrees and at 10 a.m. it was 80 degrees, it probably is safe to assume that at 9:30 a.m. it was about 75 degrees. If, however, you need 30 credits to graduate at the start of the semester and 15 credits to graduate at the end, it is not safe to assume that somewhere around mid-semester break you need 22.5 credits. Measurements that occur in stair-step fashion are appropriately represented in bars. Measurements that occur in linear fashion are appropriately represented in fevers.

Occasionally either chart is appropriate. Charting the daily close on the Dow Jones Industrial Average as a line ignores the rises and falls that occur between each day's close. If, however, the graphic's "chatter" or source line states that daily closes are charted, a fever chart can still be appropriate because the daily close charts a general trend, even if hourly variations fail to show up in that trend.

On the other hand, charting unemployment by decade is too big a leap even with a note in the "chatter." Trends in joblessness are more accurately expressed as month-to-month or year-to-year trends. Five-year readings are better expressed as bars than as fever lines. In short, the only rule is common sense. Minor non-linear anomalies in data do not require use of bar charts, particularly if a large amount of data, recorded at commonly used intervals, is involved. The only absolute is that, when in doubt, a bar chart is always right whereas a fever chart carries no guarantees.

When the precise interval of the readings is significant, but not enough to warrant use of a bar chart instead of a fever, dots denote when the readings were taken. As Figure 12.14 explains, dots indicate that observations were made at only some of the implied intervals. Without such dots, a fever chart implies that readings were taken continuously or at intervals corresponding to the labels on the horizontal axis. If the axis indicates that the years involved were 1992, 1993, 1994, 1995 and 1996, dots are unnecessary if the measurements were, in fact, taken in each of those years. If, however, readings were taken only in even-numbered years, dots might be needed.

12.14 **Dots or no dots:** What they mean

Exactly these points
Probably the points in between

EXAMPLE
Readings taken at intervals

All grid intersections **equally reliable**

EXAMPLE
Continuous readings or averages

Dots indicate exactly when specific readings were taken.

Technically, a fever chart consists only of a line and, perhaps, the dots on it. In this book and in the information design industry, we also apply the term "fever" to charts that fill the area beneath the fever line. As Figure 12.15 explains, filled fever areas mean something different than unfilled fever lines. An unfilled line indicates a specific reading (the temperature at noon was 55 degrees), whereas a filled area indicates that all amounts from zero to the top of the line are included (last year the company had $55 million in earnings). Temperatures aren't additive; 55 degrees isn't composed on one side of town as 25 degrees and the other side as 30 degrees. Quantities like $55 million, however, can be broken into components; $25 million came from one product, whereas $30 million came from the other. Unfilled lines are appropriate primarily with temperatures and other readings on arbitrary, non-additive scales. Only quantities, values and other additive totals may be appropriately represented with filled areas. When in doubt, a fever line is always right. A filled fever area, like fevers in general, carries no guarantees.

Theoretically, there's no problem with "cutting" the scale on an unfilled fever chart that reports arbitrary scalar data like temperatures. A temperature of 98 degrees is not twice as hot as a temperature of 49 degrees, so it's unnecessary to show the reading's relationship to zero. In most cases, however, a "cut" scale, in which a portion of the distance from the data line to the zero point has been removed, is a graphic that tells a lie, as discussed in Chapter 5.

The argument for "cutting" a scale comes in the case of a quantity that exists in a narrow range—the Consumer Price Index, for example, which starts at a large base, then moves in small increments with regard to that base. The argument is that to show changes in the index, some of the always-present area between the data line and zero must be elided. In fact, the argument is specious on its face. If change is what's important, why not chart the change instead of the data? If consumer prices rise by one percent in 1995, three percent in 1996 and two percent in 1997, economists and politicians will talk about how inflation—the rate of change in the Consumer Price Index—slowed from 1996 to 1997. Prices still went up, but they went up at a slower pace. By charting the rate of change instead of the base index, the visual metaphor begins to match the accepted verbal metaphor for what happened (see Figure 12.16).

Fever charts are among the easiest graphics to "tune" to match expected levels of reader involvement. "Chartoon" proponents, such as Nigel Holmes, advocate use of visual humor—charted puns that add to a graphic's vividness by making a joke out of its data metaphor. A chartoon might depict the rising cost of college as a data line that also serves

12.15 **Filled or unfilled:** What it means

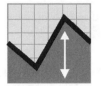

All values between the line and zero

EXAMPLE

Quantities or other additive values like dollars

These values only, not including values below the line

EXAMPLE

Readings on an arbitrary scale like temperatures

Unfilled lines are used for numbers, such as temperatures, that are measured on arbitrary scales.

12.16 **Graphics and politics:** Rates of change

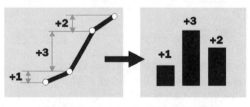

Consumer prices or the national debt

. . . quantities that always seem to be rising

Inflation or the budgetary deficit

. .`. rate of change of rising quantity

Raw data might be appropriate as a fever, but rates of change require bars. Be careful in labeling such charts to make it clear that while a fever might deal with prices, a rate-of-change bar chart deals with inflation.

as the tassel for a cartoon graduate's mortar board, atop which the words "Send money" have been spelled out in tape. The problem is, in attempting to increase vividness by way of humorous data metaphors, readers all too often see the vividness but miss the metaphor. With metaphorical simplicity low, even uninvolved readers have trouble identifying the point, and chartoons end up being stylistic visual "shouts" instead of informative tools.

Chartoons aren't the only way in which fever charts may be adorned. Figure 12.17 shows three variations of the original graphic from Figure 12.12. At left is the ultimate in metaphorical simplicity; at right, the ultimate in technical data metaphor; in the middle, a modified balance of the two. All are simpler than the icon and three-dimensional filled fever chart used in the original. Technically, each represents a different type of chart. To a statistician or mathematician, only the graphic at right is a true fever chart, which shows only a line connecting various data points. By shading the area under the fever line, the other charts could technically be known as area charts. In reality, however, all three accomplish the same purpose. For systematic readers with personal stakes in the topic, the graphic at right offers somewhat greater precision and detail. For heuristic readers without strong personal stakes, the graphic at left gives a quicker, "big picture" view.

12.17

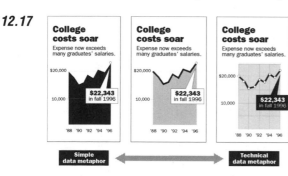

When more than one method of charting is statistically sound, the choice of which to use often becomes a matter of whether the graphic needs a precise metaphor to appeal to personally involved readers or a simpler metaphor to appeal to personally uninvolved readers.

Even the more visually vivid graphic originally shown in Figure 12.12 can come in different forms. If the headline for an overall package duplicates the graphic's headline, a modified version of the graphic can be seamlessly integrated into the headline-text-and-graphic package as shown in Figure 12.18. It is important for graphic designers to keep such possibilities in mind and not create graphics as works-in-themselves but as potential elements in integrated design packages, as explained more fully in Chapter 17.

12.18

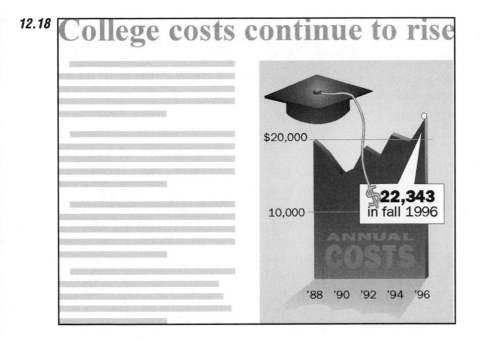

An information graphic is one element in an overall information design. Designing graphics so that they can be integrated with text and headlines is an important goal.

In creating fevers, many information designers still use a manual method of creation, which they contend takes less time than firing up a charting program and removing the "chartjunk" from its output. Manually charting a fever works much the same as manually charting bars: Start with your pre-drawn "graph paper" backdrop, chart the data and then delete the backdrop. If you're charting a line-and-fill fever, take advantage of your computer's power by drawing the data line once, duplicating it and using one copy as the line and the other as the fill, as shown in Figure 12.19. If you wanted to add three-dimensional characteristics to the data area, follow the same basic steps as in Figure 12.7 in the previous section.

12.19

Even when manually charting data, keep in mind that the computer can do much of the work for you. The duplicate command is a big time-saver.

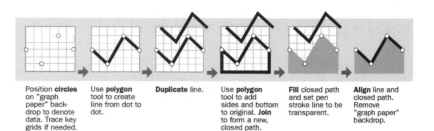

Position **circles** on "graph paper" backdrop to denote data. Trace key grids if needed.

Use **polygon** tool to create line from dot to dot.

Duplicate line.

Use **polygon** tool to add sides and bottom to original. **Join** to form a new, closed path.

Fill closed path and set pen stroke line to be transparent.

Align line and closed path. Remove "graph paper" backdrop.

Once you have decided on an approach, charted the data and picked a key point to highlight with a pointer box, the remaining question is what to do with the other values. Remember the concept of the visual inverted pyramid from Chapter 3: The main point is told by a pointer box, and the secondary point is told by the general trend demonstrated by the data line. The actual numbers underlying each point become minor supporting details, elements from the bottom of the visual inverted pyramid. True, they are necessary parts of the graphic, but they should not attract so much attention that they obscure the main and secondary points.

As shown in Figure 12.20, the more points that are labeled, the less need there is for a system of grid lines or abbreviated grid lines called tick marks. Material at the bottom of the visual inverted pyramid may appropriately require effort on the reader's part to obtain. Rather than emphasizing such information the way you must with main points, you can leave supporting details to be divined by your graphic's readers from other clues. The more clues that are provided by other elements, the fewer new clues you must provide. Thus, if few or no data items are labeled, a grid featuring full horizontal lines may be needed. If a representative handful of the data items are labeled for some other purpose, only tick marks may be needed. If all data items are labeled, even the need for tick marks goes away.

Grids, ticks and other scale items all add to a graphic's clutter, reducing its metaphorical simplicity. Determine whether each potential scale item is really needed before inserting it into a graphic by rote. In the cases in which you do insert such an element, feel free to use medium grays and smaller than usual point sizes to help push it to the bottom of the visual inverted pyramid.

Full horizontal grid
if no data labeled

Horizontal ticks
if some data labeled

No grid or ticks
if all data labeled

No zero line
for bar charts

The more clues to meaning that are supplied elsewhere, the less the need for cluttersome scales.

If the zero point is obvious because that's where all the bars in a bar chart start, there's no need for a zero line. Similarly, there rarely is a need for vertical grid lines. Axis labels at the bottom should do the trick, as should changes in the slope of the data line at each plotting point.

Labeling each data point solely for purposes of establishing a scale is the worst option. Labels at each point interfere with easy comprehension of the main and secondary points, reducing your ability to focus readers' attention on essential items. Drawing full graph-paper grids or even just the X and Y axis lines likewise tends to be counterproductive.

Whatever scale clues you determine to be necessary, you must also consider which increments to use in creating your scale. Generally, common, round numbers are the most useful scale items. Although a charting program might create grid lines at 4, 8, 12 and 16, we know that 5, 10 and 15 are more "user-friendly" breaking points.

In general, only one to three grid lines or ticks other than the zero line are needed. The fewer, the better. Moreover, it isn't necessary to use grid lines or ticks that exceed the value of the largest item charted unless that item is very close to reaching that level—more than 75 percent of the way there from the previous grid line or tick, for instance.

Unless there are only two grid lines or ticks, specific labels are needed only on every other grid line. Two labels are really all you need. Unless only one other line is labeled, the zero line, while present, need not have a label specifying that it represents zero.

Where to position labels or tick marks was the subject of considerable debate between artists and mathematicians in the 1980s, when Nigel Holmes insisted on putting them on the right side of a chart, as near as possible to the key point. Unless you want to be called by a mathematician in the wee hours of the morning—yes, they have been known to do this—it is a good idea to put such marks on the left side, where the Y axis normally would be if you had drawn it in.

Refer to numbers just as you would in text, following standard wire service style. Use "scientific" notation with large numbers (12 million, not 12,000,000), and prefix decimals with a leading zero (0.5 not .5). Align the numbers as discussed in the section on tables and demonstrated in Figure 11.24 in the previous chapter.

Abbreviations that go beyond standard text style are used in chart scales. Years may be abbreviated as '96 and '97, instead of being spelled out as 1996 and 1997. Percentages are used as numerals and symbols in all cases (14%) instead of being spelled out (14 percent). Months may be reduced to just their first letters if all 12 are charted (J F M A M J J A S O N D) or to just three letters if only a few are charted (May Jun Jul Aug Sep). Note that periods aren't needed. Financial quarters of a year may likewise be expressed as roman numerals (I II III IV) or as Arabic numerals with the letter Q (1Q 2Q 3Q 4Q), provided that a full range is supplied.

If your audience can grasp the meaning at a glance, an abbreviation is superior to spelling out the full name. The key phrase here is "at a glance." Reliance on keys and overuse of non-standard, quasi-scientific notation should be avoided. Notations such as "all figures in thousands" or "x1000" fail to work because readers may miss the footnote explaining the notation system and become confused as to what the true values are. They can't get the information at a single glance; understanding requires a double take. That's particularly so because the human mind doesn't work in scientific notation for numbers smaller than 1 million. We clearly understand what 560 means. It's not so clear what 56 tens means.

DO

- **Highlight one key point.** Use a pointer box to reiterate that main point verbally.

- **Include icons.** Only include them, however, if they help identify the subject matter and do not overwhelm the main point.

- **Consider the data implications of the chart you create.** Use fever lines, filled fever areas, data dots or bars only when they are appropriate for telling the data you hope to convey.

- **Reduce "chartjunk."** Use only minimally necessary grids, tick marks and labels. Make use of abbreviations, smaller point sizes and grays to fade such information into the background.

DON'T

- **Let your fever grow unchecked.** As with bar charts, a typical fever needs to be no more than two inches wide. The smaller the chart, the better. Use the same sort of height-to-width and spacing ratios that help keep bar charts at a reasonable size.

- **Distort relationships.** Do this by "cutting" scales inappropriately or by using height-to-width ratios other than moderate ones.

- **Use label keys.** Spell out what the scale is clearly, if quietly. Avoid notation systems that include footnotes like "all figures in thousands."

Pie Charts

We hate to tell you this, but all the time you spent in your high school geometry class was wasted. In mathematics, pi is equal to 3.1415926535897932384626, plus or minus a few decimal places. In the information design world, pie is always equal to a simple, round number: 100 percent.

Pie charts like the one in Figure 12.21 depict how one or more quantities relate to the whole. Although this shows how each of the quantities relate to one another—a comparison normally made in bar charts—never forget that the main purpose of a pie is to show the relationship to the whole. Percentages in pie charts must, therefore, always add up to 100. You may end up a tenth of a percentage point or two off because of rounding, but that's an inconsequential difference easily explained in a footnote. If, however, the sum is way off—say, for example, if multiple answers were allowed in a survey—a pie chart no longer is appropriate. One of the most common mistakes made by mathematically disinclined information designers is to automatically think a pie chart is called for just because a number is expressed as a percentage.

12.21

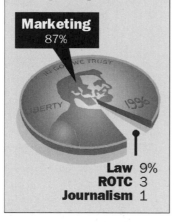

Ferengis study sales

Marketing is the most common major for Ferengi college students.

Marketing 87%

Law 9%
ROTC 3
Journalism 1

Although pies compare more than one component quantity to the whole, the visual inverted pyramid requires that only one of the quantities receive top billing. How to create a penny pie chart is detailed in Figure 12.29 at the end of this section.

Pie charts, particularly those based on oval shapes, are among the most difficult charts to create technically. Some drawing programs enable you to create arcs (or circle fragments) by editing a circle and displaying the degrees the arc passes through. Because each percentage point is equal to 3.6 degrees (100 percent equals 360 degrees), a pie can be created manually with such programs and a calculator. Many programs, however, do not allow this. In such cases, a separate charting program is a virtual necessity unless the percentages involved are quite simple. Charting errors are common when information designers create pie charts with no more accurate tools than their eyeballs.

One way around using a charting program is to create a circle grid much like the "graph paper" backdrop created in the previous section. Even with easy access to charting programs, some information designers prefer to create pies manually using circle grids. Create your grid by drawing lines that bisect a circle every 18 degrees—the equivalent of five percentage points. Duplication and rotation commands can automate this effort, as explained in Figure 12.22.

12.22

Holding down shift to constrain, draw a perfect **circle** and a line bisecting it.

Duplicate the line and **rotate** the duplicate 18 degrees (the equivalent of 5%).

Repeat until you go all the way around, then **align** all objects to their centers.

Even though charting programs create pies almost automatically, some information designers prefer manual means using an easy-to-create circle grid.

Your finished grid, with or without the labels added to Figure 12.22, can be a guide in drawing the slices of a pie chart, as shown in Figure 12.23. Many designers keep a circle grid, a graph paper backdrop, bars of standard proportions, blurb boxes, mock headlines and other elements that they save as a stationary template. They can then create new graphics very quickly, using pre-established tools.

To create a pie slice using a circle grid, start by drawing a polygon that begins and ends at the zero mark on the grid. Go from the zero mark to the center of the circle to the value you want to represent and then go back to the zero mark, as shown in Figure 12.24, in which a slice representing 43 percent is

12.23

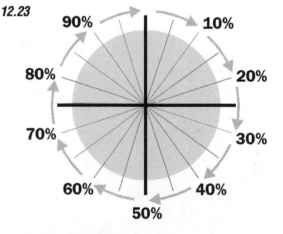

Using a circle grid like this one to manually create pie slices reduces the designer's guesswork to a minimum. You may have to approximate how far 43 percent is away from the 40 percent and 45 percent lines, but in a small graphic, that error margin is tolerable.

being created. After the polygon is closed, activate the bezier points at the origin and the destination, and adjust the curvature of the polygon so that it matches the curvature of the circle. The result is a closed arc, suitable for filling as a pie slide. If you don't create a closed arc, you won't be able to change the shading of pie slices to make key slices stand out.

12.24

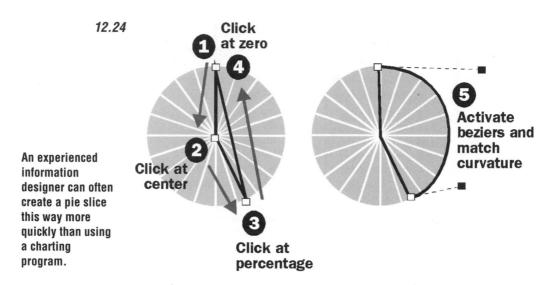

An experienced information designer can often create a pie slice this way more quickly than using a charting program.

Another advantage to creating pie slices as closed arcs is that it gives you latitude over which type of pie you plan to use, as shown in Figure 12.25. You can use all your slices and create a full pie chart within an imaginary "pie pan." You can remove important slices from the imaginary pan and specifically display them as a partial pie chart. You also can use an exploded pie chart in which one key slice is pulled away from the others to give it added emphasis. Rotating the pieces around their center point also allows you to rearrange them so that different wedges appear at the top.

12.25

Not all pie slices have to be displayed the same way. Partial pies leave out non-essential slices, whereas exploded pies emphasize key slices by moving them away from lesser slices.

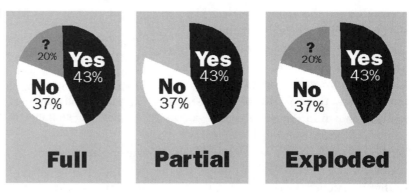

Creating pies as separate, closed polygons also facilitates a practice that probably is greatly overused. With all the slices grouped, you can quickly "squish" the pie vertically to make it look as if it were being viewed from an angle. Our sample graphic in Figure 12.20 about the study preferences of Ferengi students is a classic example of a "squished" partial pie. In Figure 12.20, the perspective doesn't cause any problems, but in some pies, as researcher Prabu David has found, it can. Modest gains in vividness from added perspective can exact a tremendous toll on data metaphor, rendering values very difficult to compare. Figure 12.26 offers a clear example, showing how a five percent slice in one part of a squished pie barely resembles what should be an identical five percent slice in another part.

12.26   # Distorting the pie
          # may distort reality

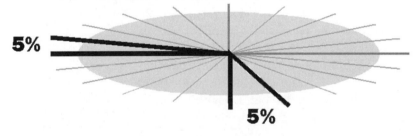

Adding perspective can reduce accuracy in pies.

When properly used, perspective can be a valuable tool, as can partial pies and exploded pies. All are powerful means of addressing the other common error in pie charts: excessive clutter. Small, almost irrelevant categories can become so cluttersome that a pie chart's main point might be overlooked. Such non-essential data can be eliminated in partial pies or forced to the visual background in exploded pies that take advantage of perspective.

Figure 12.27 shows what happens when a pie becomes sliced too thin. With only two or three reliable shadings between pure black and pure white, there aren't enough shades to handle more than four or five slices to a pie. Moreover, a multitude of slices means not only that a pie goes a lot further on your dinner table but also that a pie chart takes a lot longer to read—too long to be effective as an entry-point graphic.

12.27

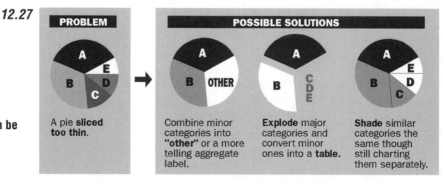

A variety of techniques can be employed to unclutter a cluttered pie.

PROBLEM

A pie **sliced too thin**.

POSSIBLE SOLUTIONS

Combine minor categories into **"other"** or a more telling aggregate label.

Explode major categories and convert minor ones into a **table**.

Shade similar categories the same though still charting them separately.

When confronted by a thinly sliced pie, the first thing to look for is categories that can be combined. "Very good" and "good" often can be combined, as can "poor" and "very poor." Likewise, a list of expenditures that includes defense, debt and 15 domestic categories can be condensed to simply defense, debt and domestic. If you're trying to show expenditures on specific domestic programs, you probably need a separate pie to break that out. Even if there isn't a good way to group categories, you always can resort to the old standby of labeling a group of the smallest categories "other."

As in Figure 12.20, you can break small slices into a separate table while letting major categories remain in an exploded, partial pie. If you don't want to lose data by combining categories, you should shade similar categories the same so that you visually put them together even if separate figures on the graphic keep them apart.

One technique you don't want to resort to is using keys or odd bitmap shadings. Keys, as explained in Chapter 3, render quick readership impossible. Bitmap shadings—crosshatches and the like—confuse the eye with extraneous lines, reproduce poorly and look about as stylish as a herring-bone leisure suit.

Other clutter can be removed by limiting how the data are labeled. If the actual number is important—$900 billion for defense, $50 billion for all else—use it as part of the data label. Don't worry about also listing percentages for those items; that's what the visual data metaphor of the chart conveys. Likewise, in most cases the numbers themselves belong in smaller type than the words that explain what each slice represents. Refer to Chapter 3 for more on this point.

Pies, like fevers and bars, can become very confused when multiple items are tracked simultaneously. Clear labeling, aggregation of small categories into larger ones and, if all else fails, separation of each item into a separate graph are the appropriate remedies. Clear labeling means not only applying item labels to each charted bit of data but also adopting shades that differentiate one item from the next, as done in Figure 12.28. Note how each fever line, each bar and each pie slice bears the name of the company whose data are being charted. Note, too, that shading is consistently used so that each company can be differentiated from the others, without having to read the label. Effectively, a key has been created, but labels applied directly to the data make the key so self-evident that it is unnecessary to have an inefficient box at the bottom, showing how to decipher the charts.

12.28

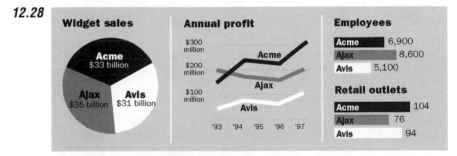

Every line, bar and pie slice should be labeled when data from more than one entity are being charted. Moreover, shading should differentiate one entity's charts from the others'. This combination of fever, bar and pie charts takes that requirement one step further by adopting a consistent shading scheme that carries over from one chart to the next.

Although we've talked about oval-shaped pies, no cosmic edict requires that all pies be round. The pie chart's circle metaphor, first used by William Playfair, is preferred because circles automatically convey a sense of completion—a message that is important to convey when comparing the parts to the whole. Other metaphors, however, also accomplish this. The most common is the one used in the "where your tax dollar goes" graphic, which divides a dollar bill in proportion to the amount of money spent in various categories. Although that graphic has become cliché, the technique of dividing something other than a circle is still fresh enough to merit consideration. Variations in which a quarter, a dime and two pennies are used to signify that 37 percent is spent in one category, while a dime and three pennies are used to signify that 13 percent is spent in another, are among the most promising. Technically, these veer away from being pie charts and serve more as pictograms, which are dealt with later in this chapter.

How Figure 12.21 Was Constructed

12.29

Using bezier, draw Lincoln in silhouette.

Draw facial highlights as light **polygon.**

Create type.

Flow type to match path of circle.

Apply radial fills, position items and **group.**

Rotate grouped penny.

Skew perspective.

Add light stroke **line** to create "edge."

Duplicate ellipse and darken. Off-set it down and left. **Send to back.**

The pie chart in Figure 12.21 requires some skill to duplicate Abraham Lincoln's face with bezier lines, but the rest of the chart, including the realistic three-dimensional effect, is easy to create.

Create polygon matching slice to be masked.

Add polygons needed for 3-D.

Position atop grouped penny and **group.**

Put atop planned background and add **shading** as desired.

DO

- **Highlight one key slice.** Highlight in a much darker or brighter shade than the others and use a pointer box with it to reiterate the main point verbally.

- **Simplify data.** Condense the number of slices to no more than five.

- **Augment pies with tables.** Do this to report data from what otherwise would be very small slices.

- **Label effectively.** Make each slice's name, not its number, stand out. Use actual numbers, not percentages, in data labels because the pie itself will provide clues as to relative percentages.

- **Include icons or three-dimensional treatments.** Include these however, only if they help identify the subject matter, provide a valuable metaphor and do not overwhelm or distort the data.

DON'T

- **Try to report everything.** Pies are for conveying the big picture, not details. Too many slices obscure that picture. If you are drawing lots of lines from data labels to the slices, your pie is too comprehensive and not sufficiently focused.

- **Bake too big a pie.** A typical pie need be no more than two inches wide. As a rule, the smaller the pie the better, provided it has enough surface area to allow labels to be applied without keys or a need for lots of lines leading from slices to their labels.

- **Distort relationships.** Don't "squish" a pie so much that it makes what should be identical slices no longer look identical.

- **Use visual clichés (such as slicing up a dollar bill).** If you really want to slice up currency, pick a denomination other than $1. The more unusual the bill, the better.

Area Charts

Although deciphering them can be a puzzle, there's nothing puzzling about what area charts are. Areas are nothing more than fevers with a complex. Not only are they fevers; they also think they are pies.

Rather than present a single fever line (or separate fever lines charted with the same zero point), areas present multiple fever lines all at the same time, each using the other as its zero point. Typically, there's an overall line plus one or more component lines within it, as in Figure 12.30. Because this allows for the simultaneous display of large amounts of information, including pie-like relative percentages for each component area, area charts can be extremely powerful. This same complexity, however, can make them difficult to understand. In fact, so many readers may have trouble understanding them that they should be used sparingly. Figure 12.30 is among the simpler of area charts. It could function on a business page or in an annual report, where readers are accustomed to looking at complex charts. In another setting, however, it might be completely misunderstood.

How do you read it properly? The dollars brought in by sales (the top line) include both the dollars spent on costs and the dollars retained as profits (the component lines). Without labels on those areas, the uninformed might assume that costs and profits are charted as separate lines, both extending to zero. Once you understand what's really shown, you see not only that Scrooge Inc.'s sales have risen dramatically but also that its costs have remained relatively stable, allowing most of the increased sales to be translated directly into profits. The graphic uses this information to make and support a very powerful main point about the impact that the hiring of a new chief executive has had.

12.30

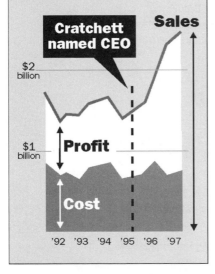

Area charts are among the most data-intensive of graphics and the hardest to use effectively.

A key element in designing a successful area chart is building in visual clues to explain to readers that the chart is not simply a multiple-line fever. Note in Figure 12.30 how range arrows are used to denote which portion of the chart is represented by each label. Profit, for example, is clearly indicated to be the area between the sales line and the cost line, not the distance between the sales line and zero. In the first year, profit was about $0.9 billion—the difference between sales and cost—not $1.8 billion, which might have been true had this not been an area chart. If you find yourself tempted to use an area chart, go overboard on labeling so that you make sure readers understand exactly what is shown.

Another key to designing successful area charts is in determining which component goes where. By using cost as the lower component, Figure 12.30 is able to make its point about costs remaining constant. Had it been the upper component, distorted by radical variations in profit, this point might not have come across as clearly. If the number of data sets or the fact that all of them vary pose additional problems, you probably should avoid an area chart altogether and instead create separate fever and pie charts to get the points across clearly.

Area charts are serious statistics. They almost always require use of a charting program and are best used in situations in which readers have some degree of statistical literacy and strong enough personal stake in the subject matter to be willing to invest the time needed to glean the information. Because such situations occur only rarely, area charts are something you usually will avoid.

DO

- **Simplify complex data.** Determine all data relationships before starting and craft the chart to present as much information as possible at a glance without being overloaded by details.

- **Label liberally.** Use range arrows to make it clear that this is an area chart, not just multiple fever lines.

- **Consider using separate fevers and pies.** Don't run the risk of confusing readers with this overly complex graphical form.

Pictograms

12.31

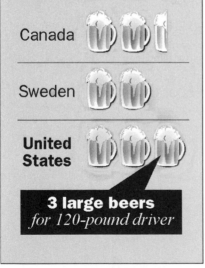

Intoxication limits vary

U.S. traffic rules allow higher blood-alcohol contents for drivers.

Canada

Sweden

United States

3 large beers
for 120-pound driver

This pictogram is deceptively simple. It simultaneously charts blood-alcohol level and the volume of alcohol needed to create it, then depicts the results with icons that provide both a data metaphor and a topical metaphor.

Pictograms, like the one in Figure 12.31, are deceptively simple but can be powerful graphics. Essentially, they are nothing more than bar charts or pie charts that use icons instead of bars and pies, but therein lies their strength. Without reducing organization or simplicity, they make iconic elements, which normally serve only to further vividness, and do double-duty in conveying data metaphors. As a result, pictograms "read" extremely quickly and probably are among the most memorable of graphics. The only challenge in creating them is not to weaken their simplicity with needless adornments.

Such adornments often include keys. Most pictogram creators use keys to explain that one icon equals a certain number of items being measured. Nothing is inherently wrong with using a key if the icons are clear and unambiguous and can be understood before consulting the key. Problems develop, however, when more than one type or size of icon is used. It's better to have one icon, duplicated several times, and perhaps divided into pieces to represent fractional quantities, than it is to have separate icons for different items— separate icons 20-ounce and 10-ounce beers, in the case of Figure 12.31.

Inoffensive as pictogram keys might be, they usually are redundant. A pictogram bar chart comparing nuclear arsenals might say that the US has 10,000 warheads, symbolized by 10 bombs, while Russia has 9,000 warheads, symbolized by nine bombs. Such a structure—with "10,000" next to 10 icons, and "9,000" next to 9 icons—makes it abundantly clear, even without a key, that each bomb stands for 1,000 warheads. Adding the key only dilutes the message. Remember, too, that what a graphic shows is relationships between data. If specific numbers are more important than relationships, an agate table is a more appropriate venue.

12.32

Pictograms based on single symbols instead of multiple icons, such as the one in Figure 12.32, are less common, even though you will find one in the stock market listings in your newspaper each day. The most common mistake designers make in creating such pictograms is to forget that the visual should be proportional to the quantity reported, not merely an icon of its category. How big to make the Up and Down arrows and the "unchanged" box should vary with the numbers to be represented.

NYSE yesterday

449
gainers

97 unchanged

293
losers

This gainers-and-losers stock market graphic is part bar, part pie and part pictogram.

DO

- **Keep icons simple and small.** Icons should be easily recognizable as representative of what you are measuring.

- **Highlight the main point with a pointer box.** Highlight the point just as you would in any other graphic.

- **Avoid keys.** Instead, make the relationship of the icons to specific quantities be intuitive by carefully labeling what's going on in a pointer box.

DON'T

● **Use other icons.** Other icons could distract from the value of the icons used as data metaphors.

● **Enlarge or reduce icons to show fractional quantities.** Half the width and half the height makes one-fourth the area. A half-size icon would properly signify one-quarter of the original value, yet designers and many readers might be confused into thinking it represented one-half. It's better to use a regular icon, cut in half, as was done in Figure 12.31.

Use of Charting Programs

For those who don't trust their hand-eye coordination or their ability to do math in their heads, charting programs are invaluable assistants in creating graphs. However, because they require mastering another program and the task of moving material from one program to another, information designers tend to use charting programs only on major graphics involving lots of numbers.

When you open a spreadsheet or charting program, the first screen is a ruled columnar pad that enables you to enter the raw data. Type the *X* axis data labels in the first vertical column and the *Y* axis data measurements in the second vertical column, as shown in Figure 12.33.

12.33

	A	B	C
1	1992	73,607,000	
2	1993	65,109,000	
3	1994	88,067,000	
4	1995	75,401,000	
5	1996	141,000,000	
6			
7			
8			

Data from the graphic in Figure 12.1 is entered in tabular fashion into a Microsoft Excel spreadsheet.

Highlight the squares into which you have entered data, then invoke the program's Chart command, which in Microsoft Excel is under the Insert menu. Once you find the Chart command, most programs like Excel give you a choice as to which type of chart you wish to create. A typical dialog box is shown in Figure 12.34. You must take care to select an appropriate type. The software won't stop you from making a mistake unless the type you select requires more data than you highlighted. It is best to select something other than the 3-D version of the chart you want. Most charting programs create a lot of "chartjunk." The 3-D versions they create notoriously are full of it.

12.34
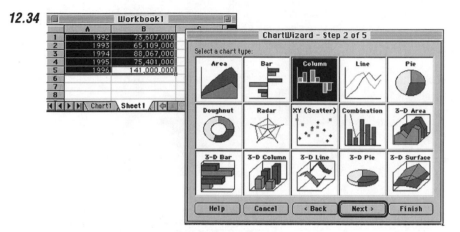

Excel's "ChartWizard" asks you a series of questions that let you determine what kind of chart will be created. DeltaGraph and other charting programs work much the same.

It is best to decline your charting program's offer of creating a headline, axis labels, keys, data labels and other accoutrements. Use the program only to create the basic chart, including grids. Create all other aspects of the graphic in your drawing program. When your charting program displays its finished chart (see Figure 12.35), select the entire charted area, copy it and paste it into a new document in your drawing program. You then can begin tracing over the charted elements or eliminating "chartjunk" and adjusting line widths and shadings to match what you normally use in graphics.

12.35

This is Excel's chart of the data in Figure 12.1 at the beginning of this chapter. Note the improper height-to-width ratio, the exaggerated spacing between bars and the large amount of "chartjunk." These must be removed when you copy this image and paste it into your drawing program.

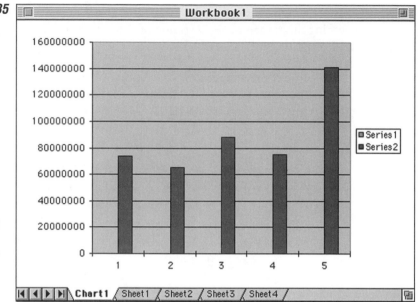

Maps

An atlas contains maps of great detail: every road, every river, every city, even county lines, time zones and strange little dots and numbers that someone, somewhere is supposed to be able to use to figure out exactly how far it is from one place to the next.

Information graphics contain maps, too. Unlike atlas maps, however, graphic maps offer specifically targeted information, not everything anyone could ever conceivably want to know. If a road is important, it's listed; if not, it's ignored. A river is shown only when it is the focus or provides an essential landmark. No more than one or two key cities (plus, perhaps, one other for reference) are highlighted. Topography, mileposts or other accoutrements that atlas maps possess are normally missing.

In short, graphic maps—like all other information graphics—follow the visual inverted pyramid style. Rather than serve as complete references, they serve as hierarchically organized messages, making one clear main point and one or more secondary points and (only after these points are presented) offering additional supporting details.

Maps functioning as information graphics take on several forms:

- **Locators** show where something is or will be in relation to something else.
- **Insets** identify a point or region iconically.
- **Data maps** report where different statistical facts or quantities occurred.

- **Schematics** explain how to get from Point A to Point B, using simplified geography.

- **Sequences** (discussed separately in Chapter 15) chart an event across space and time.

This chapter explores each of the basic map forms in detail and offers some specific pointers on general cartographic style. But before getting into the details, some overriding points about graphic maps in general need to be clarified.

Unlike cartographic maps, graphic maps, although they still must be in proportion, do not require a specifically stated scale. Nor is it always necessary to include a compass indicator. In the visual inverted pyramid approach, such items, depicted in Figure 13.1, are supporting details and are, therefore, optional.

13.1

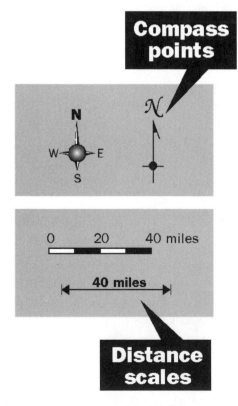

The freedom to leave out such normally vital items carries with it a responsibility: graphic maps must be created so that readers are not deceived by proportions or orientations so unusual that a compass pointer or a scale would be necessary. In other words, North must always be at the top, and sufficient landmarks must be included so that readers can tell at a glance, without consulting a scale, roughly how far apart things are.

Readers are so conditioned to seeing North as up that even a compass pointer showing North as being some other direction is likely to be ignored. As a result, in all graphic maps, North should be up, and the little compass pointer indicating North becomes optional. Likewise, a map that requires a scale to be understood has failed as a graphic. Graphic maps, like all graphics, seek to convey the big picture, not minute details. If a reader needs a key to

Although required in atlas maps, cartographic niceties such as these typically are optional in graphic maps.

tell relative distances, he or she cannot use the graphic at a glance. The map probably focuses on too small an area or fails to contain enough reference points.

There's nothing wrong with using a set of compass points or a distance scale in a graphic map, as long as it is kept small enough so that it doesn't interfere with the telling of the main and secondary points. Something is wrong, however, if a graphic has to include either item to make it understandable.

Another essential characteristic of graphic maps is their use of pointer boxes to highlight a single main point. Even in a tiny inset map, the graphic's reason for being must be clearly stated in both a point box and (in the case of all but insets) a headline. A graphic without a stated reason for being is no longer a graphic. It's merely an icon, decorating text.

MAPS *at a glance*	
Best suited for:	Expressing **geographic** relationships
	Labeling topics by place
Least suited for:	Topics for which **location or path** is **insignificant**
	Listing **specific** details
Answers the question:	**Where**
	Occasionally, **how**
Often used as:	**Entry points** within text
	Occasionally, secondary visual elements
Typical size:	**1 to 3 inches** wide
	Occasionally, somewhat to very much wider
Key challenges:	**Simplifying** information (Chapter 3)
	Accurately and predictably depicting geography (see this chapter)
Key techniques:	Visual **data metaphors** (Chapter 6 and this chapter)
	Drawing techniques (Chapters 8, 9 and this chapter)

13.2

Burglary linked to bombing

Police contend that items taken from a quarry at Marion, near where one suspect lived, were used in the Oklahoma City bombing.

Suspect's farmhouse

DICKINSON COUNTY

MORRIS COUNTY

MARION COUNTY

Blasting caps stolen

Marion Lake

56

Marion

Hillsboro

77

HARVEY COUNTY

50

To Oklahoma City

BUTLER COUNTY

Locators, like other well-designed graphics, should tell more than just one thing.

Locators

True to their name, locators answer the question, "Where?" But the answer should not be just a one-place reply. If they are true to the visual inverted pyramid approach, they go beyond the main point and offer secondary points and supporting details that help tell an overall story.

The locator in Figure 13.2 is a perfect example. It not only tells where a set of blasting caps were stolen. It also illustrates how close the theft was to the suspect's home. Finally, it indicates that the theft occurred in what is an almost straight line between the suspect's home and the site where the suspect allegedly used the stolen detonators in one of the worst tragedies of 1995. Such a graphic does a lot more than answer the small question of "Where?" It begins to answer bigger questions, as graphics are intended to do.

Examine Figure 13.2 in the visual inverted pyramid approach. The main point, covered by the headline and the pointer box, is that there was a burglary near Marion in which blasting caps were stolen, and that authorities think this theft may be related to the bombing of the federal building in Oklahoma City. The secondary point, covered in the chatter and in boldfaced references, deals with the proximity of the theft to the home of one of the bombing suspects and to what could have been the route from his home to the site of the bombing. The supporting details, offered without elaboration, indicate that all this happened near what residents of the area know to be a popular recreational lake, not far from the intersection of several major highways and nearby Hillsboro, known for its ethnic heritage. People seeing the map might realize that they had been in the area before, by listing one of these attractions.

Type sizes and weights, pointer boxes, chatter and shading are used exactly as they are in a bar chart or a fever chart—to hierarchically organize information. The single largest challenge a designer faces in creating a locator is to make certain it justifies the space and attention it occupies. If the space of a locator cannot be justified, an inset (see next section) might suffice.

Although creating a locator requires considerable work, it affords little opportunity for artistic latitude. North is always up. Geographical boundaries may not be reshaped. Height-to-width ratios must not be altered. Practically the only choices involve how tightly focused on a given geographical area the graphic should be.

Generally, the area depicted by a locator should be as small as possible while allowing for sufficient landmarks to make the site recognizable by a typical reader. That requires exercising judgment regarding what a typical reader might know of the area. Figure 13.2 might be appropriate for publication in the *Wichita Eagle,* just a few miles from the area, but inappropriate for the *St. Louis Post-Dispatch,* several hundred miles away.

Judgment can be summary in some cases. A map like the one in Figure 13.3 is **never** appropriate, even though one

13.3

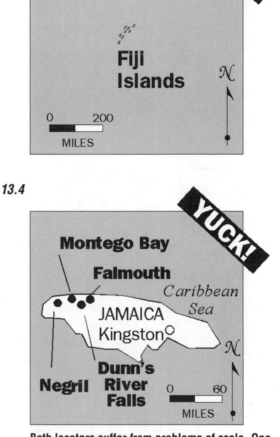

13.4

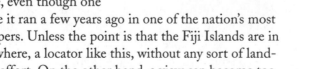

Both locators suffer from problems of scale. One has too narrow a scale, without appropriate landmarks; the other provides such a distant landmark that important relationships between other sites are obscured.

almost exactly like it ran a few years ago in one of the nation's most respected newspapers. Unless the point is that the Fiji Islands are in the middle of nowhere, a locator like this, without any sort of landmark, is a wasted effort. On the other hand, a view can become too broad, as in Figure 13.4, adapted from the same newspaper. The point of the story that Figure 13.4 accompanied was that it was better to stay

13.5

Copy the image,
drawing one square's
worth at a time

Tracing an image is an imprecise art, but using a grid to keep the item properly proportioned reduces the imprecision.

in Falmouth or Montego Bay than in Negril if you planned to visit Dunn's River Falls. The map did not bother telling why it located all these sites. Adding Kingston as an unnecessary landmark made the point almost completely contrary to what the text said. With such a broad view, all the places looked much too close together.

The only other technical problem in creating a locator is in physically drawing the map. Thanks to computer technology, that's easier than it's ever been.

The old-fashioned, non-computerized way—one still practiced by many graphic designers—involves use of a "graph paper" grid like the one you created in Figure 12.5. Draw a grid on top of a reference map, put a similar grid on your computer screen, then duplicate, square by square, each curve of the reference map onscreen. Although this procedure, shown in Figure 13.5, is hardly high-tech, it does have the advantage of being surprisingly quick, does not require the use of a scanner, and can be nearly as accurate as physically tracing a scanned image if the grids are carefully followed.

A better idea is to scan the map from a good atlas, place the scanned image in your drawing program and trace the lines you need.

Better yet, you can start with an online service such as the US Census Bureau's TIGER map service, as shown in Figure 13.6. TIGER enables you to create maps of any area of the United States in any scale imaginable. You can zoom in on an individual block, zoom out to the entire continent, or select virtually any view in between. The relatively simple but comprehensive user interface allows you to specify a location by name, by zip code, by longitude and latitude, or simply by clicking on a base map and its "zoom in" and "zoom out" buttons. In addition to streets, highways, lakes, rivers, political boundaries, time zones and a host of other geographical data, TIGER also charts income levels, average age and an ever-increasing wealth of other census data, broken down by governmental unit, census tract or both.

The list of data available grows monthly. Best of all, you can download the finished map onto your computer so you can adapt it electronically as needed.

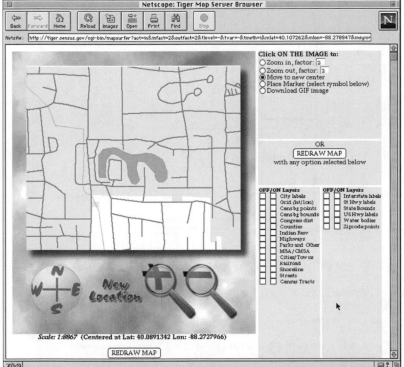

The US Census Bureau's online TIGER map service at *http://tiger.census.gov* **offers a wealth of highly configurable geographic and demographic data.**

After you have downloaded a base map from TIGER or imported one via your scanner, simply follow the procedures in Figure 13.7 to construct your locator. Start with a large version of the image (so it is easy to trace precisely) and use your pen or polygon tool to draw in the few key features you need. Remember that graphic maps show only what's important, not every conceivable piece of map information. After drawing all the streets you need, set the street lines to a thick, dark stroke, group them and duplicate the grouped items. Reduce the line width on the duplicated group by one point, change the stroke to a light color and align the original and duplicate groups atop each other, creating the illusion of having drawn each block instead of each street. Decide which portion of the map you will use and mask off the rest of

it with white rectangles (or paste it inside a cropping square, if your
program allows). Apply labels, a headline, chatter and a point box as
needed, and you're done.

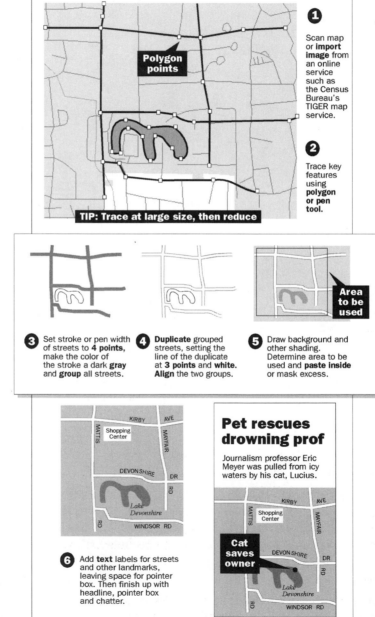

**How to create a
locator, from
original scanned
or downloaded
image to finished
product.**

As with any drawing created by human hand-eye coordination, there typically are minor imperfections. Thanks to the computer, you can hide these by making pen lines lighter or transparent and by increasing the use of shadings instead of solid blacks and whites. This process has the added value of sending the map into the "visual background," making it seem to be "behind" the bold blacks and whites you use to designate key locations and make your main point.

DO

- **Highlight key locations** by listing them in larger, bolder type.

- **Use a pointer box** aimed at a single location to make the locator's main point verbally.

- **Include a reference point** to establish scale. Make certain the reference point is not so distant that its inclusion obscures small but significant distances between other points. At the same time, consider the graphic's audience in deciding what reference points are likely to be most recognizable.

- **Follow inverted pyramid style.** If there's nothing to say after the main point has been made, consider using an inset (see next section) instead of a locator.

- **Follow cartographic style.** Maps don't need a key because readers are conditioned to expect certain symbols and certain typography to mean certain things. Stick to that system, which is outlined at the end of this chapter.

DON'T

- **Fritter your locator's impact away with detail.** If Walden Pond isn't a key site or a recognizable landmark, don't include it.

- **Include icons** other than standard cartographic symbols, which also are outlined in the last section of this chapter.

- **Let maps get too big.** A typical vertical locator need be no more than two inches wide, and a typical horizontal locator need be no more than three inches wide. As a general rule, the smaller the better, provided there's adequate space to highlight key locations and provide one or more reference points.

- **Distort reality** by altering height-to-width ratios, by putting North anywhere but at the top or by otherwise altering geography.

Insets

Insets are to locators what mug shots are to photographs—smaller, simpler and dramatically less informative. A mug shot tells what a person looks like, but it says nothing about what he or she does. An inset tells where something happened, but it says little about why it might have happened there or what else might be happening in that area.

Insets like the one in Figure 13.8 act almost like icons. They identify a region in general terms without providing a secondary point or supporting details. They are useful when a more detailed graphic is unnecessary, most likely because readers would be so unfamiliar with the area depicted as to make reference points meaningless. Still, as Figure 13.8 shows, even an inset attempts to convey a main point. Without a main point, the inset becomes nothing more than a decorative icon.

13.8

This inset might be used to tell the story of Figure 13.2 in a distant publication.

In many ways, insets are the buck privates of the graphics army. There is more of an opportunity to use them, and less of a payback when they are used. But, just like army privates, they tend to be of greater value when they are not used alone. Placed under the command of a fully commissioned locator, a lowly inset can transform what otherwise might be an inappropriate graphic into one that truly can inform.

Using an inset alone, as in Figure 13.8, sacrifices the important secondary points of the original blasting caps graphic. However, adding an inset to the original graphic, as in Figure 13.9, conveys the original graphic's points without the concern that the readers will understand its scale. The inset gives readers a second, broader perspective from which to view the locator, making it appropriate even in areas not in close proximity to the theft.

Insets are appropriate additions to almost any locator. Designers must be careful, however, not to use insets as an excuse for making a locator out of something that really merits only an inset. Only if there are secondary points and supporting details is a locator called for. If only a main point is to be conveyed, an inset is perfectly capable of conveying it.

DO

- **Use insets on their own** when a full locator would offer no meaningful secondary points or supporting details.

- **Use insets with locators** if readers are unlikely to be familiar with the locator's reference points and you don't want to lose track of the secondary points and supporting details it conveys.

- **Severely limit** the geography depicted in an inset.

- **Include a main-point pointer box** if the inset stands alone.

DON'T

- **Let your inset get too big.** A typical inset is about an inch wide. Any wider and a locator may be needed instead.

Data Maps

Data maps, like the one in Figure 13.10, not only answer the question, "Where?" They also answer the question, "How much?" Using progressive shading, a data map graphically indicates the category to which each of several sub-areas with a larger area belong. Numerical data is put into ranges, and each area is shown to reside within similar or different ranges.

13.9

Adding an inset to a locator extends the locator's reach by offering readers a second perspective from which to view the graphic.

13.10

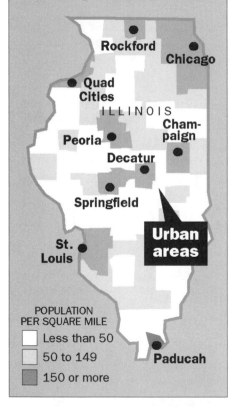

Urban Illinois is more than Chicago area

Eight downstate areas also have high population density, according to 1990 census.

ILLINOIS

Rockford

Chicago

Quad Cities

Champaign

Peoria

Decatur

Springfield

Urban areas

St. Louis

POPULATION PER SQUARE MILE

- Less than 50
- 50 to 149
- 150 or more

Paducah

All information for this data map was obtained from the Census Bureau's TIGER map service online.

Complicated? Not really. Data maps are things you see all the time. When Willard Scott tells you how hot it's going to be in Florida and how cold it's going to be in Minnesota, chances are he's doing so while pointing toward a data map. When you picked up your newspaper the morning after the presidential election and saw a map showing which states voted for Bill Clinton and which voted for Bob Dole, you were looking at a data map.

Data maps are extremely powerful tools, enabling information designers to present massive amounts of data in a very small space. Very often they also enable readers to see patterns that would not otherwise be apparent. Looking at an election map, you can easily see where each party has its greatest base of strength. Looking at an isotherm weather map—the type that uses color bars to report expected daily highs—you can see fronts of cold and warm air battling across the continent.

Making a data map like the one in Figure 13.10 is no more complicated than making any other graphic map. The only differences are that you usually need to draw a few more lines and you have to think a bit about exactly how to divide the data.

One of the significant limitations on data maps is posed by the printing process. As discussed in Chapter 10, presses may not reliably reproduce more than two distinct shades between solid black and solid white.

That's no problem if a graphic is to show whether a state voted for Clinton or for Dole—two choices, two colors. But it the graphic is to report continuous data such as unemployment rates, per-capita income or, in the case of Figure 13.10, population density, the numbers underlying the graphic must first be gathered into discrete categories.

Two factors affect how numbers should be divided. First, there is a tradition of dealing with round numbers—even multiples of 5, 10, 25, 50 and 100, for example. In Figure 13.10 the categories are divided at 50 and 150. The other tradition is to divide categories so that roughly equal numbers of areas fall within each category. A four-way division is known as the quartile approach.

Clearly, how categories are drawn can radically affect the "spin" a map places on data. Seeking the middle ground, as in the height-to-width ratio of bar charts, is in order. Unfortunately, there is no easy-to-remember ratio governing data division. Trial and error, along with a conscious effort to avoid extreme "spins," often suggests the best alternative.

Imagine that you're teaching a class. One student got a final grade of 98 percent. Two got 90.5 percent. Three got 89.5 percent. And so forth. Where do you draw the line for an A? The top student obviously performed much better than the next two, while the three behind them were almost as good. It would seem unfair to draw the A line at 90 percent, since it would diminish the achievement of the one truly outstanding student while discounting the achievement of those who got very close to that level. By the same token, 90 percent is a standard cutoff, and you really don't think the class deserved six As. What do you do? This question has plagued educators for generations. Some resort to a purely automatic approach: 90 percent is 90 percent, and that's the cutoff. Others, perhaps to impress people with their statistical knowledge, "curve" all grades by awarding them on the basis of how many standard deviations the students are away from the class mean. (That's the system MIT uses, for example.) Still others try to give roughly equal numbers of As, Bs, Cs and so forth. While this technically isn't "curving" the grade, that's what most students think a "curve" means, and it is very similar to the quartile approach described above. Which is the right answer? There isn't one. Hard as it may be to accept, you simply have to use your best judgment and consider the implications of all your actions.

Whatever divisions are chosen, shadings should be applied progressively, with the lightest shade for the category with the lowest numbers to the darkest for the category with the highest numbers. The same rule is true in color graphics as well as black-and-white. Examine the color weather page of *USA Today* or another newspaper to see how temperatures are handled progressively in color, from frigid blues to sweltering reds.

Finally, when producing a data map, make certain that readers can see at a glance which areas mean what, without having to consult the map's key. A pointer box clearly identifying one or more extreme areas should suffice to set the tone. Details of the actual numeric division—a supporting detail in the visual inverted pyramid approach—may then safely be left in a traditional data key, as in Figure 13.10.

DO

- **Divide data logically and ethically,** using round numbers as breaking points, attempting to get equal numbers into each category, avoiding "outlying" values and striking a middle ground in the "spin" created by shading schemes.

- **Use progressive shadings,** consistently going from lightest (least) to darkest (most).

- **Include a pointer box** to establish the general orientation of the key. Also, include a full key, but do not expect readers to see it at first glance.

- **Severely limit** non-essential information.

DON'T

- **Use more than four shades.** Typically, solid black, solid white and two shades in between are all that can reliably be reproduced as distinctly different tones.

Schematic Maps

A map without geography? Why not, particularly if it tells the story better than one that features geography.

Schematic maps like the one in Figure 13.11 give only passing acknowledgment to actual locations and distances, stressing instead the turns or stops necessary for traveling from one location to another. Often schematic maps are used because real geography is too confusing to report because some stops appear to be too close together while others appear to be too far apart. This problem may exist whether the map in question reports how to get from one part of town to another on the subway or from one planet to the next for a space probe.

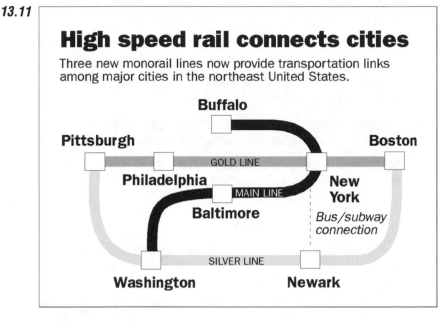

High speed rail connects cities

Three new monorail lines now provide transportation links among major cities in the northeast United States.

Schematic maps are a mainstay for explaining stops and interconnections of public transportation systems.

Schematic maps are deceptively simple. For a schematic to work well, sites must go **roughly** where readers would expect to find them, even if it's nowhere near where they actually would be on a non-schematic map. The key is to think more of time sequences than location sequences, and to set aside enough space so that each turn, stop or transfer can be clearly articulated. In Figure 13.11, for example, it geographically is almost impossible to go from Boston to Newark without going through New York. However, the way the transit system is run, if you get on a Newark-bound train in Boston, you won't be able to get off it in New York. The schematic map makes this clear while a geographic map would leave riders confused—and, in all likelihood, quite angry when they found they had to go all the way to Newark on a train that they thought would take them to New York.

In many regards, schematic maps are to other data maps what illustrations are to photographs. The more abstract they look, the better they are. Otherwise, people may begin confusing them with literal depictions of reality. Footnote-size references stating that a map that otherwise looks very geographic is in fact schematic are insufficient to take away the overall impression that an accurate, non-schematic map is being attempted. If you schematicize map data, make it so clearly schematic that, while things may still seem to be **roughly** where they're supposed to be, no one assumes that the map is accurate to scale.

DO

- **Use schematics when geography confuses,** not just when you don't feel like being accurate with your measurements.

- **Locate sites thoughtfully,** making things "seem" to be in the right place even as you expand or contract distances to better describe flow.

- **Design the map and its routes abstractly** so as not to confuse readers who might take the schematic for a literal map.

DON'T

- **Use schematics when literal graphics would work better.** Schematics are a last resort, valuable in only a few select situations when depicting flow is more important than depicting relative locations.

Cartographic Style

In the front pages of your favorite atlas you probably can find one or more pages devoted to explaining what each of the symbols on the ensuing maps means. There's no space for such exposition in a graphic map. Even if there were, it wouldn't be in keeping with the visual inverted pyramid, which disdains the use of keys for all but supporting details.

In graphic maps, little effort is made to differentiate between the population of cities depicted. Rather, graphic maps differentiate among cities on the basis of their relative importance to a story. A tiny town shows up in bold 10-point type if it is the most important site. A nearby major metropolitan area may be in light 8-point type if its reason for being on the map is merely to offer a supporting detail, such as to explain what major city the key city is near.

Aside from such use of typography to convey main and secondary points, there are several conventions governing how supporting details are presented typographically on maps. Following these conventions enables maps to avoid having to devote space to keys the way atlases do.

By convention, sites tend to be identified in standard capital and lowercase letters, while regions (countries, states, nations and continents) tend to be identified in all capital letters. Extra space often is used between the letters of the name of an encompassing region—a continent, when nations are shown; a nation, when states are shown; a state, when counties are shown. Conversely, italics often are used for the names of constituent areas within such an encompassing region.

Round dots signify cities, except when precise municipal boundaries are needed. City names appear as close to the dots as is practical.

Although sans serif type typically is used for sites and regions, italicized, serifed type often is used for rivers, lakes, oceans and other bodies of water. Examples of all these styles appear in Figure 13.12.

13.12

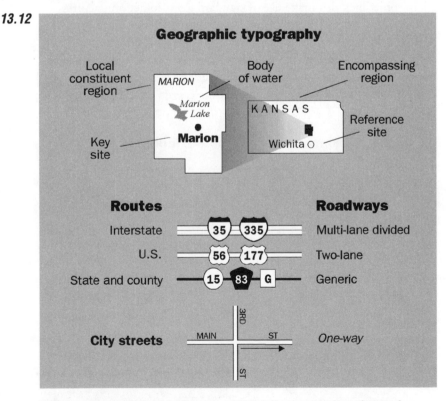

Graphic maps don't need keys because they follow conventions that readers have been conditioned to expect.

Also in Figure 13.12 is an explanation of how to identify roads, streets and highways. In casual conversation, people often speak of "Highway 66" or "Route 66." Actually, each highway in the United States goes by a more formal name — US 66, for example. Any freeway or turnpike may be a superhighway, but almost all Interstate routes are. Most other primary roads are US routes, and most secondary arteries are state, county or township roads.

On road signs and on maps, the different designations for highways are symbolized by different shields in which the route numbers appear. Moreover, on maps, limited-access freeways and toll roads often are symbolized by broad, divided lines, but other routes are symbolized in a more basic fashion.

Shields and numbers traditionally are placed in the middle of these lines. In contrast, street names within cities are by convention capitalized and placed along the top or right edges of the streets.

Maps sometimes also make use of standard icons to denote facilities one might expect to encounter while traveling. Many of these are derived from icons created out of Otto Neurath's 1920s Isotype movement. A collection of some of the more common ones appears in Figure 13.13. On many computers, specialty fonts such as Carta may contain icons of this nature, making it unnecessary to redraw them.

13.13

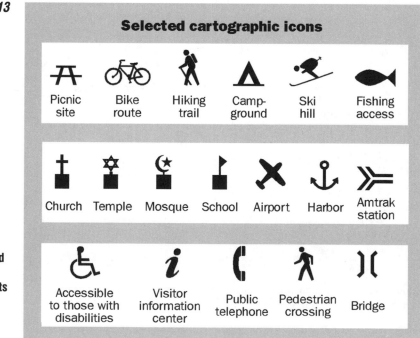

Icons may be used without a key to mark salient points of interest or importance on a map.

Diagrams

Glances organize. Charts convey information symbolically. Maps depict large-scale reality on comprehensibly smaller scales. Illustrations render the abstract imaginable.

Diagrams, a hybrid of all four, employ elements of each. Whether symbolic or realistic, they depict reality in organized ways on manageable scales that seek to make complicated spatial or systematic concepts as understandable as possible. Relationships may be conveyed with realistic or abstract symbols. Either way, the symbols are first purged of unneeded details.

In many regards, diagrams are one of two ways (illustrations, discussed in Chapter 16, being the other) in which graphics do what photographs cannot. Whether explaining an entire ecosystem or simply how to open a bottle, realistic diagrams eliminate the non-essential clutter that a photograph might contain so that attention can focus on key points. Non-realistic diagrams similarly use elementary symbols or imaginary perspectives to show abstract relationships or inner workings that photographs cannot.

Diagrams come in several varieties:

- **Depictions,** like maps, depict realistic systems in simplified fashion.

- **Schematics,** like charts, depict abstract relationships symbolically.

● **Instructions,** like glances, highlight key elements of simple, concrete relationships or procedures.

● **Cutaways,** like illustrations, show inner workings that otherwise cannot be seen.

There's an adage in information design:

If it's real, photograph it.

If it's abstract, illustrate it.

If it's measurable, chart it.

Keep these pointers in mind. In most cases, they prevent you from wasting your time trying to do something that is best done another way. Unfortunately, diagrams typically exist in the gray areas of the adage. Often, they convey how a real item or system functions in unfathomably abstract ways. They document one-step sequences that cannot otherwise be frozen in time or they depict interrelationships like a chain of command or family tree. When diagrams also attempt to do this across time, they advance to the category of sequence graphics, explained in the next chapter.

For diagrams and sequence graphics, the same pointers that guide the creation of graphs, maps and glances apply. Information should be organized and clearly stated to convey a main point. Non-essential facts and imagery should be avoided, unless they add to vividness and readers are expected to be uninvolved. Real or symbolic representations of spatial or functional relationships should be employed wherever possible. Vivid light versus dark typography and shading should be employed extensively, right up to, but just short of, the point at which it confuses.

Specifically, a diagram should have a main point, which should be highlighted by shading, restated in a pointer box and unencumbered by non-essential visuals or data. Images should be bold and either clearly realistic or universally simple and metaphorical. Additional information should be provided, but at a lower level in the visual inverted pyramid, often without specific references or explanations. This is in keeping with what a chart does with its secondary points and supporting details. (Refer to Chapter 3.)

Information designers not skilled as artists often look upon diagrams as impossible tasks. Actually, object-oriented drawing programs make it easy to draw sophisticated images. Every diagram you'll see on the next few pages is easily created by even a novice information designer with little or no artistic skill. In most cases, step-by-step instructions show you when to use the tools and techniques you already have explored. Don't forget that after you've done your best in an object-oriented drawing program, you can always export your work to a bitmap paint or photo program for additional "touches" that complicated blends, blurs, perspectives and filtering allow.

DIAGRAMS *at a glance*

Best suited for:	**Comparing** spatial or hierarchical relationships
	Highlighting key **components and interactions**
Least suited for:	**Literal depictions** that could be done photographically
Answers the questions:	**How** and **what**
	Often, who and why
Often used as:	**Secondary visual elements**
	Occasionally, visual centerpieces
Typical size:	**Four inches** wide or wider
	Occasionally, somewhat narrower
Key challenges:	Creating **schematic** data metaphors (see Chapter 6 and this chapter)
	Simplifying information (Chapter 3)
Key techniques:	**Drawing** techniques (Chapters 8 and 9)
	Evaluative typography, particularly **pointer boxes** (Chapters 3 and 10)

Depictions

Depiction diagrams are like road maps. The difference is that they depict ecological or methodological systems instead of transportation systems. Depictions explain the different parts of a thunderstorm, the camera angles used in filming a TV family's dining room (didn't you ever wonder why everyone sits on the same side of the table), the floor plan for your dream house or, as in Figure 14.1, the differences between natural and artificial environments.

14.1

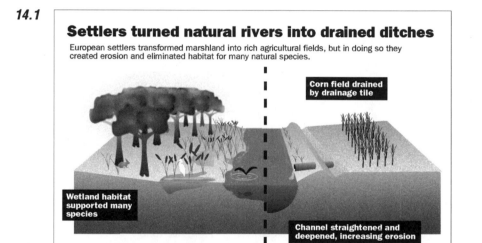

Settlers turned natural rivers into drained ditches

European settlers transformed marshland into rich agricultural fields, but in doing so they created erosion and eliminated habitat for many natural species.

Corn field drained by drainage tile

Wetland habitat supported many species

Channel straightened and deepened, increasing erosion

This panoramic diagram draws its strength from cutaways (discussed later in this chapter), from realistic imagery (see Figure 14.2) and from simplicity— that is, from careful selection of exactly which items to depict and which to leave out. Together, these focus the reader's attention on important differences that might be obscured in photographs, which naturally would be cluttered with nonessential items.

The key to a successful depiction is to capture the essence of the system while not getting bogged down in its details. Farm homes, fences, roads and other non-essential elements of the artificial ecology on the right side of Figure 14.1 are ignored. This allows the reader's attention to be drawn more quickly to how the area has been clear-cut, drained, dredged and channelized—the essential elements of the artificial system. At a glance, the reader sees that efficient agriculture has replaced a richly diverse ecosystem.

Realistic imagery is used to make the graphic "read faster"—that is, to make its points come across more quickly. By the same token, truly real images, such as those from a photograph, are avoided because they tend to include irrelevant details that detract from the main point. The graphic thus uses both visual data metaphor and simplicity of meta-phor, allowing it to appeal both to uninvolved and involved readers. This is one of the greatest strengths of a depiction.

Reversed blurb boxes highlight main points, while secondary points and supporting details are left to be discerned by readers who, tempted by the main points, choose to ponder the graphic further. Note the stillness of the water, evidenced by a ripple created by the bird in the left portion of the drawing. A meandering creek would be likely to flow more slowly than a channelized, dredged ditch. That's a relatively minor point in the graphic, secondary to the lack of biological diversity. A reader would have to discern this difference rather than have it directly cited. By hierarchically ranking information, specifically stating the most important while leaving the rest to be discerned, the graphic becomes organized—an important quality for readers with a personal stake in the topic.

At the same time, the graphic's realistic imagery and bold, main-point blurbs provide a visual vividness that interests readers who don't have a personal stake in the topic. Diagrams are among the few graphics that can simultaneously appeal to heuristic and systematic readers.

Depiction graphics need not be large panoramas of nature like Figure 14.1. They also may depict much smaller systems—the proper and improper bagging of burgers, fries and soft drinks in a fast food drive-through, for example. In most cases, however, depiction graphics are more useful in explaining the key differences between systems than they are in explaining how a system operates. Such explanations typically are left to process graphics, a type of sequence graphic explained in the next chapter.

The difference between depictions and processes is important to note. A depiction explains what the system is, not how it works. A process graphic explains the procedure, not the resultant system. This may be an arbitrary distinction. And, in fact, it is. Making such a distinction, however, ensures that your graphic possesses a clear focus and, therefore, is organized as tautly as possible.

Depictions tend to be among the most visual of graphics. A depiction may at first seem to be an impossibly complex artistic task. With a little practice, however, it's easy to break a complete scene into simple components and build it gradually, taking full advantage of drawing programs' power.

Figure 14.2 breaks Figure 14.1 down into its component shapes. Each shape is a simplistic polygon or path, not much different from a casual doodle.

One set of leaves was drawn and then re-scaled, flipped horizontally and copied twice. The three leaf areas were then placed atop a drawn trunk and grouped so that the finished tree shape could be duplicated 10 times to create an entire forest out of only two original shapes—the original leaf area and the trunk.

A single oval for a cat tail was drawn, duplicated, rotated and placed atop a stem to form one cat tail plant. All 13 of the cat tail plants were then created using re-sized and horizontally mirrored versions of the original. Delete two of the cat tail seed pods and you have the corn stalk, which was duplicated 35 times to make an entire field.

In short, all the plants in the drawing were the result of just four original shapes—the leaf area, the tree trunk, the plant stem and the corn ear/seed pod. Duplication, reflection and re-sizing did the rest.

The top of the water and the land plus the cutaway portion of each of them also had to be drawn. A few minor additional areas to provide details and shading and—violà!—you have a finished sketch.

How Figure 14.1 Was Constructed

14.2

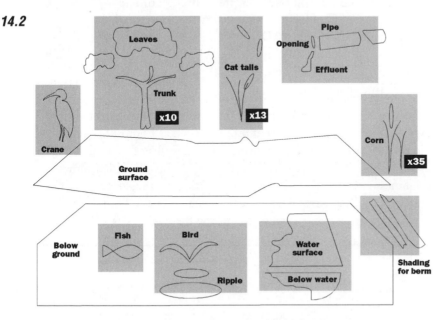

Each of the elements in Figure 14.1 were constructed as a simple polygon path with Bezier curvature. A computer's ability to let you refine an individual shape with Bezier curves, experiment with graduated and radial shading and duplicate the same images makes it easy for even a non-artist to draw realistic-looking features. Step-by-step instructions for single images not unlike the components of this diagram are provided in Figures 14.5 and 14.7.

The key to realism in a sketch such as this is the elimination of pen or stroke lines around each shape, which are replaced by realistic shading. Imagine Figure 14.1 with all the shapes unfilled, as they are in Figure 14.2. Not nearly so realistic, huh? Generally, it's best to shade items **before** putting them in position on the drawing and before duplicating them. Some programs, notably FreeHand, enable you to designate a particular shade as, say, "dark leaves." Then you can go back and change that shade, automatically updating every figure into which you have placed it. This is a powerful tool that is rarely used to its maximum benefit.

This book won't explain all the nuances of creating appropriate shading patterns. The simplest and easiest thing to do is to find something that looks like what you're trying to draw, look at it under a bright light that you can bring quite close to the object, and observe which areas are lighter and darker as you rotate the item through different perspectives. Practice as you did in Chapters 8 and 9 when trying to draw a cardboard box and other shapes. Do it often enough and you'll be able to predict how to shade something without having to stick a replica of it under a light. Our minds almost innately understand the subtle nuances that shading possesses.

After working with a drawing program, you can augment your work by exporting it into a photo or paint program such as Photoshop. Techniques such as blurring and texturing can add realism to your drawing. A useful feature of Photoshop is its feathering command, which allows brightness, contrast, texturing or other altering commands to take effect gradually, much as a radial fill expresses itself gradually. Some high-end drawing programs are beginning to include these effects as well.

DO

- **Use realistic images,** carefully shaded without pen lines to appear three-dimensional.

- **Highlight the main point** with a blurb or pointer box, just as you would in any other graphic.

- **Remove non-essential elements.**

DON'T

- **Use depictions when process graphics are needed** instead. Depictions simplify reality so a main point about the overall system can be conveyed. Process graphics instead explain how each element within the system works.

- **Use depictions when photographs are needed** instead. Once again, depictions simplify reality so a main point about the overall system can be conveyed. If reality need not be simplified for the reader to grasp the main point, use a photograph instead.

Schematics

At the opposite end of the symbolism-to-reality scale reside schematic diagrams, like the one in Figure 14.3. Rather than attempt to accurately (albeit simply) depict real-world systems, schematics use abstract data metaphors to explain component parts and relationships. Among the most common schematics are genealogies (or family trees), organizational charts, circuit diagrams and blueprints.

14.3

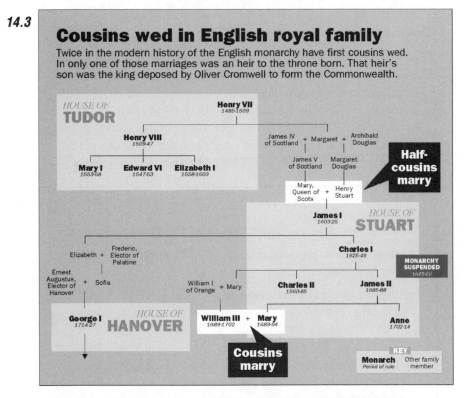

Cousins wed in English royal family

Twice in the modern history of the English monarchy have first cousins wed. In only one of those marriages was an heir to the throne born. That heir's son was the king deposed by Oliver Cromwell to form the Commonwealth.

Schematics like this genealogy represent detailed relationships with simple data metaphors. Pointer boxes and shaded areas make a main point, while other shading areas organize the secondary points.

Obviously, the relationship of parent to offspring, president to vice president and resistor to capacitor are abstract to begin with. Floor plans, on the other hand, can be portrayed either abstractly, as a schematic, or realistically, as a depiction. The difference between the two explains what a schematic does versus what a depiction does.

The choice between depicting a floor plan (or any other scene) as a two-dimensional schematic or as a three-dimensional depiction comes down to what it is you want to show. If your goal is to explain how the room in the floor plan "functions" as a "system"—that is, what it would be like to live in it—a 3-D view that contains sofas and other furniture would be in order. If, however, your goal is to depict the specific relationships between elements of the room—how far the window is from the door, how long a trip from the sofa to the fridge takes—a map-like schematic of the floor plan would work best. Realism lets you relate to the item in its entirety; symbolism lets you measure the relationships between items within that reality.

With schematics, it is particularly important to convey a main point. As with tables and other glances, hierarchical organization is what makes a schematic a graphic. Without organization, it's no more than tabulated agate with a few connecting lines that's impossible to use as a quick source of information. Remember: Graphics are powerful tools for conveying essential messages in a hurry. Unorganized, they no longer merit the type of attention they command.

DO

- **Use simple, universally understood symbols** to express relationships.

- **Highlight the main relationship** with a blurb or pointer box, just as in any other graphic.

- **Remove all non-essential elements.**

DON'T

- **Use schematics when depictions are needed** instead. Schematics explain relationships within systems while depictions describe the overall system.

- **Use schematics to convey only details.** A schematic without a central mission is nothing more than an agate table. Always make sure you can say specifically what the graphic tells ("a new hierarchy has eliminated middle management"), not merely what it tells about ("how the new hierarchy is organized").

Instructionals

Much like depictions, instructional graphics feature simplified yet realistic images of actual objects. Unlike depictions, they tell not how an entire object works but how an important action involving the object occurs.

As shown in Figure 14.4, instructionals frequently tell how such things as Tab A are inserted into Slot B. A realistic image of the object is employed along with arrows, pointer boxes and other visual clues as to how the action occurs.

14.4

Acme's caps now child-proof

It's may be a bit harder for you to open our new medicine bottles, and we hope you'll like it that way. In response to federal guidelines urging child-resistant packaging, Acme has modified its containers so that tabs must be aligned to open.

Twist top to align tabs

Instructional diagrams are highlighted depictions of reality, without the clutter that reality might otherwise produce.

Instructional diagrams differ from sequence graphics in that they report on one action, not a complete sequence. Instructional graphics therefore are typically more realistic and less schematic. Sequence graphics, because they report on several interactions, eliminate as much non-essential visual vividness as possible. In fact, sequence graphics are often composed of one or more instructional diagrams, with the imagery in each diagram simplified to minimize visual confusion.

Obviously, realism is important in creating an instructional graphic and nothing contributes to realism more than shading. As you saw in Figures 14.1 and 14.2, shading transforms simple shapes into realistic drawings. Figure 14.5 offers step-by-step reminders of how this is done. A simple medicine bottle is created out of a rectangle. An oval forms the bottom of the bottle, two identical ovals form the top and bottom of the lid and a rectangle represents the lid's depth.

How Figure 14.4 Was Constructed

14.5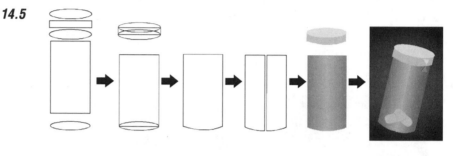

Draw needed **ovals** and **rectangles**.	Bring them into position.	Use **bezier** to modify rectangle to match curvature.	Use **knife** tool to split modified rectangle into halves.	Apply **graduated shading** to accentuate roundness.	Move items into position, **rotate** and add details as desired.

How Figure 14.4 was constructed hints of shading's role in three-dimensional drawings. There's more on that topic in Figure 14.7

If graduated or radial shadings hadn't been needed, standard fills could have been applied to the original shapes, and pen or stroke lines simply removed. However, to abut two graduated shadings into a single, non-radial shading that is light in the middle and dark on the edges, you may first alter a single polygon to match the overall shape created by the multiple outlines. If your program does not allow a doubly-graduated fill, you must then divide the shape into halves so you can graduate the shading toward the center of both halves, then reposition the halves so they abut.

A simple depiction might not go to the trouble of making the bottle seem three-dimensional. In an instructional graphic, however, the realistic reference points offered by dimensionality make this advisable. Some programs make non-circular three-dimensional blends as easy to use as standard radial and graduated fills. In other programs, however, it may be necessary to use outlines that have been grouped and filled separately as guides for drawing single or mirrored polygons. Such polygons can be used to create special fill effects, such as a simulation of the semi-transparent roundness of a cylinder like a medicine vial.

14.6

DO

- **Use realistic images,** carefully shaded without pen lines to appear three-dimensional.

- **Highlight the main action** with a blurb or pointer box, just as you would in any other graphic, adding arrows and other schematic indicators of motion as needed.

- **Remove most non-essential** elements but retain enough associated items to give the central image needed realism and vividness.

DON'T

- **Use instructionals to convey multiple steps.** Sequence graphics, with less detailed imagery, don't run the same risk of losing track of multiple main points amid all the realistic visual detail.

- **Use instructionals when photographs are needed** instead. As with depictions, instructionals simplify reality so that a main point can be conveyed quickly. If reality need not be simplified for the reader to grasp the main point, use a photograph instead.

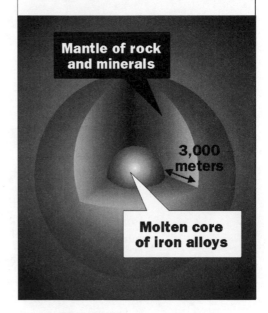

Eon's center is melted metal

Scientists speculate that 3,000 meters beneath the surface of Jupiter's newly discovered moon, Eon, is a molten metal core similar to Earth's.

Mantle of rock and minerals

3,000 meters

Molten core of iron alloys

Cutaways let you see inner workings that a photograph cannot depict.

Cutaways

Cutaways, like the one in Figure 14.6, create unique perspectives that enable you to view inner workings that cannot otherwise be seen. Essential to their success is their ability to convey two scenes realistically while also slicing away a portion of one of them to reveal the other.

As shown in Figure 14.7, shading once again is the most important technique, that provides the biggest clues to the three-dimensional nature of an object.

How Figure 14.6 Was Constructed

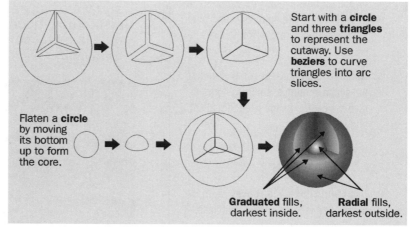

Start with a **circle** and three **triangles** to represent the cutaway. Use **beziers** to curve triangles into arc slices.

Flaten a **circle** by moving its bottom up to form the core.

Graduated fills, darkest inside.   **Radial** fills, darkest outside.

Shading enables readers to see one round sphere within another round sphere.

What extends toward us tends to be brighter; what falls back away from us tends to be darker. As clichés go, things either step forward into the spotlight or fall back into the shadows.

Although you should avoid clichés in writing, remembering them can help you create cutaways. In Figure 14.7, the central core and the overall moon both are filled radially. If real spheres had been present, the area closest to us would have be the surface of each sphere's front side. Thus, the centers of our 3-D circles are shaded the lightest and the edges the darkest.

"Slices" cutting into the moon go from the outer surface to the center are filled in graduated fashion, from light on the outside to dark on the inside. The angle of the graduated fill is shifted so that the lightest area is always along the surface and the darkest is always at the core, regardless of whether the lightest is at the left, bottom or right of the slice.

Perhaps even more so than other diagrams, cutaways require simplicity including the elimination of all but the most essential visual elements. With two visuals to convey simultaneously, details often get in the way. Only those most necessary should be included.

Regardless of such simplicity, cutaways should convey more than a single main point. Supporting details, such as the 3,000 meter distance between the surface and the core in Figure 14.6, may still be presented, if they do not obscure the main point.

DO

- **Take care to keep both scenes realistic.** Not only must the item in the cutaway be faithfully rendered with careful shaded and no pen lines, but so too must the outer image and the slices in it that reveal the inner image.

- **Highlight the main action** with a blurb or pointer box, just as you would in any other graphic, adding arrows and other schematic indicators of motion as needed.

- **Remove all but the most essential elements** so as not to obscure the main point.

DON'T

- **Use cutaways to replace two graphics.** Cutaways show the relationship between the outside and the inside. If only one of them is important, then focus only on it. If both are important in their own right, use two graphics instead.

- **Use cutaways just because they are artistic tours de force.** If it's important, for example, to know what's inside a baseball, do a cutaway. But if it's just the opening of baseball season and you want to produce some sort of graphic—any sort of graphic—about baseball, don't choose a cutaway of a baseball just because you think the drawing would look neat.

Sequences

Maps, glances and diagrams that travel through time assume a new identity, becoming one of the most common yet diverse of graphical forms: the sequence graphic.

Sequences come in two basic varieties:

- **Time lines,** like glances, organize text. Like charts, however, they do so against a visual data metaphor of time passing.

- **Processes,** like maps and diagrams, show interactions that occur across both space and time.

The two look as different as can be but share several common challenges, the most important being simplification of information. A time line shouldn't be an exhaustive chronology. A process graphic shouldn't be a complete set of instructions. Rather, each must reduce the information it conveys to its essence, simplified almost to the point of oversimplification.

This simplification makes sequence graphics among the most difficult to create. Not only must the topic be thoroughly understood so that decisions can be made about what to include and what to leave out, but the information must be arranged so that it can be presented in similar installments. Each entry in a time line or a process graphic is like a separate act in a play. Unfortunately for information designers, many real-world topics don't neatly fit that kind of treatment.

Imagine trying to construct a time line of World War II in Europe. To present a historically meaningful view, you would need to show the end of World War I, the crushing reparations that Germany was ordered to pay, the decline of the German economy to the point at which a firebrand such as Adolph Hitler could take over, the misdeeds he committed and finally the outbreak of war itself. The problem is, most of the events are clustered around a very few years with huge gaps between them. What we Americans view as the war in Europe—from D-Day to Germany's surrender—was barely more than a year in length. More than three years before the start of that period is when the US entered the war. More than two years before that is when most of the early events of the war occurred and Hitler rose to power six years before they happened.

How do you deal with such rat-in-python problems? You can't just space things out evenly and let the years fall where they may. Ethically, that would make your graphic tell a lie by making events seem to be in closer proximity to each other than they really were. You wouldn't want to add meaningless events just to pad out the empty areas. That would do little more than obscure the truly significant points.

Unfortunately, problems such as these have no easy solution, and they don't occur just with information design. Have you ever watched one of those "This Old House"-style programs on television to learn how to do some home improvement? First, you measure the cabinet, then you clean the old countertop, and finally you apply the new Formica. Some guy in a flannel shirt drones on about each of these points, then whips out a bunch of tools and after a quick fadeout he's pointing to a finished cabinet top. That's like giving a friend directions that go into infinite detail about how he should get out of his garage and where he should park once he arrives but that fail to say a word about how to get to the place he's seeking.

The problem is one of scope. Sequence graphics, like all graphics, should tell a story. In most cases, however, they should tell only a part of the story, not its entirety. Preferably, they will tell the most impor-tant part, but regardless, they shouldn't try to tell it all. That's what the TV carpenter does that ticks us off. We all know or can figure out how to measure and clean things. What we need him for is to explain how to use those fancy tools he owns—and possibly how to do the job without them. In trying to explain to us the forest of knowledge about his project, he fails to let us see the most essential grove of trees.

A sequence graphic about how to build an atomic bomb might not be able to simultaneously cover the processing of plutonium, the creation of trigger mechanisms and the physics that cause bombs to work. It can, however, begin to explain one of these areas while hinting that the others exist. Your first challenge in producing a process graphic is to determine what limited area can be managed.

SEQUENCES *at a glance*

Best suited for:	Explaining processes and causal relationships
	Establishing chronological reference points
Least suited for:	Topics for which **causality is unimportant**
	Quantitative comparisons
Answers the questions:	**When, why** and **how**
Often used as:	**Secondary visual elements**
	Occasionally, visual centerpieces
Typical size:	**4 to 6 $^3/_8$ inches** wide or wider
	Rarely, somewhat narrower
Key challenges:	**Simplifying** information (Chapter 3)
	Creating schematic data metaphors (see Chapter 6)
	Evaluative typography, particularly **pointer boxes** (Chapters 3 and 10)
	Occasionally, **drawing** techniques (Chapters 8 and 9)

Time Lines

Learning history is what time lines, like the one in Figure 15.1, are all about. Time lines don't just present background details about issues. They help explain the issues and give readers necessary reference points from which to judge current developments.

15.1

This time line about the continuing strife in Rwanda and Burundi attempts to explain nearly 500 years of inequity between the principal combatants.

As Figure 15.1 indicates, neither the Hutus nor the Tutsis are indigenous to the Rwanda-Burundi region, but the Hutus have been there much longer. For nearly 400 years, the majority Hutus were peacefully ruled by the minority Tutsis. For the next 60 or 70 years, however, both were subjected to colonial rule. The Hutus eventually overthrew their colonial rulers in the 1960s, and the Tutsis, who hadn't been involved in the fighting, saw the revolt as an opportunity to reassert their old monarchy. The Hutus, having won freedom on their own, resisted. It may be a bit oversimplified, but thanks to a time line you now finally have an idea why the Hutus and the Tutsis are at war. If accompanied by a pie chart showing that both Rwanda and Burundi are 85 percent Hutu, the graphics would make a very significant contribution toward answering a question that day-to-day news coverage about the carnage in Africa hasn't answered.

Time lines don't always have to look back to explain issues and give readers reference points. Some, like our Smallville Savings & Loan time line, repeated here as Figure 15.2, look both backward and forward. There even is a variant of the time line, called a schedule graphic, that routinely reports such things as when a sports team will play or, in the case of Figure 15.3, when another event will be conducted.

15.2

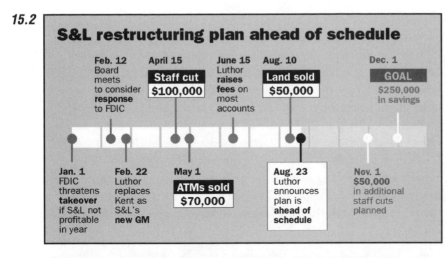

S&L restructuring plan ahead of schedule

Feb. 12
Board
meets
to consider
response
to FDIC

April 15
Staff cut
$100,000

June 15
Luthor
raises
fees on
most
accounts

Aug. 10
Land sold
$50,000

Dec. 1
GOAL
$250,000
in savings

Jan. 1
FDIC
threatens
takeover
if S&L not
profitable
in year

Feb. 22
Luthor
replaces
Kent as
S&L's
new GM

May 1
ATMs sold
$70,000

Aug. 23
Luthor
announces
plan is
ahead of
schedule

Nov. 1
$50,000
in additional
staff cuts
planned

This time line shows both the past and the future. Note how future entries are symbolized in different fashion from past ones.

15.3

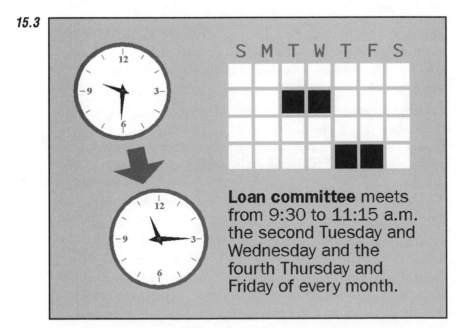

Loan committee meets from 9:30 to 11:15 a.m. the second Tuesday and Wednesday and the fourth Thursday and Friday of every month.

This schedule graphic, part of the time line family, uses another type of temporal metaphor to report on times of day and days of the month.

Figures 15.1 through 15.3 appear different, but underlying each is a consistent visual metaphor representing time. Note, in Figure 15.1, how the centuries pass evenly—500, 700, 900 and so on—with each century labeled in bold type. Also included is a hash mark: two vertical lines that interrupt the scale, much as the rising scale of a fever or bar chart might be elided to show a change. The remaining entries—1920, 1940, 1960, 1980 and 2000—are 20 years apart, not 200 years. To reflect the change, an elision mark is used and the entries shift from boldface to italic. Both preserve the integrity of the graphic while simultaneously getting around the problem of having too many entries in too short a time. Figure 15.2 similarly shifts its typography so that the future portion of the time line is faded, which differentiates these entries.

Figure 15.3, although not a time line in the classic sense, presents two strong data metaphors for time—clock faces indicating the starting and ending time for each meeting and a calendar indicating which days the meetings are scheduled for.

Editorially, time lines are much like glance boxes, requiring decisions on what to include and what to discard. Artistically, they are like graphs, using consistent scales and a visual data metaphor to record a quantity—the passage of time.

Time lines typically spread out horizontally, but they can run vertically as well. One reason they don't often do so is because such a configuration makes it more difficult to link each piece of text to the appropriate point along the time line. Horizontally, slight jogs from a data entry to its point on the scale are possible, as shown in Figure 15.1 with the "Germans establish colonial rule…" and "Hutus attempt to overthrow…" entries.

One of the secrets to creating a professional-looking time line is to minimize the visual "weight" of such jogs. Note how full-blown pointer boxes, with their tornado-like tails, are avoided in Figures 15.1 and 15.2. Had pointer boxes been used instead of simple lines and dots, the two graphics might have looked like scenes from the movie *Twister*.

While that secret helps with looks, the next one helps with information. One of the secrets to producing an informationally effective time line is not to treat each entry as if it were of equal importance. Notice in both Figures 15.1 and 15.2 how some items are allowed to appear in normal text, while others have more vivid backgrounds. This, plus the use of punched bold, gives readers the visual "hooks" they need to be able to process the information in an organized fashion. They see key turning points before they see the background leading up to them. This allows a time line to possess hierarchical organization while also presenting simple data metaphors and visual vividness.

Adding photographs or icons to a time line is one way to increase its vividness. Unless the time line is very large, however, it is difficult to insert photos or icons larger than postage-stamp size. A rule of thumb in photo usage is that if a photograph focuses on an individual person, that person's face should be no smaller than a penny or dime. The more complex the image, the larger it needs to be. Obviously, a time line that includes photographs or other icons could quickly swell to immense dimensions.

Note how, in both Figures 15.1 and 15.2, the date of each event is downplayed. What's important is not that something happened from 1898 to 1903, but the actual event—the German establishment of colonial rule. "Germans" is boldfaced and the specific years, as elements further down on the visual inverted pyramid, are left to be discerned by approximate means. We all know that time passes. What the graphic needs to stress is what happens, not the sequence of one year to the next.

DO

- **Use constant scales,** with time increments progressing evenly.

- **Include visual clues** whenever the scale must be "cut" (that is, whenever it switches to a different set of constant increments) or whenever it changes from the past to the future.

- **Highlight key words** with punched bold and key events with dramatic shading, larger or bolder type or other visual magnets.

- **Remove all non-essential elements** and focus on the most important part of the story.

- **Include iconic imagery** such as photographs but only if there is sufficient space to display it.

DON'T

- **Use overly vivid links** from data to the time line. Simple lines rather than tailed pointers suffice.

- **Emphasize dates.** The data metaphor of the time line itself gives readers a general idea what happened. What's important to highlight textually and visually is exactly what happened. The "when" can be discerned in general terms from the metaphor.

Processes

Is it really important to have a special type of graphic, with specialized rules, to explain processes?

A week ago, I visited a new discount store and picked up a package of cheap disposable razors manufactured under the store's house brand. I tried them out and promptly decided that I had been ripped off. Try as I might, I just couldn't get the razors to give me anything approaching a close shave. After trying five different razors, each of which proved equally dull, I decided to throw the whole package away.

As the package was sailing from my vanity into my bathroom waste-basket, something caught my eye. On the back of the package was a little graphic with a sketch of a razor and arrows going backward and forward. It looked like an instructional diagram, explaining how the razor pivoted to match the contours of the shaving surface—a mean-ingless bit of puffery that I had ignored. This time, however, I chose to read the tiny accompanying text. To my surprise what the package designer was trying to create was not an diagram of how pivoting worked but rather a process graphic showing the razor's safety cover. Slide the cover back and the blades are exposed. Push it forward and they are covered to prevent accidental cuts. The reason all the razors had been so darned dull was that I had been shaving with the safety cover in place.

OK, so I'm not the brightest person in the world and maybe I'm a little too cheap for my own good. But so are the people who will see the graphics you produce. Had the package designer presented information about the razors' retractable safety covers properly—as a process graphic showing each step, with one sketch showing the cover in place and another showing the blades exposed—instead of creating a single image that looked like a pivoting head, I would have seen it a lot earlier. Had he or she used pointer boxes, headlines and other devices rather than compose his text in tiny, four-point type, I might have got the message. That, in turn, would have eliminated a lot of mumbled profanities about the retailer who sold me a package full of "dull" razors.

The right graphic for the right task, eh? When the task is explaining a procedure step by step, there's no graphic better than a process graphic, like the one in Figure 15.4. Properly used, process graphics explain everything from how to remove a razor's safety cover to how Nobel Prizing-winning advances in microbiology occur.

15.4

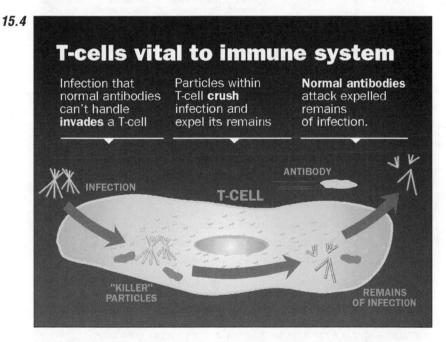

This process chart is basically a depiction diagram with arrows indicating the sequence of events.

Depiction process charts like Figure 15.4 accomplish this by superimposing onto a diagram the sequence in which a process occurs. Typically, arrows take the reader from one step to the next in a smooth-flowing path. Labels, blurbs and pointers are added along the way to make sure the process is clear.

Process graphics also may be created out of graphical forms other than depiction diagrams. I need not show you an example of a process graphic created out of instructional diagrams; several dozen of them are scattered throughout this book. Every time an explanation of how to draw some shape was offered, as in Figure 15.5, what you found yourself looking at was an instructional process graphic.

15.5

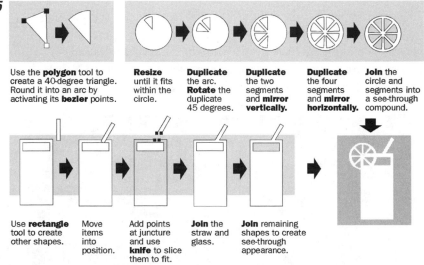

Use the **polygon** tool to create a 40-degree triangle. Round it into an arc by activating its **bezier** points.

Resize until it fits within the circle.

Duplicate the arc. **Rotate** the duplicate 45 degrees.

Duplicate the two segments and **mirror vertically.**

Duplicate the four segments and **mirror horizontally.**

Join the circle and segments into a see-through compound.

Use **rectangle** tool to create other shapes.

Move items into position.

Add points at juncture and use **knife** to slice them to fit.

Join the straw and glass.

Join remaining shapes to create see-through appearance.

Remember Figure 12.11? It and other figures like it throughout this book are instructional process graphics.

Process graphics also may be based on map graphics, as shown in Figure 15.6, or based on glance boxes, as shown in Figure 15.7, a rerun of the Smallville Savings & Loan graphic we created in Chapter 2.

Notice how, in each case, arrows and other visual clues are used to move the reader from one point to the next. Not only does the graphic contain all the things that made it a glance box, map or diagram. It also contains sequence references that make it a process graphic.

Sequence references tend to be strongest if they employ visual data metaphors like arrows rather than text-based instructions like numbers. In some graphics, numbers are needed so that there's no ambiguity about the graphic moving in sequence from one point to the next. But such situations tend to suggest that the graphic is weakly conceived. Figure 15.4, for example, could have been designed in a circular manner, which probably would be more technically accurate than the left-to-right progression that is used. Avoiding the ambiguity of such a design, however, requires the numbering of each point, thereby eliminating a chance for left-to-right arrows. Readers with personal stakes in the topic might not need such a metaphor, but other readers do. Moreover, if kept simple (arrows alone rather than arrows and numbers, for example) even the systematic readers with personal stakes in the topic benefit.

Process graphics essentially are flow charts (which, in fact, is what a schematic diagram becomes when it is transformed into a sequence graphic). "A" leads to "B" leads to "C." If "C", then "X." If not "C", then "Y." Flow charting and symbolic logic are sciences in their own right. Process graphics simplify these sciences by using icons of relationship (arrows) instead of complex symbolism. In a graphical flow chart, arrows replace such symbols as a triangle of dots standing for "therefore" or differently shaped polygons standing for different types of procedures.

For a process graphic to work, all of the requirements of the original graphical form must be met. The map must be simple and accurate. The glance must be reduced to its essence. The diagram must show the big picture, with extraneous clutter removed (see Figure 15.6).

The added requirements of a process graphic must then be met. Primary among these is the establishment of a clear, intuitive sequence that fits well within the visual inverted pyramid approach (see Figure 15.7).

15.6

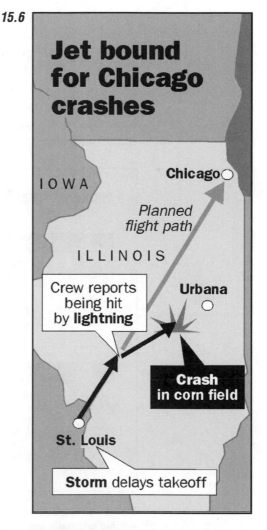

When geography and sequence both are important, a map becomes a process graphic to tell the story.

In Figure 15.6, for example, we see a main point—"Crash in corn field"—denoted by a bold, reversed pointer box. We see secondary points about a storm delaying takeoff and the crew reporting a lightning strike. Geographic reference points provide supporting details, but an unstated subtext is there, which an attentive reader is likely to pick up on. After the plane was struck by lightning, it veered from its planned course. This supporting detail makes the process map go far beyond merely locating what happened. We now get a hint of what may have caused the crash. The lightning strike may have damaged the plane's navigational systems, throwing it off course. The graphic doesn't directly say that; investigators hadn't made an official statement about a cause. By charting the information as a process graphic, however, we can see a possible cause underlying the facts.

15.7

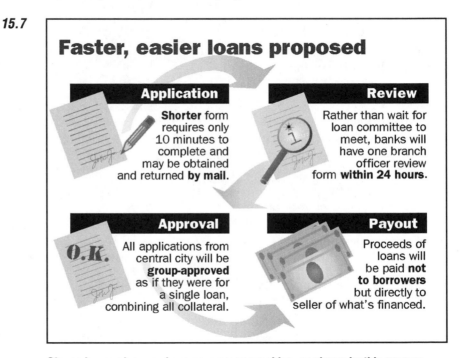

Faster, easier loans proposed

Application
Shorter form requires only 10 minutes to complete and may be obtained and returned **by mail.**

Review
Rather than wait for loan committee to meet, banks will have one branch officer review form **within 24 hours.**

Approval
All applications from central city will be **group-approved** as if they were for a single loan, combining all collateral.

Payout
Proceeds of loans will be paid **not to borrowers** but directly to seller of what's financed.

Glance boxes also may become process graphics, as shown by this process graphic originally presented as Figure 2.5.

Causality is the one key hue that process and other sequence graphics bring to our information design palettes. Better than any other graphical form, they answer the questions of "how" and "why."

DO

- **Base process graphics on other graphical forms** such as maps, diagrams and glance boxes, adhering to all the rules for creating those forms.

- **Add simple, iconic indicators of sequence,** such as arrows, proceeding in left-to-right and top-to-bottom fashion.

- **Avoid numbering each step** unless it is necessary to prevent ambiguity. In such cases, first consider whether the overall design could be altered to avoid this ambiguity.

DON'T

- **Use process graphics to explain the unimportant.** Process graphics are powerful tools and are quite time-consuming to create. If the portion of the process being explained does not help tell the overall story, don't bother.

- **Try to explain everything. Keep process graphics simple.** Handle nuances that graphics cannot depict in accompanying text or with footnotes.

Chapter

Illustrations

Everything you've read in this book so far deals with how to take concrete pieces of information and, using the simplest of computerized tools, communicate that information visually. That's about to change, but don't worry. The topic we're about to undertake belongs in a book about information design only because it tells you what you **shouldn't** do, not because it tells you what you should do.

As we embark on this brief discussion of illustrations, let me warn you up front that I have no plans to show any of the winning entries in this year's Society of Newspaper Design illustration contest or to analyze classic illustration against some Aristotelian standard of ethos, pathos and whatever else Aristotle thought up while in the throes of sucking on Greek grapes.

Every sample graphic you've seen so far was intentionally created using the most basic of techniques. With a bit of patience, a self-critical eye and some time spent practicing, you should feel confident in your ability to re-create every one of them even if you haven't had an art class since grade school, are using a computer that was state-of-the-art 10 years ago or have an aversion to mice that extends to the mouse of your computer. In fact, I encourage you to try. Part of the unusual approach I have chosen for this book includes attempts to stress simple, attainable goals rather than wowing you with the wonderful creations of the field's best and brightest. We don't hand people who are learning to use the written language a copy of *Moby Dick* and tell them, "Do it this way." We shouldn't teach people to use visual language by showing them only great works of art.

When talking about illustrations, such an approach to teaching information design doesn't work. Why? Basically, because illustrations are not part of information design. In fact, they're not even information graphics. They are, as *The Times* of London's Harold Evans calls them, "flavor" graphics.

Illustrations don't deal with concrete information, as glances, graphs, maps, diagrams and sequences do. Rather, they deal in the more ethereal world of emotion. They set a tone, spark the imagination, interpret the abstract and convey feelings. Photography does this through documenting reality. Illustration does it without being bound by reality's limits.

Creating a good illustration requires artistic expression—including technical knowledge about space, texture, line and composition. It would be impossible for you, within the span of a few pages, to learn enough about those qualities to emerge with any confidence in your ability to commit art at will. So, rather than examine how to create an illustration, let's examine what an illustration is **not**:

- **An illustration is not a depiction.** Depictions deal in facts—verifiable, concrete information. Contorting a depiction artistically into a cartoon-like or stylized illustration does not make the depiction become an illustration. It remains a depiction, albeit a bad one, because the vividness of the artistic style overwhelms the organization and data metaphor. Illustrations aren't fancy substitutes for depictions. They are alternatives to be employed only if depictions are impossible. From a communications perspective, if concrete information is available, it's better to sell the steak informationally then to sell the sizzle artistically. Anything else is an abdication of communications' responsibility to provide just the facts, ma'am.

- **An illustration is not a giant icon.** Icons are universally understood tokens that refer to specific items or concepts. Illustrations are works of art, whose meaning varies with each viewer's differing emotional response. Clarity, valued in icons, is disdained in illustration. An illustration's message may end up being more powerful. Its interplay with its viewers' emotions gives it the potential to make truly profound statements. An icon simply cannot do that. Its strength is its efficiency. An icon drawn huge is barely more efficient than it would be at a small scale.

● **An illustration is not a photograph.** True, photography plays on
emotions just as illustrations do, but illustrations deal with the
abstract, while photography deals with reality. A drawing that
looks like something readily seen in reality isn't an illustration at
all; it's a rendering of a photograph or a depiction that an artist
neglected to organize visually. Why go to the trouble of drawing
something when a photograph would be more believable or a
depiction would be more informative? The goal of art is emotion.
The goal of graphics is information. A drawing that contains
neither is either bad art or a bad graphic—typically, both.

All of this, of course, begs two questions: Are illustrations inherently
bad? And if they so rarely are needed, why bother wasting our time
with this discussion?

First, illustrations aren't bad. Great illustrations, like great poetry, have
their place, but in information design, your concern is getting your
message gets across, not with entertaining your audience. Once in a
while an illustration can be offered to accompany text based on its
prosaic qualities. Powerful communication is initiated this way, but for
routine communication, illustration is no more necessary than the
transmutation of news stories into blank verse.

Unfortunately, most information designers are asked to create illustrations far more frequently than such a guideline would suggest. To the
visual illiterates of the world, anything that isn't text is art. They
ignore, possibly because of the marginalization dating to Gutenberg's
time, the entire field of information design—the field this book
specializes in. As a result, information designers are called upon to
create what artistic designers should be creating instead—if, in fact,
such works of art are even warranted.

The result is designs that don't work informationally or artistically:
icons that convey no message, overly stylized sketches that fail to
convey reality or images that require organization to function efficiently but get hung up in technical niceties of drawing.

The real reason for bringing up illustration in a book on information
graphics is to suggest a course of action among information designers:
the elimination of the word "illustration" from their vocabularies.

All too often, particularly at newspapers, illustration serves as a lazy journalist's way out. Rather than finding the information needed to create a depiction or meeting people performing tasks that can be photographed, such journalists sit in their offices and pontificate on reality without learning the facts or contacting anyone.

Resulting illustrations can attempt to play on emotions but suffer without the emotional substance of good artwork, without the informational substance of good graphics and without the humanitarian substance of good photography. They are, in short, insubstantial, out of touch and inherently biased—three failings that have increasingly dogged journalism since the revolution in computer technology made illustrations easier to create.

By banning "illustration" (and the companion phrase "photo illustration") from the workplace vocabulary, not only will you force yourself to create more informative graphics and encourage more realistic photojournalism, you will also go a long way toward establishing a standard that helps an entire industry recapture the respect of its audience.

ILLUSTRATIONS *at a glance*

Best suited for:	Depicting abstract concepts
Least suited for:	Depicting reality that could be photographed
	Conveying flavor rather than information
	Substituting for information that could be charted
Answers the question:	None, deals more in feelings than facts
Often used as:	Visual centerpieces
Typical size:	6 3/8 inches wide or wider
	Rarely, somewhat narrower
Key challenges:	Delicately balancing subtlety and recognition
	Avoiding stereotypes
Key techniques:	**Drawing** techniques (Chapters 8 and 9)
	Emotive **typography**

Chapter **17**

How Graphics Fit into Integrated Designs

Something's wrong with this chapter.

The information is all here.

It just doesn't seem to fit together.

What's wrong?

The Medium

The Techniques

The Forms

The Profession

> A well-designed package should be more than the sum of its parts, each delivering separate pieces of an overall message.

> A well-designed package should integrate text, photos, graphics and design into a single informational thrust—an all-out invasion on the reader's senses that isn't artificially separated into subparts.

Just as sentences in a passage of text should not be separately boxed, whoever takes the photograph, designs the graphics, writes the text and assembles the layout for any informational package should act in unison to make each element an integral part of an intricately orchestrated campaign.

The most obvious reason that an informational choir isn't singing in harmony comes from myriad borders delineating exactly who tended to what part of the package: little black lines around the photo, little black lines around the graphic, wide lines of whitespace around the headline, wide lines of whitespace around the text.

Nothing is inherently wrong with borders around graphics and photos, or with frames of white around headlines and text. Often, however, they symbolize boundaries that have been drawn around each creative task by otherwise dedicated professionals who have become more worried about the separate, specialized dish they prepare than the informational meal the reader will consume.

Potluck design is light-years away from the easy integration of text and visuals found in the writings of Renaissance authors. Moreover, failure to adopt the Renaissance-inspired "graphics without borders" mind-set has many less obvious, but more important, effects: photos that seem unrelated to the headlines adjacent to them, graphics that repeat verbatim the headlines or first paragraphs of story text, visuals that seem to tell stories markedly different from those told by non-visual elements.

As communications professionals, we know that many specialists contribute to the informational meals we prepare, just as many chefs and cook's helpers slave over the food we order at expensive restaurants. We don't expect a restaurant meal to mix cuisines erratically, regardless of how creative the individual dishes might be. Why should we be any less forgiving of informational packages that fail to work together?

The Maestro Concept

Making each element work together is a concept that goes by many names. The *Chicago Tribune*, a pioneer of this approach among newspapers, calls it the centerpiece concept. Design consultant Mario Garcia refers to it as the WED approach—a marriage of Writing, Editing and Design. Communications researcher Ann Aumon calls it integrated editing. Perhaps none have a better name for it than educator Buck Ryan who, in noting similarities to orchestra music, calls it the maestro concept.

Ryan's description is most fitting because it, unlike the others, approaches the goal with an eye on how to achieve it. Producing an integrated, well-orchestrated package, Ryan advises, requires enlisting the support of all the involved professionals from the first day any work on the project is performed. The more cohesive the unit preparing the meal, the more cohesively prepared the meal will be.

The worst design in Ryan's view, and in the view of an increasing number of design professionals, is design that is committed after the fact—after the text has been written, after the photographs have been shot and, in some cases, after the graphic has been created. Writers, editors, photographers and designers all need to adopt proactive approaches, rather than continuing to be shackled by assembly line thinking that technology should have liberated us from long ago.

In our computer-assisted society, an individual should have the technical skills needed to take photographs, write headlines, create graphics and design pages in addition to writing text. Books like this are written to encourage that. The fact is, however, many in the communications industry work only in narrowly specialized areas. This can be good because it allows development of finely focused expertise, but it's bad if that focus prevents the overall goal from coming into view.

The maestro concept is valuable because it shows you how to work within a system of specialization yet simultaneously emphathize with how readers are likely to view your production as a whole: photo first, headline next, graphic third, text last (see Figure 17.1). If the first three fail to convey meaningful information, chances are slim that readers will ever reach the fourth, which, all too often, is the starting point where all design decisions are made.

17.1

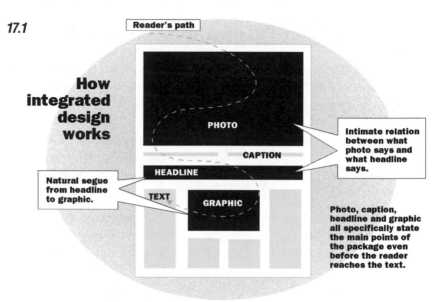

Readers typically get to the text last.

The maestro concept calls for the creation of teams of professionals—photographers, writers, editors, designers—all assembled under the leadership, not of a supervisor, but of a team member. The team directs not only how the finished work is presented but also how the original concept for the package is executed before any writing, photography or research has begun.

The concept is deceptively simple. If, for example, the project is an exploration of how shopping malls have become the new main streets of our society, particularly among the elderly, the team works together on all aspects of the visual and written elements. All team members are involved in research, and compromises are a key ingredient as the project moves from research to execution to display.

If the writer finds five individuals who are worth focusing on but the photographer finds that only one of them photographs well, the package is recast to focus on that individual. If narrative stories focusing on individuals are included along with broad statistics covering large groups, the writer and the designer work together to have those stories compliment each other.

Even before the first reporting is done, each team member makes sure that the topic can be told well in his or her particular milieu. Each member also has the added responsibility of deciding how to advance the chosen topic in a different way so that this is possible. The photographer seeks out one individual to follow, while the graphics editor goes after the broader story and the writer picks up threads of each.

When all is done, the headline writer works with the others to create a headline that plays off the photo and the graphic, not just off the first few words of the text. If the finished package begins with a large photograph of an elderly person socializing in a mall, the headline need only say "America's New Main Street," to get the point across. The graphic need not include an icon and may not need its own separate headline; the package's overall headline and photo may suffice. The text can then immediately begin the tale of the photographed subject in a narrative style.

How to Conduct a Maestro Session

The key to making the maestro concept work is the elimination of a four-letter word: turf. The team is assembled not to figure out how to package the story, how to illustrate the story or how to create graphics to accompany the story. Rather, it is assembled to *tell* a story—a story that consists of much more than just text. The story is the entire package—photos, captions, headline, graphic and text. No one player on the team is any more important than any other in shaping how the story will finally be told. The headline writer, the graphic artist, the photographer or the writer may come up with the original idea. At various points in the process any one of them may temporarily lead the way. If the story suddenly has to change directions, the text may have to be rewritten to accommodate a photo or graphic, or a photo and graphic may have to be redone to accommodate the text. None of these is automatically assumed to be superior to the others.

Obviously, this can be a messy proposition when strong-willed professionals are involved. That's one of the reasons why supervisors, contrary to Ryan's original plan, generally are left out. Supervisors tend to be even more turf-conscious than staffers and often automatically defend the views of those they supervise. Discussions of that sort usually lead nowhere. If all involved learn of the project at the same time, the entire project begins on virgin turf and the strategies need not be crafted from a defensive, combative perspective. Deep down, most professionals want to do a good job. If cooperating with colleagues from different specialties makes this more likely, so be it. Negative confrontations are unlikely when a sense of true professional cooperation is allowed to take over.

Essential to a maestro approach is the establishment of a track record for story teams. If your organization can find a group of professionals who already work well together and are set up as a team to handle a pilot project, skeptics of the approach could see tangible results that might win them over.

Be careful, however, in advertising this to non-writing staff members. The maestro approach does not mean that photographers, designers and editors are suddenly let in on the writing process and given a voice where they used to have none. With that voice comes responsibility. The non-writing members are required to offer ideas on what to research and may have to conduct some research themselves. They are being included not just to make sure mistakes aren't made. They must be willing to contribute to some of the work that, in the past, only writers performed. That means they must begin casting about for ideas themselves rather than simply wait for ideas to be handed to them. They no longer are just traffic cops; they must take responsibility for designing an effective traffic flow.

No hard and fast rules govern how to conduct a maestro session. In fact, the best maestro sessions don't even have a maestro. Rather, they are more like creative jam sessions, where each professional shares equally without anyone serving as leader. Everyone in the group must realize from the outset that the first sign of failure is when any one of them begins questioning who has final authority. Votes of this committee, like those of a jury, must be unanimous. Failure to arrive at a unanimous verdict isn't the fault of the dissenters or the majority. It is the fault of all.

Maestro teams need not be set up by supervisors or officially endorsed by management. Anyone at any level within an organization can get the ball rolling, without even mentioning that maestroing is going on. A casual walk across the office'to chat about what a colleague with a different specialty is working on is as good a starting point as any. Bring a third colleague with yet another specialty into the conversation and you have the beginnings of a very promising maestro team. Just make sure you get there before turf has been staked out and that you are helpful without being intrusive as the brainstorming progresses.

Ten Steps to Better Overall Design

Whether assembled via the maestro process or through traditional means, information graphics remain only one part of a finished page. Helping you present better pages as a whole is a 10-step checklist (often called the Ten Commandments of Design). These 10 steps offer simple guidelines for creating more effective pages that include informational graphics.

✔ **Text**   For normal text, use a 10- or 11-point serifed Roman such as Times. For graphics and captions, use a contrasting sans serif like Helvetica, at least as large. Limit italics to short phrases. Use bold, not italics, to show emphasis. Don't alter leading, tracking or horizontal or vertical scale significantly; instead use type designed for such purposes.

✔ **Width**   Set type no wider than twice the width of the lowercase alphabet (about 18 picas or three inches for most 10-point type) and no narrower than one time that width (about 9 picas or 1.5 inches in that type size). Use the optimum width, halfway between those, for everything except rare, special items of a less informative and more narrative nature.

✔ **Visuals**   Each page needs one and only one dominant visual element—a photo, graphic or artwork in the top half of the page that is at least 1.5 times the size of the next-largest visual, and at least the same size as the next-largest headline-text-and-visual package on the page.

✔ **Display**   Every text element needs a headline; every photo, a caption; every four inches of type, an entry point—a pull quote, facts box, subhead, photo or graphic. Non-textual entry points should never interrupt the vertical flow of text. Use run-arounds or position them at the tops of columns.

✔ **Layout**   Headlines should go immediately above and across the full width of text to which they refer. A caption, explaining the main point of the entire package, should go immediately below each photo in a different width than accompanying text. Text should begin immediately beneath the left edge of a headline.

✔ **Modules**   Each headline-text-and-visual package should be bounded by a visible or invisible rectangle, with photos, headlines or both spanning the entire top of the rectangle. Irregularly shaped modules (or "doglegs") should not be used. Neither headlines nor visuals should abut except in photo layouts. Modules should be of varying shapes and sizes, either exactly the same as neighboring modules or radically different. Avoid near-miss symmetry.

✔ **Spacing**   A consistent, fixed amount of space—horizontally and vertically—should be used between elements within a module. Varying amounts of space may be used creatively on outside edges. Don't trap white space inside a layout; let it flow around the layout.

✔ **Headlines**   Use different weights not different faces, save for the possibility of a single "accent" face used sparingly—certainly no more than a handful of words per page. Otherwise, rarely use more than three fonts (headlines, text and captions) in any single publication. Capitalize consistently, preferably as would be done in a sentence, not a title. Vary sizes. Keep bigger sizes at top, smaller sizes at bottom.

✔ **Use it or lose it**   If a visual doesn't meaningfully inform or organize, discard it as useless decoration. Each visual should tell a story, not merely illustrate or decorate. Never alter a photograph's reality or weaken it by overprinting, blocking out or cropping non-rectangularly.

✔ **Catch-22**   The goal is effective, ethical communication. If violating any of these rules furthers that goal, by all means violate them. But do so only if you can fully defend your action on those grounds, not on grounds of art or style.

Graphics, Design and the Law

Paul Newman, Sally Field, O.J. Simpson and you. You're the cast in a startling new drama about to unfold in America's board rooms, newsrooms, and courtrooms.

The time: the 21st century, just a few short years away. The plot: Information designers have replaced investigative reporters as the primary targets of libel suits. The title, if you will: *Absence of Graphics Malice.*

Far-fetched? Perhaps. But an era in which graphics are regarded as among the most noticed and persuasive parts of a printed page—and in which lawyers seem obsessed with litigating the known universe—are libel cases involving information designers really that unlikely?

Already the visual has surpassed the verbal as the source for some of the most celebrated defamation suits in television news. Can the printed page, just emerging into a truly visual era, be far behind? And if so, will lawyers and information designers be prepared?

Thanks in no small part to a certain double-murder trial, more has been written on how graphics affect the practice of law than on how the law affects the practice of graphics. To-wit, here is an attempt to balance that coverage.

Are You Liable for Libel?

Basic communications law applies to more than just text. Just as headlines and photo captions can become targets of libel actions, so too can a graphic if it negligently or, in the case of public figures, recklessly misstates truth in ways that can damage reputations.

Any portion of a medium's content, isolated from the rest of that content, can cause defamation. Just because a graphic or a design isn't a traditional news story doesn't allow it to escape the rigors of libel. Headlines, file photos, even lines saying what topic is next in a series of stories have been the targets of successful newspaper libel cases, even when non-defamatory truth was reflected in accompanying text. The fact that the "whole story" appears in text, or is told via a footnote, does not take away from a graphic element's capability to libel independently from the rest of the page.

A graphic that, for example, inadvertently shows a company's sales falling instead of rising just before its initial public stock offering could be actionable, even if the accompanying headline and story stated otherwise. Moreover, because of the added attraction, memorability and believability of graphic elements, a plaintiff might successfully argue that visual defamation was *more* damaging than verbal defamation. A publication confronting such an allegation could be forced to defend itself against its own internal research attesting to graphics' power.

Certain graphic images can possess special protection akin to what is allowed in hyperbolic satire. In a series of cases, graphical images, as works of art, have been regarded less as factual presentations and more as expressionistic viewpoints. Such graphics are free to offer visual parodies or satires as broad expressions of societal comment and criticism, whether they come in the form of political cartoons, satirical depictions of buildings, or outrageous use of photographs. (For a complete discussion, see Laura Cohen's "Beyond Silberman v. Georges: Shielding the Artist from Claims of Libel," *Columbia Human Rights Law Review*, 1986.)

The key is to make sure that the satire is clearly a parody, not just a slight exaggeration of the truth. Add a rat and leaky roof to your sketch of an apartment complex and you may be sued. Sketch the entire complex as if it were a giant cardboard box and you may be protected for engaging in satire. If art is viewed more as an idea than as a fact, artistic defamation is difficult to prove. As Supreme Court Justice Lewis F. Powell Jr. noted in *dicta* (an off-hand, non-binding comment) in the landmark case *Gertz v. Robert Welch Inc.*: "Under the First Amendment, there is no such thing as a false idea."

Images presented as fact, not satire, receive no such protection, of course. Nor does the textual, tabular, or charted material contained in non-satirical graphics. Although few cases have arisen, such material would most likely be treated as if it were normal text—with the possible effect of the graphic having more impact. Even an inadvertent juxtaposition—material intended for one topic being associated with another one—could lead to collectable libel.

Libel Checklist

✔ Is it fair and accurate on its own, without relying on footnotes or the text?

✔ If it artistically exaggerates, is it clearly satire based on opinion, not facts?

✔ If file photos are used, are the subjects completely unidentifiable, either directly or by background clues, or are they provably still involved in the activity shown?

The Too-Graphic Graphic

Privacy invasions committed in graphics also could be regarded as more serious than those committed in text.

Imagine a graphic depicting the injury sustained by John Wayne Bobbitt when his spouse sliced off a certain key appendage. A defense of newsworthiness from the artist could be used against a tort alleging disclosure of embarrassing private facts (*Sidis v. F-R Publishing Corp.*). The disclosure, however, could be deemed to "outrage the community's notion of decency" (*Diaz v. Oakland Tribune Inc.*), leading a jury to find against the artist. Any sort of medical graphic, particularly from a case such as Bobbitt's, could pose this kind of peril.

Information designers also must take special care when selecting file photographs to use as icons within graphics or designs, even if the images are altered digitally. If, despite alteration, the subject of the original photograph remains identifiable, even to only one person, a successful action could be brought. If, for example, a person is falsely portrayed as being a welfare recipient because that person's silhouette is used to accompany statistics on welfare, action could be brought for libel if someone recognized the silhouette. If the depiction was merely embarrassing, not damaging, a privacy tort could be brought for placing the subject in a false light. The latter could be the case if a habitual welfare recipient, currently not on the dole, were to be wrongly associated with the current welfare list.

Defamation can occur by implication alone, even if no faces—silhouetted or otherwise—are seen. A photo of a house, with its address carefully removed, in a graphic about crack houses could produce a successful libel suit if only one person recognized it and associated it with the homeowner. A major newspaper recently averted disaster when it scuttled plans to use a photo-illustration, staged with models, about pedophilia among priests. Although none of the subjects were real priests, the blurry background of the photo contained enough information for parishioners to identify it as being the altar area of a particular local church. The priest serving that church, and the church itself, could have brought a successful libel action.

Libel cases involving use of republished photos are fairly common (*Martin v. Johnson Pub. Co.*, for example), particularly in broadcast journalism. Common law torts of false light, where embarrassment but not defamation is the result, are much less common. The tort is not allowed in all states and is tried under varying standards. Recent court cases, however, indicate a growing willingness on the part of the judicial system to guard individuals' privacy.

Scanning Your Way into Court

A more common concern in graphics and design is copyright infringement, particularly involving images appropriated by digital scanners. Graphics creators seem obsessed with the idea of taking old images and transforming them into new expressions by using today's manipulation tools.

Within the legal community, debate has raged over whether such appropriations for creating Post-Modern art constitute a "fair use" under federal copyright law. In one celebrated case (*Rogers v. Koons*), a sculptor replicated a picture postcard of a couple holding puppies, making only small variances from the photo and specifically telling his craftspeople to create the sculpture "as per photo." In an equally celebrated case (*Campbell v. Acuff Rose Music Inc.*), a rap group, 2 Live Crew, sampled portions of a 33-year-old recording to create a parody of the original work. The puppies sculptor was found to have violated the postcard photographer's copyright, although the rap musicians were found to have made fair use of the original recording.

After those rulings, legal commentators suggested the existence of judicial confusion over handling Post-Modern appropriation of copyright material. A different test with clear-cut applications to graphics and design was proposed: the principle of economic substitution. Under this legal theory, advanced by Michael C. Anderson and Paul F. Brown in the *Loyola University of Chicago Law Journal* in 1993, what matters most is whether the secondary use acts as an economic substitute for the original. The purchaser of the sculpture could have gone to the postcard photographer and commissioned him to supervise the rendering of his work into three-dimensional form by the same craftspeople who did the work for the sculptor. On the other hand, a re-issue of Roy Orbison's original recording would not have had the same audience as did 2 Live Crew's parody of it. Commentators advancing this theory use similar logic to rationalize other seemingly contradictory fair-use decisions.

If a graphic or design was questioned for its appropriation of copyright artwork, an economic substitution defense could have strong results. Clearly, most information graphics serve different economic purposes than the sources of commonly appropriated copyright material, such as "clip art" packages, encyclopedias and other reference works.

Failing such a defense, a graphic that appropriates copyright material could be defended on more traditional grounds that the appropriation was creative and advanced learning. In light of graphics' informational role, this is a particularly strong argument. Moreover, appropriated images such as maps or diagrams might be more factual than creative, allowing greater latitude for appropriation. In many cases, what is appropriated might also involve only a portion of an image—something less than its essence. Such use is commonly allowed.

Several copyright cases involving graphics and design have been decided on these grounds. A pitching form based on a wire service's box scores was ruled creative for its selection of which categories to include (*Kregos v. The Associated Press*). A racing form that reprinted track results in "purely functional grids that offer no opportunity for variation" was "mechanical," "conventional" and "garden variety," and therefore ruled illegal (*Victor Lalli Enterprises v. Big Red Apple Inc.*). A minority telephone directory, drawing most of its listings from a broader directory, was ruled creative for its "unique organization" of the longer original list into a list of only minority companies (*Bellsouth Advertising and Publishing Corp. v. Donnelly Information Publishing Inc.*).

Copyright Art Checklist

✔ Is the copy incapable of substituting economically for the original?

✔ Is the original so newsworthy that copying it, after its initial release, would be in the public's interest?

✔ Is the copy used to create a new and different artwork?

✔ Is only a minor portion of the original used?

Just the Facts, Ma'am

Clearly, copyright law governs not only appropriation of art but also appropriation of how data are presented—an even more prevalent practice than artistic appropriation in modern information graphics. Although it can be argued that news items based on statistical reports are original news creations, not subject to the originator's copyright, what of graphics that appropriate all or substantially all of a copyright report's statistical database and serve a purpose other than journalism?

As defined by the US Constitution and noted in several Supreme Court rulings (most notably *Basic Books Inc. v. Kinkos Graphics Corp.*), the goal of copyright law is free dissemination of information. It establishes mechanisms that ensure due compensations for those who create, but it does so expressly as a way of furthering dissemination.

Consistent with the theory of economic substitution, this concept bodes well for information graphics. Although a case can be made against a graphic that appropriates an income-tax service's proprietary tax-preparation worksheet, thereby depriving the firm of potential business, most graphics do not deprive copyright holders of potential compensation unless they are copied from rival organizations.

Economic substitution theory gives rise to several interesting, hypothetical tests of fair use, particularly in cases involving appropriation of maps and other graphical guides. It might be safe to appropriate much of, for example, a graphical guide to fishing spots to use as a map accompanying a report on a drowning of an angler in a lake. If, however, the appropriated package were promoted and sold as a special report on fishing, the appropriation would seem much less justified. The closer an appropriated product comes to substituting for the original, the more likely is it is to have difficulty with copyright law unless the newsworthiness of the material is overwhelming, as it was with the Abraham Zapruder film of the John F. Kennedy assassination in *Time Inc. v. Bernard Geis Associates*.

What about situations with less than overwhelming news value—the type of situation that most non-journalists and even some journalists commonly face? Say an organization issues a moderately newsworthy, factual report containing statistics. Its entire database must be reproduced to be meaningful, but there exists only one way to present the information—with the same charts or tables used in the original version, for which the writer obtained copyright protection so that it could be sold on the basis of its informational value. A summary of tax rates among suburbs of a large urban area is a classic example of such a report.

Defenses of overwhelming newsworthiness, creativity in making the appropriation, and lack of economic substitution of the appropriated version for the original would be precluded. Appropriation in such cases could be deemed an unjustifiable infringement, but only if the original material actually qualified for copyright protection.

In a landmark database case, *Feist Publications v. Rural Telephone Service*, the US Supreme Court in 1991 abandoned earlier principles that factual compilations were suitable for copyright because of the amount of work that went into creating them—a doctrine known as "sweat of the brow." Instead, Justice Sandra Day O'Connor wrote that creative editing, organization, or display of information is required before copyright protection may be granted.

In essence, what O'Connor itemized is exactly what a good information graphic should possess: creative ordering of data. Use of someone else's information in one's own organization and display would be permitted. Moreover, copying someone else's organization and display when there is no other practical way to present such information, as in Feist's appropriation of Rural's telephone book listings for use in a another telephone book, is permitted because the original, in lacking creativity, cannot qualify for copyright.

Implications of this ruling are far-reaching. When appropriating someone else's information, an information designer may be protected by making choices about what portion of the information to appropriate. At the same time, he or she may be protected by having so few choices to make that the appropriation must occur in total. Data items themselves are not protected. If there is only one way to present the data, the presentation strategy may be freely appropriated as well.

Copyright Chart Checklist

✔ Are the data presented in a creatively different way?

✔ If presented as in the original, is there only one practical way to present this kind of information?

✔ Do any of the items on the copyright art checklist apply?

Everyday Examples

- **Use of pre-drawn "clip art"** in a graphic might be readily defended on grounds that its new use was creative and that it did not serve as an economic substitute for the sale of clip art packages. Using one clip art package, however, to put together another clip art collection you would sell as such would be prohibited. An electronic "font," by way of analogy, is typically protected by copyright. Acquiring a font without payment of copyright fees may be unjustified, but using a font that has been properly acquired to produce a new work requires no royalty fees to the font's creator as long as the new work does not amount to creation of a font-like product—an alphabet poster, for example.

- **Digital manipulation of appropriated photographs** can be defended as being creative, provided the intent is not to deprive the copyright holder of typically accorded resale rights, as might be the case in reusing a work-for-hire (or "stringer") photograph. Increasingly broad latitude is given to use of copyright material in creative Post-Modern collages, provided that the strength of the material is a new creation, not the appropriated original, and that the new creation does not diminish the potential market for the original. The more an image is enhanced digitally and the more it is mixed with other elements to form a new creative whole, the more likely its appropriation will be justified. Making Andy Warhol's Campbell's soup cans the cover art for a soup cookbook, even if a nifty headline were applied, would be another matter altogether.

- **Copying of commercially sold products such as maps** can be defended on several grounds: The boundaries of a geographic area are factual, not creative and therefore cannot be protected. Duplication of the method of presenting such information, if deemed to be done in the only way that is practical, is likewise defensible. Care must be taken, however, not to duplicate "enhancing" features that make the original different from other, similar presentations. Appropriation of a map showing the route of Interstate 99 between Feldonville and its intersection with US 86 in Adamstown might be defensible, but appropriation of the map's locations of motorist call boxes and service stations along the route would be less defensible. These are features that make the original unique.

- **Charts, tables and other images** may be directly appropriated intact from copyright sources if they present newsworthy information in a way that does not compete economically with the original. They also can be used if the original's lack of creativity makes it unsuitable for copyright protection. The chart appearing in a corporation's annual report could be lifted intact and placed in a stockbroker's report on the company's stock, provided no creative, artistic elements were in the original graphic.

- **Reusing creative work for a purpose similar to the original function** is likely to create the greatest difficulty. Appropriation of a Santa Claus sketch from a greeting card company's new line of Christmas wrapping paper might be permitted in a news story about wrapping paper or a graphic detailing Santa Claus myths. (No, Virginia, we weren't saying he's completely mythical.) If used generically in a promotional item to wish readers of a newspaper a Merry Christmas or to advertise a Christmas sale, the holder of the original copyright might be justified in objecting. Duplicating the original to accomplish a similar purpose could diminish the value of the original. Who among us, save for a few quirky journalists, would want to wrap Christmas presents in paper featuring an image, the novelty of which already has been consumed by a publication's self-promotion?

- **When straying from information into promotion,** information designers must exercise considerable care. What might be allowed in a newsletter, newspaper or magazine might not be allowed in a souvenir reprint, on a T-shirt or in an advertisement. When a graphic is offered as part of a product that is sold not as a news product but rather as a routine commercial item, economic substitution theory undermines fair-use defenses. Moreover, with a commercial product, individuals retain under privacy law the ability to control whether they wish to be associated with the venture. Businesses have much the same right under trademark law. In privacy law, this is known as the right of publicity. While the newsworthiness of a local sports hero's accomplishments might make it permissible for a newspaper to show her photograph on the front page, her rights of publicity make it impermissible for the same paper to put her likeness on a souvenir reprint of the front page without first securing her permission. Similar restrictions exist when creating material for advertisements and other commercially, rather than journalistically, inspired endeavors.

Chapter **19**

Graphics' Role
on the Internet

Graphics represent the present for information design. But what of its future?

Graphics' role in traditional communications is assured to grow as desktop publishing expands the capability of non-artists and non-programmers to become visual communicators. In all industries, people with skills in graphics are in extreme demand even as positions in other specialties are being eliminated. Graphics is such a hot field that a *New York Times* recruiter recently joked that a potential *Times* employee could earn a job offer in two ways: "Win a Pulitzer or know something about graphics."

Another way a candidate could interest the *Times* is to know something about an even hotter field of communications: online publishing. Nearly one-fourth of the 1996 journalism graduates of Northwestern University went to work in online publishing. That's particularly impressive when you consider that less than half of all journalism graduates ever find work in the publishing industry.

Growth of online publishing has been dramatic and swift. Before 1993, fewer than a dozen newspapers world-wide were published electronically. That year, the number rose to 20. In 1994, it reached 78. Since then, the number of online newspapers has increased by an average of 50 each month, reaching 511 midway through 1995, exceeding 1,000 early in 1996, and swelling to more than 1,600 by year's end. And that's just newspapers. Add in more than 2,400 magazine and broadcasting sites plus countless corporate, organizational and amateur sites, and you have a trend that only someone in Antarctica could miss. Truth is, even that person couldn't miss it. Among the publications now online is the *New South Polar Times* (http://139.132.40.31/NSPT/NSPThomePage.html), a newsletter about the goings-on at the very bottom of the world.

Striking differences can be noticed between the online and print versions of publications that are produced in both forms. While the 10 most popular online news sites all carry graphics on their front pages in print, none of them does so online. Graphics, a hot field in traditional communications, are getting a cold shoulder online.

Is this a sign that online readers or journalists don't care about graphics' impressive ability to be more quickly processed, more memorable and more believable than text? Hardly. Many of those creating online sites come from graphics backgrounds. Online reading is, if anything, the ultimate in skimming, where graphics should play a major role. Rather, technology—graphics' simultaneous friend and enemy—once again has created problems. And the first problem is bandwidth.

Being online offers tremendous capabilities for visual communication, but only if users possess the right equipment and connections. Stores overflow with high-speed Pentiums, Power Macs and 33.6 kbps modems. But even these are not fast enough to give traditional graphics their due. In fact, the Internet today runs so slowly that one-third of all users report that they routinely disable the capability of Internet browsers like Netscape Navigator and Microsoft Internet Explorer to receive photos and other graphical files.

The nature of the medium is the root of the problem. Online pages are transmitted digitally—bit after bit, byte after byte, in sequential order. Print is produced in analog; five inches of text or five inches of graphic reproduce equally fast on a rotary press. The adage about a picture being worth a thousand words remains true online. The human mind still sees online images in analog, and processes and remembers them more easily as a result. However, the medium itself, requiring digital transmission, imposes a bandwidth penalty that more than offsets the natural advantages of using the visual channel. The thousand words that a picture might replace could very well have been transmitted in a lot less time.

The second problem is file formats. Online, graphics are presented as GIF or compressed JPEG files, in formats designed to allow photographs to be transferred with less of a bandwidth "penalty" than might be imposed by more typical TIFF and EPS formats. GIF compromises by allowing for only 256 colors or shades of gray. JPEG compromises by reducing image resolution and looking for duplicative patterns, much as compression programs like PKZIP or StuffIt do with files on a PC or a Mac. Neither is an object-oriented language the way EPS is. Lines, shapes and, in particular, text are stored and transmitted as bitmapped images. This may be fine for a photo, but for a graphic containing text, bitmapping can render letters unreadable. If you've experimented with a scanner to create graphics, you know that scanned photos look fine, but that scanned text often is distorted and jagged. That's exactly how a GIF or JPEG graphic shows up online.

Today's online graphics are much like the graphics in Gutenberg's day: boxy, one-piece elements that don't mix well with text, which, in contrast, can be manipulated letter by letter. As a result, they often are confined to the same fate that graphics received in Gutenberg's day: marginalization. Typically, if an online graphic is provided, readers must click its title before seeing it display. As a result, the graphic loses whatever value it might have for attracting attention. Its organization and metaphorical simplicity suffer because of the bitmap format. In the end, it is hardly worth the effort.

Technology will eventually catch up and allow online graphics to be created in an object-oriented format like EPS. In the meantime, graphics can be created through simple, albeit time-consuming, ways as something other than one-piece elements that don't mix with text. The secret is translating the graphic into the Internet's native tongue— HyperText Markup Language, or HTML.

HTML is an simple coding scheme by which browsers like Netscape and Explorer know what to display. It is not a page design language, and thus has only limited capabilities. But in some ways, that is a blessing. The less there is to do, the less there is to learn:

Beginner's Guide to HTML

Basic Formatting

Each page must follow a basic format so browsers know how to handle it.

<HTML><HEAD><TITLE> Title of your page goes here **</TITLE> </HEAD><BODY>**

Rest of your page, including headlines, goes here **</BODY></HTML>**

Controlling Typography

Your page will look different on different browsers. Your control is limited to:

Boldface	<B>	Word(s) to appear in bold </B>
Italic	<I>	Word(s) to appear in italic </I>
Typewriter font	<TT>	Word(s) to appear in monospaced font </TT>
Rule across page	<HR>	
Headlines	<H1>	Largest headline </H1>
	<H2>	Second largest headline </H2>
	<H3>	Third largest headline </H3>
Indented text	<BLOCKQUOTE>Material to be indented </BLOCKQUOTE>	
Bulleted list	<UL><LI> First item	
	<LI> Second item	
	<LI> Last item </UL>	
Pre-set spacing	<PRE> Section with tabs, columns, and so on </PRE>	
New line	Start a new line after this. 	
New line + leading	Add a blank line in addition to starting a new line. <P>	
Show a GIF graphic	<IMG SRC="File" ALT="Word(s) in lieu of graphic" HEIGHT= Size in pixels WIDTH= Size in pixels >	

Jumping from Section to Section or to Other Pages

You cannot always specify fonts, sizes or spacing, but you can call for them:

Link to a file	`<A HREF="File">` *Description your readers see* `</A>`
Label a location	`<A NAME="Label"></A>`
Link to a label	`<A HREF="#Label">` *Description your readers see* `</A>`
... in different file	`<A HREF="File#Label">` *Description for readers* `</A>`

Deciphering an Online Address

```
http://vinny.csd.mu.edu/tribune/tribune.html =
method://computer.owner.type/directory/document.type
```

By convention, we tell a Web browser we are looking for a Web page by beginning the address with `http://` and following that with the name of the **computer** on which the Web page is located, followed by the computer **owner** and the **type** of system. Thus, the address `http://www.newslink.org` means that the page we seek is located on the WWW computer at NewsLink, which is an organization. If it were `http://vinny.csd.mu.edu` the site would be on Vinny Carpenter's computer in the Computer Science Department at Marquette University, which is an educational institution.

Unless the file is named index.html and located in the base directory of the server, we also must identify in which **directory** the file can be found and what the **document** is named, followed by its **type** (almost always html). The address `http://vinny.csd.mu.edu/tribune/tribune.html` means that the file we are looking for is the "tribune" directory and is called "tribune.html." Note that capitalization matters. If the file had been named index.html and stored in the server's base directory, a relatively shorter URL (or Universal Resource Locator) such as `http://www.newslink.org/` could have been used instead.

In HTML, when jumping from page to page within a directory or when calling in a graphic from within the current directory, only the **file name** needs to be used: `<a href="stats.html">`. To link to another computer, you must use the **full URL**: `<a href=http://www.newslink.org/stats.html>`.

Advanced Codes You Can Safely Use

Some browsers will not display these but will not malfunction if they are present:

Centered text `<CENTER>` Material to be centered horizontally `</CENTER>`

Background image **Modify BODY command in basic formatting to read:**

`<BODY BACKGROUND="`GIF file's name`">`

Color of all text **Modify BODY command in basic formatting to read:**

`<BODY TEXT="#`2200CC`">`

with colors designated in hexadecimal RGB format

(2200CC is flag blue, CC0022 is flag red, 000000 is black)

Square bullets `<UL TYPE=SQUARE><LI>` First item

`<LI>` Second item

`<LI>` Last item `</UL>`

Image run-around `<IMG SRC="File" ALT="`Non-graphical description`"`

`ALIGN=`Left or right`>`

Font and size `<font size="`1 (small) to 7 (large)`"` FACE="Typeface`">`

Typefaces must reside on reader's computer. Use Helvetica, Courier and Times safely. Others may not work.

Controlling Page Layout

One of the few ways to control spacing is with tabulation commands. Set up your page a maximum of 580 pixels wide to accommodate all monitor types.

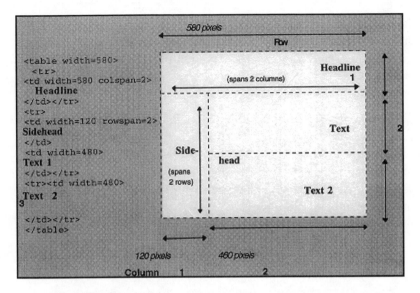

Begin table   <table width= # of pixels border=weight of rule, if any>

Repeat for all rows in table:

Begin row   <tr>

Repeat for all cells in row:

Define cell width   <td width= Overall width

If cell spans row   rowspan= Number of rows spanned

...or column   colspan= Number of columns spanned

Align vertically   valign= Top, center, or bottom

Align horizontally   align= Left, center, or right

Enter cell data   > Cell data </td>

End row   </tr>

End table   </table>

Armed with these simple commands, it's tedious but not difficult to create an online graphic. One of the secrets is using the IMG SRC (or image source) command, which lets you display a GIF image. This command enables you to rescale the image by entering additional parameters, in pixels, for its height and width.

Create a GIF image that is nothing more than a solid 10-by-10-pixel square and store it as bar.gif. Using the rescaling feature of the IMG SRC command, you can then create bars of varying sizes for a graphic, in proportion to the data. For example, by dividing the data by five your could create a bar chart like the one in Figure 19.1 charting the number of online newspapers:

```
4/94 <img src="bar.gif" height=10 width=4> <b> 20 </b>
<br>

1/95 <img src="bar.gif" height=10 width=16> <b> 78 </b>
<br>

9/95 <img src="bar.gif" height=10 width=94> <b> 471 </b>
<br>

6/96 <img src="bar.gif" height=10 width=267> <b> 1,335
</b> <br>

3/97 <img src="bar.gif" height=10 width=340> <b> 1,700
</b> <br>
```

A chart such as this can easily be dressed up with a GIF icon at the top, a background GIF, various font sizes, and a table format. Add a headline as well as the top-and-bottom-of-page HTML commands, and you have a workable, if not elegant, online graphic, like the one in Figure 19.1. You can even make the graphic come to life by using "animated" GIF89a files. Your chart's bars can grow or change colors, or the icon you put atop them can spin and morph. To "animate" a GIF, a shareware program such as GifBuilder is the only tool you need.

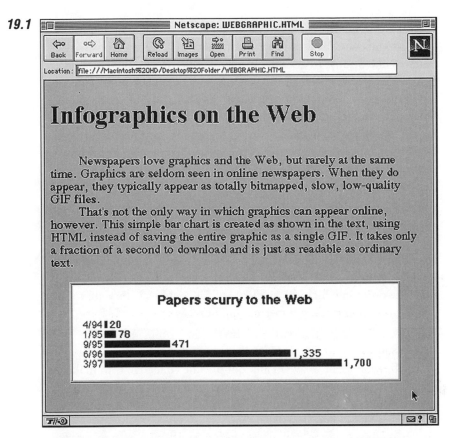

19.1

The previous HTML code produces a graphic that looks like this in Netscape Navigator 3.0.

Information design, however, has a higher calling online that the creation of mere graphics. The entire experience of visiting an online page is similar to that of reading a graphic. The lessons you have learned about how to design a graphic in print carry over well into how to design an online site in hypertext.

"Hypertext structures make bowls of spaghetti look like models of good organization," writes Howard Strauss of Princeton University. Authors like Strauss frequently condemn hypertext on such grounds. Yet the design of hypertext, in allowing readers to click highlighted sections to summon or skip over details, is similar to the "entry point" behavior found in graphics readership. In fact, even some of the tools are the same. "Punched bold," for example, is one of the currently *en vogue* ways for presenting text in cyberspace. People who know how to create graphics have a definite advantage when it comes time to move material from print online.

In creating a graphic, a designer practices (probably without knowing it) something known as nonlinear storytelling, another *en vogue* method online. Graphical "stories" possess beginnings, middles and ends. They only thing they don't possess are narrative elements that hold the story together the way transitions do in text. Readers determine the order in which the elements of the graphical story are read, just as they do in reading hypertext online.

Bill Skeet, chief designer with Knight-Ridder's online media laboratory in San Jose, California, likens hypertext design to charting a map in which readers can weave in and out of. The challenge is to make the map easy to follow while simultaneously ensuring that key points are not overlooked. This is precisely the same challenge that an information design faces in creating a graphic.

To writers, the nonlinear nature of hypertext may seem contrary to what they have been taught. As you learned in Chapter 3, "Getting a Point Across," however, such techniques may be more akin to traditional, inverted pyramid writing than one might suspect. Inverted pyramid writing stresses the value of concise information and the stripping away of excess details. It includes only the most important and discards the rest. Exact titles, times, geography and other minor facts included by rote in normal text (including wire service text that supposedly passes for inverted pyramid) are not allowed to interfere. In essence, inverted pyramid style employs what amounts to a historically appropriate telegraphic style.

If thoughtfully used, online hypertext takes telegraphic efficiency to its logical conclusion, treating each fact within text as if it had its own headline. Rather than turn a story into a single inverted pyramid, hypertext writers create many, small pyramids, each representing a separate facet of the overall story. Readers can choose to read only the hyperlink headlines for some, the full text for others.

Imagine, for example, how the tragic story of the Oklahoma City bombing could be told in hypertext. With a chart showing how the hyperlinks would unfold, the story could look like this:

19.2

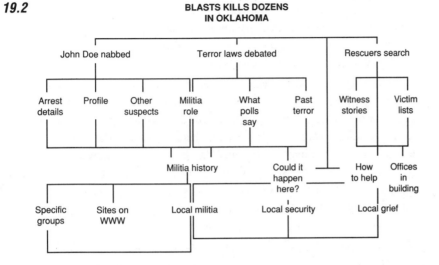

BLASTS KILLS DOZENS IN OKLAHOMA

Take a moment to follow the story as you would have on the day of the tragedy. For each reader, the path is likely to be different, but the overall design should still be familiar. Hypertext's basic logic mirrors the strategy behind how pages of related stories are assigned and laid out in print. Its structure is similar to a classic outline's—minus, of course, the Roman numerals. It mimics the pattern, revealed by Eye-Trac, with which readers examine printed pages.

In essence, hyperlinks are to online publications what "entry points" are to newspapers in print. They enable skimmers and scanners to gain some knowledge of a topic, even if the topic does not initially seem to interest them enough to read it. The biggest difference between online hypertext and the design of printed information is that the main piece of text is likely to be shorter and the supplementary pieces more numerous. This change is one that Eye-Trac researchers long ago urged for print design. On a typical 85-square-inch computer monitor instead of a 560-square-inch broadsheet page, the need for shorter text is even more pronounced. Topic count and, therefore, appeals to skimmers would decline markedly, and aversion to long texts would increase greatly, if text were not somehow broken up.

Exactly how to break up a story has developed into a small science. At the *Chicago Tribune*, Leah Gentry began referring to it as "deconstruction and reconstruction." Others, such as Chip Scanlon of the Poynter Institute, have referred to it as creating "dozens of miniature inverted pyramids floating around in cyberspace." Whatever the terminology, the process generally involves identifying and breaking out each factoid into a separate hyperlink—a time-consuming re-editing that is affordable only for major projects.

Contrary to what many believe, hypertext does not reduce a reader's ability to comprehend what he or she is reading. In laboratory studies, readers exposed to hypertext were expected to have lower comprehension than readers exposed to linear text. Reading comprehension theory predicted that hypertext would break down the coherence of text, reducing comprehension. However, readers who could have chosen to follow hypertext non-coherently chose instead to develop their own strategies for maintaining coherent structure to the text. The human mind's almost effortless ability to organize isolated facts was demonstrated. If key points were highlighted, subconscious organization and comprehension were made easier.

Hypertext also is the preferred means of navigation for online readers. In analyzing the navigational techniques employed by hundreds of online users, researchers found a preference for hypertext over other navigational devices. Moreover, how a reader uses hypertext is directly related to the user's purpose for being online.

Hypertext use typically falls into one of three categories: directed searches for specific goals, general browsing of sources for items of interest, and purely random browsing. Put another way, online readers tend to be active information seekers, habitual skimmers of efficient sources, or classic Internet surfers that take whatever they find. The middle group—the casual, habitual browsers—is the key. Others come and go, but this group keeps coming back. That's why they are the people that you, as the operator of an online site, want to attract. If your site is well-designed, its predictable efficiency will go a long way toward establishing their return visits.

Structured in outline form, hypertext should facilitate information gathering by enabling readers to access data more quickly and easily than traditional narratives. This, in turn, increases the medium's predictable efficiency. At the same time, it imposes few obstacles on information seekers, while offering serendipitous topics for surfers to investigate.

Presenting material in hypertext enables a writer to make each hyperlink a clue to the importance of the entire package, even if it is not read as a whole. For such a strategy to work, however, the information contained in each link must communicate effectively in its own right. A chain that begins with "City Council meeting" and continues to "action on bus fares" and "reasons for action" yields little for the skimmer to gather. All it says is that the City Council did something about bus fares. One that begins "bus fares to increase" and continues with "action divides City Council" and "subsidy cuts blamed" is far more useful. The gist of what happened is communicated and skimmers uninterested in transit yet interested in ancillary topics, such as subsidies, know that the story contains material of interest.

Hyperlinks, in short, are no different from headlines for graphics or text in print. Rarely should they serve only as a label. The only kind of users who would prefer label headlines, or label hyperlinks, is the active information seeker. For such a person, labeling could make retrieval easier, but true information seeking occurs only rarely. When it does, the highly motivated information seeker is probably willing to put up with minor inconveniences in exchange for getting the needed information. The casual skimmer, on the other hand, is well served by headlines and hyperlinks that are informative in themselves. A summary of the package is gained peripherally, while specific topics can provoke specific information seeking.

Recall the four design qualities we discussed in Chapter 3: visual vividness, hierarchy, data metaphor and metaphorical simplicity. Aggressive "layering" of content by way of hypertext increases hierarchical organization. Thoughtful use of visuals, particularly if they present data metaphors in a simple manner, contributes to the latter two. Because readers will already have decided to visit a Web site, visual vividness plays less of a role online than it does in print.

An essential point in designing an online site is to remember that traditional printed material is among the most interactive forms of communication. With multiple "entry points" on each page, readers can read exactly what they want, in exactly the order they want to read it. A typical reader may read less than one percent of the news stories in a newspaper, but that's not all bad news. Most readers have only a few minutes available for reading each day. A well-designed newspaper ensures they are able to use those minutes to the greatest advantage.

Online, the challenge is no different, but in some cases it is more extreme. In either medium, the function of design is to let readers quickly find what is interesting to them and skip over what is not. Online, the tools that accomplish this are more limited. Typography is not as easily controlled and graphics carry with them bandwidth burdens. The vast information that can be presented at once on a broadsheet page is whittled considerably to fit on a much smaller monitor. Online designers must, therefore, aggressively pursue functionalities that print designers take for granted.

Suggested Reference Works

According to reference librarians at one of the nation's largest libraries, these are the first books to consult when seeking information for graphics. If your office does not already possess these, encourage your office librarian to consider purchasing these or similar works.

General and Political

Information Please Almanac. Boston: Houghton Mifflin Publishing

World Almanac and Book of Facts. Mahwah, NJ: K-III Reference Corp.

Each almanac contains an impressive mix of demographic, geographic, industrial, and historical information. If it does not have what you are looking for, chances are it will identify sources of the information you need in its credits.

The Statesman's Year-Book. London: Macmillan Publishing

This 600-page annual publication not only includes information about political officials and governmental structures but also basic demographic, technological, economic and military statistics for every country in the world.

Europa World Yearbook. Rochester, England: Europa Publishing

A similar collection of international statistics, without the emphasis on politics.

Encyclopedia Brittanica

One of the most frequently cited general reference sources, it is written more as an adult reference book than an aid to schoolchildren doing homework, as other encyclopedias now are produced for.

Aerospace and Military

Jane's All the World's Aircraft. London: Sampson Low, Marston & Co.

Complete with monthly updates, *Jane's* depicts basic performance, capabilities and dimension data for military and civilian aircraft in use world-wide. Companion volumes offer information on such things as military vehicles and weapons systems.

Climate and Weather

The Weather Almanac. Detroit: Gale Publishing

The World Weather Guide. London: Hutchinson & Co.

Each spanning more than 500 pages, these books include a wealth of climatological information, including averages and superlatives, for cities world-wide.

Demographics

Statistical Abstract of the United States: The National Data Book. Austin, Texas: Reference Press

Issued by the US Department of Commerce each September, this essential reference source is filled with official government statistics, gathered by the US Census Bureau as part of its decennial census. If you want to know what percentage of the population in Boise, Idaho, that doesn't have telephones or virtually anything else about how Americans live, this is the book to start with.

Demographic Yearbook. New York: Statistical Office, Department of Economic and Social Affairs, United Nations

Equally valuable for international information, this annual publication includes more than 1,100 pages of statistics for countries world-wide. The number of topics covered each year is augmented by special emphasis pages that focus on different aspects of demographic information. Global statistics on AIDS, for example, might be offered only every few years, making back issues important to keep.

Economics

Handbook of Labor Statistics. Washington: US Government Printing Office

Nearly 450 pages of tables about employment, earnings, prices, productivity, and other labor data gathered by the Labor Department's Bureau of Labor Statistics.

Yearbook of Labour Statistics. Geneva: International Labour Office

Similar information for other countries world-wide.

Health and Medicine

AMA Encyclopedia of Medicine. New York: Random House

Almost 1,200 pages of definitions, symptoms and treatments, this extremely useful book includes many process graphics explaining exactly how medical procedures are performed.

Sports

Rules of the Game: The Complete Illustrated Encyclopedia of All the Sports in the World. New York: St. Martin's Press

Produced by the Diagram Group, this book is a treasure trove for information designers working in newspaper sports departments.

Technology

Statistical Yearbook. Paris: UNESCO

Education, science, technology, communications and culture are the focus of this 840-page annual, presented bilingually in English and French.

References to Other Statistical Sources

Gale Book of Averages. Detroit: Gale Publishing

Intended to be a "fun" reference book, this work lists where various cities and countries rank on a wide range of issues. Seldom are any of the rankings worth using as is. Typically, only the top cities, states or nations are included. However, the book is a wealth of ideas on how things can be compared, is beautifully indexed by topic and contains information on how to find further or more recent data.

American Statistical Index. Washington: Congressional Information Service

State and Local Statistics Sources. Detroit: Gale Publications

Neither book will answer your questions, but both serve as excellent guides as to where answers can be found. Virtually every local, state and national agency that gathers statistical information of any sort is fully identified, along with information on how to reach them.

Index to Illustrations of... **series.** Syracuse, NY: Gaylord Professional Publications

Animals and plants, living things and nature's world are just a portion of the titles in the series. You won't find the illustrations themselves in these indices, but you will find references for locating graphical images published in a wide array of periodicals.

A p p e n d i x **B**

Detailed Review of Research

A book without scholarly citations is like a news story without attribution. So before we wrap up our little paperback chat about graphics, you'll have to endure a few paragraphs written in the inimitable, anti-Evelyn Woods style of scholarly journals, complete with those funky parenthetical references that pass for footnotes in research style nowadays. It's not for the feint of vocabulary and it isn't necessary if you buy what's been told to you. If not, however, here in academic-ese is the scholarly justification for the research on which most of the advice in this book is based:

Historically marginalized into an artistic pursuit (Biderman 1980), information design has re-emerged in the past two decades as a powerful communications tool (Finberg 1994; Reese 1995). Aided by technology, American newspapers have rushed to employ techniques of graphic design (Aumon 1995), but in doing have confronted research that appears openly contradictory (Bohle 1994). Confusion surrounds the few professional standards that seek to gauge a graphic's effectiveness (Feeney 1994). As a result, graphic presentations often become, rather than symphonies of proven harmony, cacophonies of unproved contradiction.

Existing as hybrids of semiotic art, designed text and visual representations of quantifiable data, information graphics can be as hard to define (Arnold 1981) as their effectiveness is to measure. Defining graphics broadly, this literature review attempts to identify factors that have been experimentally and theoretically indicated to be influences on graphics' effectiveness. Applying heuristic-systematic analysis against a backdrop of information, semiotic, Gestalt, dual-coding and reasoned-action theories, this review seeks to document a clear theoretical framework for evaluation of graphics as a justification for further research in the field.

To be effective, a graphic, like any other element on a page, must be seen, examined and understood (Koschnick 1991). Four design factors appear to be most associated with these interrelated processes, and each is theoretically indicated to appeal to different types of readers:

- **Visual vividness:** How much attention a graphic attracts is based how compelling its images and non-textual material are, regardless of their type or of whether they are in are black and white or color (Garcia and Stark 1991). This factor is important during the first second of exposure (Koschnick 1991). In such an initial phase of reading, subjects are expected to exert minimum cognitive effort. Severe time constraints typically do not permit more careful, systematic processing (Ratneshwar and Chaiken 1991). As a result, visual vividness is theoretically predicted to be expected more significant for heuristic processors than systematic processors.

- **Hierarchical organization:** Whether a reader, once attracted to a graphic, continues to examine it beyond an initial glance (Koschnick 1991) is a factor of how unambiguously it emphasizes its main points in textual highlights (Dreyfus and Mazouz 1992; Paivio, Walsh and Bons 1994). Readers casually scanning for items to process (Neuman 1981) may appreciate the predictable efficiency (Ajzen and Fishbein 1980) with which a graphic's non-linear visual hierarchy (Foltz 1993; Catledge and Pitkow 1995) prioritizes information, allowing them to efficiently scan for material of at least minimal interest (Klein 1975). Organization, therefore, is theoretically predicted to be associated more closely with systematic processing than with heuristic processing. Unambiguous hierarchy has been shown to prevent systematic processors from resorting to heuristic means (Chaiken and Maheswaran 1994).

- **Visual data metaphor and simplicity of that metaphor:** The degree to which a graphic conveys its key points as charted data or in other symbolic forms (Hart and O'Shanick 1993; Kelly 1993; Hollander 1994), coupled with the lack of complexity or high "data-to-ink ratio" of these metaphors (Tufte 1982; Bertin 1983; Tankard 1989; Akai and Nakajimi 1989; Paivio 1991; David 1992, 1994; Spence and Krizel 1994), affects how quickly and memorably the messages are understood. For readers exercising minimal cognitive effort, the natural advantage of a visual communications channel seems likely to prove important; such readers could in effect adopt a "seeing is believing" heuristic. By the same token, the more unambiguous a visual metaphor is, the less likely a systematic reader will be to resort to heuristic clues in processing it. Use of visual data metaphor thus is predicted to be associated with heuristic processing, while simplicity of data metaphor is predicted to be associated with systematic processing.

With the effectiveness of these factors likely to vary according to the heuristic or systematic tendencies of the reader, a fifth factor—**issue involvement**—becomes a key variable in determining a graphic's effectiveness. Previous research suggests that high levels of issue involvement lead subjects to employ systematic strategies while low levels of involvement lead subjects to employ more economical heuristic strategies (Chaiken 1980). Concurrent consideration of issue involvement and design strategies is, therefore, theoretically indicated to be a potential answer to the confusion that has surrounded previous efforts at measuring graphics' efficiency.

Prior to the study undertaken in response to this review, no known previous study had attempted to account for all four design variables and no known previous study had added a heuristic-systematic variable such as issue involvement. Rather, most prior research had dealt with contrasting the recall of information conveyed textually with the recall of information conveyed visually. In a few cases, metaphorical simplicity was measured as a secondary variable or controlled by design. Rarely was hierarchical organization controlled or measured. When measured, visual vividness and use of visual data metaphor were lumped together as a single factor of visuality.

The result has been a handful of studies in which results are contradictory with mainstream studies cited previously. Simple but visual graphics were indicated in one study to be no more memorable than text (Ward 1992). In another, simple background information was indicated to be comprehended equally well whether included in text or separated from text by simple but visual graphic devices (Griffin and Stevenson 1992). The potential problem with each of these studies was that they employed neither compelling visual images nor hierarchically organized material. Moreover, the data metaphors they employed were extremely weak. In short, none of what makes a graphic a graphic was employed. In one, detailed foreign affairs stories and graphics were tested on college students in "graphics" that employed minimalist devices that were more decorative than informative. Without vividness, organization, metaphor, and simplicity, correlation of a graphic's effectiveness to a composite factor labeled "visuality" was not possible.

Based on these theoretical findings, additional research, upon which this book is based on, was undertaken.

Four experimental news stories, adapted from actual published material, were constructed in standard journalistic style. Each featured a topic of varying degrees of issue involvement—one of universally high involvement, one of universally low involvement and two of mixed involvement. Issue involvement was measured both by a panel of experts and by direct questioning of experimental subjects.

Also constructed were 16 identically sized graphics, four per story. For any given story, each of the four graphics was designed to convey exactly the same information. The only difference was that each of the four employed a different design strategy, ranking high in one factor and low in the other three. The variation in design factors was attested to by a panel of graphics experts.

Four different mock editions of an actual Midwestern newspaper were then created. Each edition contained all four of the stories plus additional non-experimental matter, laid out in exactly the same manner. Accompanying each story was one of the four graphics created to go with it. In Edition 1, only graphics high in vividness were used. In Edition 2, only graphics high in organization were used. In Edition 3, only graphics high in metaphor were used. In Edition 4, only graphics high in simplicity were used. Graphics featuring different design factors were not intermixed to avoid the confounding effect of one graphic attracting attention away from another.

A randomly selected interval sample of subscribers to the newspaper was contacted in advance and invited to participate in a come-and-go research session and open house at the newspaper office, a portion of which had been converted into a comfortable waiting area. Subjects (n=150) were selected by lot to receive one of the four test editions, which were distributed as if they were that week's edition of the paper, which was due to hit the streets at the same time as the experimental sessions. Each subject was told to relax and read the front page of the newspaper as he or she normally would, then answer a brief set of questions.

After exposure to the test editions, subjects were asked to complete a demographic questionnaire and then were asked questions measuring recall of factual points conveyed only in text and factual points conveyed only in graphics. In addition, subjects' awareness of the existence of each story and graphic was measured, as was subjects' judgment as to the facilitousness of each graphic and subjects' critical recall of factual points. Critical recall was measured by testing subjects' ability to identify errors introduced into replicas of the graphics to which they had been exposed.

Control variables including standard demographics, prior experience with newspaper graphics, technical ability to interpret charted data, and confidence in that ability also were measured.

Final results of the experiment were still being tabulated at press time for this book. Preliminary results, however, indicate substantial support for the study's hypotheses regarding vividness and metaphor being associated with increased recall for low-involvement topics, and organization and metaphorical simplicity being associated with increased recall for high-involvement topics.

In other words, there's some pretty thorough research backing up what's said in this book. If you want more, watch your favorite scholarly journal for all the T-tests and multiple regression scores from this study.

A p p e n d i x **C**

Bibliography

Ajzen, I., and M. Fishbein, *Understanding Attitudes and Predicting Social Behavior.* Englewood Cliffs, NJ: Prentice Hall, 1980.

Akai, Seiki, and Yoshiaki Nakajima, "Effects of Information Conflict and Complexity in Visual Figures on Voluntary Visual Exploration, Using Structure Informational Theory," *Perceptual and Motor Skills,* October 1989, pp. 575-579.

Arnold, Edmund, *Designing the Total Newspaper.* New York: Harper & Row, 1981.

Arnold, Edmund, *Ink on Paper 2.* New York: Harper & Row, 1972.

Arnold, Edmund, *Modern Newspaper Design.* New York: Harper & Row, 1968.

Arntson, Amy E., *Graphic Design Basics,* 2nd edition. Fort Worth: Harcourt Brace College Publishers, 1993.

Auman, Ann, "Seeing the Big Picture: The Integrated Editor of the 1990s," *Newspaper Research Journal,* winter 1995, pp. 35-47.

Barton, C. Michael, G.A. Clark, and Allison E. Cohen, "Art as Information: Explaining Upper Paleolithic Art in Western Europe," *World Archeology,* October 1994, pp. 185-208.

Behrens, Roy R., review of *A History of Graphic Design* in *Print,* July-August 1992, pp. 282-284.

Bertin, Jacques, *Semiology of Graphics,* translated by William Berg. Madison, WI: University of Wisconsin Press, 1983.

Biderman, Albert D., "The Graph as a Victim of Adverse Discrimination and Segregation," *Information Design Journal*, 1980, pp. 238.

Bohle, Bob, "What Research Tells Us About Graphics," *Design*, April-June 1994, pp. 32-33.

Catledge, Lara D., and James E. Pitkow, "Characterizing Browser Strategies in the World Wide Web," 1995. Available online: http://www.cc.gatech.edu/gvu/reports/TechReports95.html.

Chaiken, Shelly, "Heuristic Versus Systematic Information Processing and Use of Source Versus Message Cues in Persuasion," *Journal of Personality and Social Psychology*, May 1980, pp. 752-766.

Chaiken, Shelly, and Durairaj Maheswaran, "Heuristic Processing Can Bias Systematic Processing: Effects of Source Credibility, Argument Ambiguity and Task Importance on Attitude Judgment," *Journal of Personality and Social Psychology*, March 1994, pp. 460-473.

Cronin, Anne, "Pulitzer Pleas: Fighting for a Spot," *Design*, July-September 1992, pp. 22-23.

David, Prabu, "Accuracy of Perception of the Different Faces of the Pie," *News Photographer*, October 1994, pp. 8-10.

David, Prabu, "Accuracy of Visual Perception of Quantitative Graphics: An Exploratory Study," *Journalism Quarterly*, summer 1992, pp. 273-293.

Davidson, Ian, William Noble, David F. Armstrong, L.T. Black, William H. Calvin, Mary LeCron Foster, Paul Graves, John Halverson and Gordon W. Hewes, "The Archeology of Perception: Traces of Depiction and Language," *Current Anthropology*, April 1989, pp. 125-156.

Davis, Angela E., *Art and Work*. Montreal: McGill-Queen's University Press, 1995.

Dowson, Thomas A., "Reading Art, Writing History: Rock Art and Social Change in Southern Africa," *World Archaeology*, February 1994, pp. 332-346.

Dreyfus, Amos, and Yossef Mazouz, *Research in Science and Technological Education*, May 1992, pp. 5-21.

Emery, Edwin, *The Press and America: An Interpretative History of the Mass Media*, 3rd edition. Englewood Cliffs, NJ: Prentice Hall, 1972.

Feeny, Mark, "Beyond the Voodoo Stick," *Design*, April-June 1994, pp. 4-31.

Finberg, Howard, "It Was Twenty Years Ago Today, Sgt. Pepper Taught the Band to Play, They've Been Going in and out of Style but They're Guaranteed to Make You Smile," *Design*, April-June 1994, pp. 12-17.

Fitzgerald, Mark, "Early Graphics on Display: Traveling Exhibit Honors Early Artisans of Newspaper Graphics," *Editor & Publisher*, March 6, 1993, pp. 18-20.

Fitzgerald, Mark, "Will Artists Become Computer Nerds?" *Editor & Publisher*, Sept. 3, 1988, pp. 10-13.

Foltz, Peter, "Reader's Strategies and Comprehension in Linear Text and Hypertext," 1993. Available online: http://psych.colorado.edu/ics/tech_rep_93.html.

Friedman, Mildred, "Opening a History," in Friedman and Phil Freshman, eds., *Graphic Design in America: A Visual Language History*. Minneapolis: Walker Art Center, 1989.

Garcia, Mario R., *Contemporary Newspaper Design: A Structural Approach*. Englewood Cliffs, NJ: Prentice Hall, 1987.

Garcia, Mario R., and Pegie Stark, *Eyes on the News*. St. Petersburg, FL: Poynter Institute for Media Studies, 1991.

Garneau, George, "Infographics: Editors Believe the Use of News Graphics Will Continue to Grow," *Editor & Publisher*, Oct. 22, 1988, pp. 44-45.

Gentry, James K., and Barbara Zang, "The Graphics Editor Takes Charge: Newspapers' New Face," *Washington Journalism Review*, January-February 1988, pp. 24-29.

Gilbert, E.W., "Pioneer Maps of Health and Disease in England," *Geographical Journal*, 1958, pp. 172-183.

Gladney, George Albert, "The McPaper Revolution? *USA Today*-style Innovation at Large U.S. Dailies," *Newspaper Research Journal,* winter-spring 1992, pp. 54-65.

Graves, Paul, "Flakes and Ladders: What the Archeological Record Cannot Tell Us About the Origins of Language," *World Archeology,* October 1994, pp. 158-172.

Griffin, Jeffrey L., and Robert L. Stevenson, "Influences of Text & Graphics in Increasing Understanding of Foreign News Content," *Newspaper Research Journal,* winter-spring 1992, pp. 84-100.

Hart, Robert P., and Gregory J. O'Shanick, "Retention Interval and Verbal vs. Pictorial vs. Figural Stimuli," *Journal of Clinical and Experimental Neuropsychology,* March 1993, pp. 245-265.

Hollander, Barry A., "Newspaper Graphics and Inadvertent Persuasion," *Visual Communication Quarterly,* winter 1994.

Hollis, Richard, *Graphic Design: A Concise History.* London: Thames and Hudson, 1994.

Holmes, Nigel, *Designer's Guide to Creating Charts and Diagrams.* New York: Watson-Guptill, 1984.

Kelly, James D., "The Effects of Display Format and Data Density on Time Spent Reading Statistics in Text, Tables and Graphs," *Journalism Quarterly,* spring 1993, pp. 140-149.

Klein, Paul, "The Television Audience and Program Mediocrity," in Alan Wells, ed., *Mass Media and Society.* Palo Alto, CA: Mayfield Press, 1975, pp. 74-77.

Koschnick, Wolfgang J., "Color Report, the Rebuttal: Recent Color Study Trends to Miss the 'Point,'" *Design,* January-March 1991, pp. 22-23.

Lalomina, Mary J., Michael D. Coovert and Eduardo Salas, *Behavior and Information Technology,* September-October 1992, pp. 268-280.

Lott, Pam, "Lockwood: A Fresh Look at the Pre-Eminent Newspaper Designer on the Eve of His First Book," *Design,* April-June 1991, pp. 4-7.

Malley, John C., David B. Meinert and Robert V. Riech, "A Guide to the Potential Misuse of Computer Graphics," *Information Strategy: The Executive's Journal,* summer 1993, pp. 39-47.

Marcy, E.J., *La Méthode Graphique.* Paris: 1885.

Meggs, Philip B., *A History of Graphic Design.* New York: Van Nostrand Reinhold, 1983.

Ibid, 2nd edition, 1992.

Menichini, Mike, "Readers Flock to Get Unpublished Persian Gulf Graphics Package," *Editor & Publisher,* Sept. 29, 1990, pp. 10-11.

Monmonier, Mary, and Val Pipps, "Weather Maps and Newspaper Design: Response to *USA Today?*" *Newspaper Research Journal,* summer 1987, pp. 31-42.

Neary, John, "Historic Messages," *Archaeology,* November-December 1993, pp. 62-68.

Needham, Joseph. *Science and Civilization in China,* vol. 3. Cambridge: Cambridge Press, 1959.

Nesbitt, Phil, "Here's Ed," *Design,* November 1988, pp. 4-16.

Neuman, W. Russell, *The Future of the Mass Audience.* Cambridge: Cambridge University Press, 1991.

Page One. New York: *The New York Times,* 1980.

Paivo, Allan, "Dual Coding Theory: Retrospect and Current Status," *Canadian Journal of Psychology,* September 1991, pp. 255-288.

Paivo, Allan, Mary Walsh and Trudy Bons, "Concreteness Effects on Memory: When and Why?" *Journal of Experimental Psychology: Learning, Memory and Cognition,* September 1994, pp. 1,196-1,205.

Parsonson, Barry S., and Donald M. Baer, "The Visual Analysis of Data, and Current Research into the Stimuli Controlling It." in Thomas R. Kratochwill and Joel R. Levin, eds., *Single-Case Research Design and Analysis: New Directions in Psychology and Education.* Hillsdale, NY: Lawrence Erlbaum Associates, 1992.

Pasternack, Steve, and Sandra H. Utt, "Subject Perception of Newspaper Characteristics Based on Front Page Design," *Newspaper Research Journal,* fall 1986, p. 29.

Patton, Phil, "Up from Flatland: Information Design," *The New York Times Magazine,* Jan. 19, 1992, p. 28.

Playfair, William, *Statistical Abstract of the United States* (an illustrated translation of Dennis Donnatt's *Statistical Account of the USA*). London: Greenland & Morris, 1805.

Playfair, William, *The Commercial & Political Atlas.* London: Debrett, 1786.

Ratneshwar, S., and S. Chaiken, "Comprehension's Role in Persuasion: The Case of its Moderating Effect on the Persuasive Impact of Source Cues," *Journal of Consumer Research,* 1991, pp. 52-62.

Reese, Nancy, "And the Band Plays On," *Design,* April-June 1994, pp. 4-31.

Shannon, Claude E., and Warren Weaver, *The Mathematical Theory of Communication.* Urbana, IL: University of Illinois Press, 1963.

Smith, Edward J., and Donna J. Hajash, "Informational Graphics in 30 Daily Newspapers," *Journalism Quarterly,* fall 1988, pp. 714-719.

Spence, Ian, and Peter Krizel, "Children's Perception of Proportion in Graphs," *Child Development,* August 1994, pp. 1,193-1,214.

Spence, Ian, and S. Lewandowsky, "Graphical Perception," in J. Fox and S. Lang, eds., *Modern Methods of Data Analysis.* Beverly Hills, CA: Sage Publications, 1990, pp. 13-56.

Tankard, James W. Jr., "Effects of Chartoons & Three-Dimensional Graphs on Interest & Information Gain," *Newspaper Research Journal,* spring 1989, pp. 91-103.

Tufte, Edward R., *Envisioning Information.* Cheshire, CT: Graphics Press, 1990.

Tufte, Edward R., *The Visual Display of Quantitative Information.* Cheshire, CT: Graphics Press, 1983.

Turnbull, Arthur T., and Russell N. Baird, *The Graphics of Communication.* New York: Holt, Rinehart and Winston, 1962.

Ibid, 2nd edition, 1968.

Turpin, Solveig A., "Beneath the Sands of Time: Petroglyphs Mark a Sacred Spot of the Ritual Landscape of Western Texas," *Archaeology*, March–April 1994, pp. 50-54.

Walston, John, "How Others Get the Facts," *Design*, March 1988, pp. 18-19.

Ward, Douglas B., "The Effectiveness of Sidebar Graphics," *Journalism Quarterly*, summer 1992, pp. 318-339.

Webster's Biographical Dictionary. Springfield, MA: G.C. Merriam Co., 1967.

White, Randall, "Visual Thinking in the Ice Age," *Scientific American*, July 1989, pp. 92-100.

Williams, Thomas R., "Text or Graphic: An Information Processing Perspective on Choosing the More Efficient Medium," *Journal of Technical Writing and Communication*, winter 1993, pp. 33-53.

Index